VANISHED

Into Thin Air

THE HOPE

OF EVERY

BELIEVER

HAL LINDSEY

WESTERN FRONT

Vanished Into Thin Air

ISBN 1-888848-43-X

Published by WESTERN FRONT LTD., Beverly Hills, CA

Interior design by Koechel Peterson & Associates,
Minneapolis, Minnesota

Manufactured in the United States of America

I wish to thank Jack Kinsela

for his invaluable and indispensable help

in the writing of this book. His extraordinary gifts

are a treasure for the Body of Christ. May the Lord

reward him for his servant's heart.

CHAPTER ONE

Our Desperate Need for Hope

*T*here is an almost universal, subconscious feeling that something catastrophic is looming in our planet's imminent future. Even Hollywood's film-makers have picked up on these phenomena as witnessed by the flood of disaster movies, which incidentally have been box office successes.

In addition, this generation more than any other is fascinated with the idea of an alien invasion of extra-terrestrials or ET's. Many people believe that there are beings of superior intelligence and power dwelling in the universe that will soon make an appearance on our planet. The numerous sightings of UFO's in the latter half of the 20th century have added both credibility and expectancy of an alien landing—if not an invasion of some kind by these ET's. Once again, Hollywood has so played on this theme with its special effects that supernatural phenomena are now rather expected to accompany the coming of these aliens. This, I believe, will have major significance in understanding 2 Thessalonians 2:9-13.

Preparing for the Unknown

There is a sense of expectancy, too, of something big happening, even though nobody seems to be able to put a finger exactly on what. It's an intangible, vaguely uneasy sense that all things are not quite as they should be. The world seems to be going through some kind of transformation, an inexorable movement toward *something*, even if that something remains undefined. There was a popular song a few years ago with the line, *"Two thousand zero zero, party over, out of time. So tonight we're gonna party like it's nineteen ninety-nine."* So, what does *"out of time"* mean? The popularity of the song proves the concept hit a responsive chord among its audience of primarily young people. But it wasn't simply the approach of the year 2000 that created this global uneasiness about the future. It has been with us for some time. Alvin Toffler wrote a wildly successful book back in 1991 entitled *Future Shock.* In it, he theorizes that the future is careening toward us, out of control, and we are all merely spectators, rather than participants, in an unfolding drama,

"Why is it that all our institutions seem to be going through a simultaneous crisis? Why is it that the health system's in crisis, the justice system's in crisis, the education system's in crisis, the value system's in crisis—you name it—why? There must be something that cuts across all of these. . . . And why is it happening in Tokyo and London and Italy and so forth? Why is there a political crisis throughout all the political countries?

"The answer is that we have sets of institutions that were designed either for agrarian life . . . as parliaments were, or . . . the Industrial Age, but no longer meet the requirements of today. And the problem used to be—it took what? Three months for a message to get from Ohio to Washington?

And vice versa? And the idea was the Senate would be a chamber for leisurely deliberation for the major issues. Well, come on! Nobody has two minutes of uninterrupted time. So the external conditions are radically changed.

"So the question is how flexible are the existing institutions themselves. We're fortunate, the Americans are lucky, because our system is generally more flexible and certainly more decentralized than the other industrial states. Which gives us a better shot. But I don't believe that the system can continue in its present form."[1]

Toffler's concern that the "system" can't continue in its present form is borne out by the obvious. The "system" is not a *system* so much as it is a living dynamic, one that is self-sustaining. His cry hits a responsive chord among his audience because most people recognize, at some level, the truth of his position.

The Fear Factor

Take a minute, and prove it for yourself. Can you picture yourself in the Year 2010? Try and imagine what the world will look like. Will America remain a sovereign nation, or will it be part of a larger alliance? What will happen to Russia? What about our social morals? In ten years or less, will television still be our main form of entertainment? Considering the way standards have

---

1 Alvin Toffler in a 1996 interview with the *Minneapolis Star Tribune*

relaxed in just the past decade, will we be watching public executions or X-rated movies during prime time? Does *anybody* have a vision of a future similar to that of say, the generation of soldiers who returned home to rebuild society following World War II? The postwar years are often referred to, nostalgically, as America's "golden years." Those "golden years" are behind us. The current generation can look forward a year, maybe a little further. Beyond that, it's anybody's guess.

Computers get smarter every day. So do we. Only a few years ago, cloning anything, even plants, remained the exclusive domain of the science fiction writer. Dolly the sheep changed all that. Today, the science exists to clone human beings. How far outside the realm of possibility is the concept of cloning human beings for use as spare parts? Or as constructed soldiers à la Huxley's *Brave New World?* What kind of world awaits us ten years from now?

What will war look like ten years from now? What kind of weapons will we have? Does it even seem *possible* that we can survive as a society long enough to find out?

In short, much of today's world is drifting along on the currents of change, without any clear idea of the course we are on.

We are living in a time unique to human history. Those people living when the Wright brothers made their first historic flight were just settling in for retirement when Neil Armstrong took his "one giant leap for mankind" on the surface of the moon. In the years since, we've developed ovens that can cook a hotdog in 15 seconds, digital television, satellites, global positioning systems, desktop computers more powerful than those that controlled Armstrong's moon flight, cellular telephones—the list is endless. And even if we were able to list all the developments of the past half century, by the time the list was complete, it would already be obsolete.

Fear of the unknown is mankind's most basic fear. And the dichotomy of this generation is the more we learn, the more we realize how little we know. And the greater the fear factor becomes, with its inevitable results of an increasing sense of hopelessness.

A great philosopher once said, "He who has no hope for the future has no hold on the present." We have to have a sure hope for the future to have stability in the present time.

This generation has no moorings to cling to and have a sense of security. All that is familiar is being swept away by the rapidity of change. This is the essence of the "Future Shock" about which Alvin Toffler wrote. We can get culture shock by traveling to another country. We can always recover our comfort zone by returning to our original culture, or at least knowing that it is still there. But the culture in which we were born is being changed so rapidly and irrevocably that it leads us into an existence that is both unfamiliar and frightening.

Examine the Evidence !

20th Century Fox inaugurated their new American all-news channel with the slogan, "We report, you decide." For the purposes of this book, we'll borrow that slogan and allow you to decide. Check it out against the historical record. Not the religious historical record, but instead, look things up in your encyclopedia. Once you have the report, so to speak, then you can develop an informed decision. Only a fool bets his future on an uneducated guess.

So let's take a look at a little of tomorrow's history, laid out thousands of years ago, and see how it stacks up with today's events. After all, if everything up to this point has hit the mark with perfect accuracy, then the odds are, those things yet to come will be fulfilled with equal precision. And "reasonable accuracy" is not what we are looking at. We are looking at a 100% accuracy rate, 100% of the time, in every category.

Birth Pangs

"As He [Jesus] was sitting on the Mount of Olives, the disciples came to Him privately, saying, 'Tell us, when will these things be, and what *will be* the sign of Your coming, and of the end of the age?' And Jesus answered and said to them, 'See to it that no one misleads you. For many will come in My name, saying, "I am the Christ," and will mislead many. And you will be

hearing of wars and rumors of wars; see that you are not frightened, for *those things* must take place, but *that* is not yet the end. For [ethnic group] will rise against [ethnic group], and kingdom against kingdom, and in various places there will be famines and earthquakes. But all these things are *merely* the beginning of BIRTH PANGS'" (Matthew 24:3-8).

The Bible outlines a precise scenario of events that would all come together in concert, at a specific point in history—a single generation, somewhere in time. That scenario culminates with a final, seven-year countdown to the Second Coming of Christ.

Hot Wars–Cold Wars

. . . and ye shall hear of wars . . .

Among the signs Jesus spoke of was the ubiquitous reference to "rumors of wars." Now obviously, He wasn't referring to someone gossiping about a war that didn't take place. So, what is a "rumor" of war? Historically speaking, a "rumor" of war is indistinguishable from the war itself, since evaluating the war from an historical perspective would necessarily include the events leading up to the ultimate conflict. There were "rumors" of war circulating throughout Europe during the 1930s, although WWII didn't officially begin until September 2, 1939. But any study of WWII would include the diplomatic and political events of the 1930s leading to the global conflagration as primary *causes*, rather than *rumors*. In this sense, a "rumor of war" would indicate circumstances in which a war was expected, but averted before open conflict erupted.

The Ultimate Rumor of War

. . . and rumors of wars . . .

The cessation of hostilities at the close of WW2 (the post-War period, remember?) was supposed to usher in world peace. We've already noted that regional conflicts continued unabated, but *global war* was rendered unthinkable by nuclear weapons—*unthinkable, but not impossible*. Beginning with the Berlin Airlift in 1948, a period of global Cold War ensued between the Soviet Union and the Western powers led by the United States.

Russia soon possessed not only the atomic bomb, but also the hydrogen bomb, curtesy of some US traitors. This forced the *unthinkable* to become *thinkable*.

A whole generation grew up glancing fearfully skyward against the day when the hands on the Doomsday Clock finally struck midnight.

The Cold War ended in "victory" for the West. The Russian Communist Party spent itself out of existence fighting "the rumor war" of Mass Destruction. The rumors of war divided the world into two spheres of influence. The final legacy of the rumors of war of the latter half of the 20th century has not yet been written. Which is, in and of itself, a validation of the Lord's prophecy. For as He warned, it was a signpost, but not an end in itself.

Out of the Ashes of Victory . . .

. . . see that ye be not troubled: for all these things must come to pass, but the end is not yet . . .

Historians divide the 20th century into "pre-War" and "post-War" periods. That means Korea, Vietnam, the Cold War, the Gulf War and the NATO War were all "post-War wars." Comparing the number of "post-War" wars ongoing around the world to the number of "pre-War" wars, it seems pretty obvious that there is a discernible rise in the instances of both "kingdom rising against kingdom" *and* "ethnic group rising against ethnic group."

Ethnic Group versus Ethnic Group

. . . Nation Shall Rise Against Nation . . .

Jesus said that *"nation* would rise against *nation"* and then, later in the same sentence, *"kingdom* against *kingdom,"* clearly indicating, by the context, that He intended to differentiate between the two. The Greek term εθνος, or "ethnos," means a race, nation, or people. On the other hand, a kingdom, βασιλεία, or "basileia," means "the territory subject to the rule of a king."

Most of the 130-plus wars raging right now are ethnic wars. The Middle East peace process is largely ethnic in nature. So is the unrest in the former Soviet republics. The NATO war against Yugoslavia's Slobodan Milosevic, although international, was an ethnic war. The term "ethnic cleansing" became part of everyday language thanks to Serbia's version of the Nazi policy of *liebensraum.*

Northern Ireland, Yugoslavia, most of sub-Saharan Africa, Pakistan and India, China and Tibet — on it goes. And they are all either ethnic or religious in nature. And let us not forget the rising tide of Muslim fundamentalism that threatens to overturn the secular regimes of Turkey, Egypt and Syria, to name a few.

Incomplete Victory

. . . and kingdom against kingdom . . .

World War I was called, at the time, *the war to end all wars.* Following its awful carnage, it was believed no nation would ever be so foolish as to make war again. But that was before we started numbering world wars. At the beginning of this century, no one dreamed that we would have to start numbering world wars.

World War II proved nothing is as certain as human foolishness, but, having once glimpsed Utopia, the world's leaders began in earnest to work toward the impossible dream of world peace. The first attempt was embodied by the League of Nations. That attempt failed dismally. As the shadow of the swastika fell across Europe, so did the globalist dream of Utopia. At least for a time.

By the time the dust cleared in 1945, war was *unthinkable!* Germany was reduced to rubble. The cream of a generation of Europeans lay crumpled in the ashes. And when power of the atom smashed the Japanese cities of Nagasaki and Hiroshima, the world knew it could no longer entertain the idea of war.

Stunted Growth

. . . and pestilences . . .

Population experts are now saying that several African countries may achieve zero population growth in just a few years. But nobody is cheering the reasons. It isn't because of careful family planning, or even a reduction in the birth rate. Instead, people are dying faster than they can be replaced. World Watch president Lester Brown told the UN "A lot of countries will not see expected population increases because of rising death rates."

In one African country, Zimbabwe, it's estimated that one quarter of the population carries the AIDS virus. In Uganda, there are already 1.7 *million* AIDS orphans.

Recent (1999) United Nations data says Botswana has a 25% AIDS infection rate, Namibia has 20%, Zambia with 19%, Swaziland with 18.5%. The UN database says there are several additional African countries with infection rates of 10% or more. In Uganda alone, there are already 1.7 million AIDS orphans. By contrast, the global AIDS infection rate steady at just under 1%.

In one of the biggest outbreaks of poisoning this century, scientists have discovered that Bangladeshi villagers are being slowly poisoned from water wells provided by foreign aid agencies. As many as 30 million people are at risk of developing cancer from the contamination.

Thirty years ago I wrote in *Late Great Planet Earth* that the Bible predicts an increase in disease in the last days. At the time, many medical doctors ridiculed my position, saying infectious diseases were virtually a thing of the past. Well, from 1980 to 1992, the death rate from infectious disease rose 60%. It's estimated that 70% of bacteria involved in infections that people get while in the hospital are now resistant to at least one antibiotic. But, since there is no national system for quickly sharing information, the true figures may not be known. One form of staphylococcus bacteria has developed immunity to our strongest antibiotic—vancomycin.

According to an official report from UNAIDS, there are close to 16,000 new infections a day at present. From the report: "New estimates show that infection with the human immunodeficiency virus (HIV) which causes AIDS is far more common in the world than previously thought. UNAIDS and WHO estimate that over 30 million people are living with HIV infection at the end of 1997. That is one in every 100 adults in the sexually active ages of 15 to 49 worldwide. Included in the 30 million figure are 1.1 million children under the age of 15. The overwhelming majority of HIV-infected people—more than 90%—live in the developing world, and most of these do not know that they are infected.

Mankind's Losing Battle with Bacteria

According to the World Health Organization, if it isn't AIDS, maybe it will be TB that will decimate the Dark

Continent. Health officials sounded the alarm that one billion may become infected by TB and 70 million may die
during the next two decades. The major problem is in poor
countries with inadequate treatment, but there is also the
threat of drug-resistant strains that have developed for
which there is no cure.

We proclaimed total victory in the war against disease
with the development of antibiotic therapy and vaccines
that wiped out many of the plagues that had formerly deci-
mated populations. But the over-prescription of antibiotics
and the development of terrifying new microbes, together
with new diseases like AIDS and hepatitis C, means we are
further behind in the fight against viral infection than ever
before. One of the most frightening discoveries is that old
nemeses of man such as TB, yellow fever, cholera, syphilis,
gonorrhea, malaria, diptheria, etc., have developed immunity to most antibiotics. Some are now incurable.

One of the signs of the last days is pestilence, or deadly,
infectious disease. Another is widespread famine. Like
birth pangs, the incidences of infection are prophesied to
increase in frequency and intensity as the time approaches.
With something close to a quarter of the African continent
dying of infection and another quarter threatened by star-
vation, it's safe to say it's pretty intense already.

Whole Lotta Shakin' Goin' On

. . . and earthquakes, in divers places . . .

It is surprising how many people deny the fact that

earthquakes are on the increase, in both frequency and intensity. I've been accused of exaggerating earthquake statistics by everyone from Gary North to the US Geological Survey. So I'll include statistics compiled *by* the US Geological Survey. Look at the totals along the bottom of the chart. Decide for yourself. *Is* 18,864 (1996) a greater number than 11,290 (1987) or not?

Water Wars?

Twenty-two countries around the world are dependent on the flow of water from other nations to meet their water supply needs. This kind of dependence can lead to international friction, escalating tensions, or worse. India and Pakistan remain on the threshold of nuclear war. At the same time, they still have to figure out ways to share water between them and Bangladesh, while their shared underground resources are diminishing steadily.

In the Middle East, the late King Hussein of Jordan negotiated fiercely over water, understanding that water is the one issue that could force his country into a regional war. Jordan shares its water supply with Israel—and that shared resource is beginning to dry up as well.

Egypt is totally dependent on the Nile for its water supply. Eighty-five percent of that river's water comes from Ethiopia.

As Ethiopia's population grows, so does its need for water. Water that Egypt already needs.

Over the last half-century, many nations have gone to war over oil. The Gulf War is a good example.

Number of Earthquakes Worldwide for 1987-1996

Located by the US Geological Survey National Earthquake Information Center

Magnitude	1987	1988	1989	1990	1991	1992	1993	1994	1995	1996
8.0 to 9.9	0	0	1	0	0	0	1	2	3	1
7.0 to 7.9	11	8	6	12	11	23	15	13	20	20
6.0 to 6.9	112	93	79	115	105	104	141	161	175	150
5.0 to 5.9	1437	1485	1444	1635	1469	1541	1449	1542	1213	1126
4.0 to 4.9	4146	4018	4090	4493	4372	5196	5034	4544	6782	8558
3.0 to 3.9	1806	1932	2452	2457	2952	4643	4263	5000	3828	4521
2.0 to 2.9	1037	1479	1906	2364	2927	3068	5390	5369	2761	2065
1.0 to 1.9	102	118	418	474	801	887	1177	779	485	267
0.1 to 0.9	0	3	0	0	1	2	9	17	9	1
No Magnitude	2639	3575	4189	5062	3878	4084	3997	1944	1367	2155
Year	1987	1988	1989	1990	1991	1992	1993	1994	1995	1996
Total	11290	12711	14585	16612	16516	19548	21476	19371	16643	18864

Over the next quarter century, nations will war over water. There are substitutes for oil. And nations can live without it, if they have to. Or at least, the populations can. There is no substitute for fresh water. A human body is 70% water. A 1% deficiency makes us thirsty. A 10% deficiency is crippling. A 12% deficiency brings death.

According to the UN, nearly 10,000 children die *every day* around the world from thirst. *A person can live a lifetime without oil, a month without food, but only a couple of days without water.* Water is the one resource that cannot be negotiated. No nation on earth would hesitate to do battle to maintain an adequate supply of water. Environmentalists say the world's population will double in the next 50 years, if the Lord tarries. The world's renewable water supply will not. It remains more or less constant. Add to that the fact that per capita water consumption is rising twice as fast as the population, and the problem becomes obvious.

What's Wrong with the Weather?

The past decade or so has brought with it a baffling change in global weather patterns. The terms *100 year flood* or *500 year storm* used to mean something, prior to the middle of the 1980s.

- The National Weather Service concluded that *July 1998 was the hottest month ever recorded.* Not just in the United States, but the hottest month in history—globally.

- In the United States, the summer of 1998's nation-wide killer heat wave claimed at least 156 lives.

- The heat wave was responsible for the wildfires that consumed huge areas of Oklahoma, Florida and Texas. But, as I said, this heat wave wasn't a local event.

- In Cairo, officials hosed down polar bears, elephants and lions. Outdoor workers in Egypt, like construction workers and street repairman, worked at night after it had cooled down to 80 degrees or so.

- In Jordan, temperatures over 118 degrees forced at least 1,000 people to seek medical treatment.

- On the island of Cyprus, the temperatures were the hottest recorded in 40 years. The only relief from the heat was the other global weather phenomenon. Flooding.

- In South Korea, unusually heavy rains caused the worst flooding on record. Flooding across Red China claimed at least 2,000 lives.

- The year 1998 brought the worst Atlantic hurricane season ever recorded. That record continues to fall with each passing season so far, and if we are as far along in the prophetic timetable as the signs indicate, that pattern will only escalate.

Global weather pattern changes, by themselves, can take credit for many of the natural phenomena predicted for the last generation before the return of Christ. The pressures created by the weight of the water on the Pacific shelf, thanks to the El Nino effect, is expected to increase the likelihood of a catastrophic earthquake sometime in the next few years along the western coast of the United States.

Dorothy's Storm Was Nothing!

National Weather Service meteorologists, in describing the F-5 tornado that flattened Oklahoma City in 1999, called it the "storm system from Hell" and a storm system "of Biblical proportions." President Clinton was also a four-term governor of Arkansas, smack in the middle of America's Tornado Alley. He said of the storm, "I've been touring tornado sites for 20 years, mostly with [FEMA Director] James DeWitt, and I've never seen a more devastating storm."[2]

The Oklahoma City tornado was 55,000 feet tall, and between one half mile and one mile wide. It packed winds *topping 318 mph*. The Fujita Scale, used to measure tornado intensity, uses the word "incredible" to describe the force of an F-5 storm. Although there *have* been storm cells of this intensity in the past century, there has been nothing on the escalating order of magnitude witnessed during the 1990s. Every F-5 tornado ever recorded has made its entry into the history books. In the movie, *Twister*, the characters playing professional tornado chasers spoke of F-5 tornado cells in hushed tones of awe.

---

2 President Clinton sound byte on CNN, May 21, 1999

Scared Silly

> "And there shall be signs in the sun, and in the moon, and in the stars; and upon the earth distress of nations, with perplexity; the sea and the waves roaring; men's hearts failing them for fear, and for looking after those things which are coming on the earth: for the powers of heaven shall be shaken."[3]

For all the technical advances of the 20th century, humanity has never been faced with so many simultaneous perils threatening our very existence. The only thing more terrifying than the concept of destruction by nuclear war, global epidemic or famine is the fear of extraterrestrial catastrophe. Every few months some astronomer will discover a killer asteroid headed straight toward Earth, only to revise his estimates shortly thereafter. But that hasn't stopped the government from spending millions planning what to do when the inevitable cosmic disaster strikes.

Spinning Toward the Abyss

The year 1999 had a weird, surrealistic feeling to it. Almost like a sense of impending doom. Look at popular entertainment as we approached the turn of the century. The most popular films dealt with global disasters. Two of that year's blockbusters revolved around the question "What if an asteroid were on a collision course with

---

3 Luke 24:25-26 (KJV)

Earth?" One movie even called itself *Armageddon* after the Biblical last days' war that ends with the Second Coming of Christ.

Politically, America was no longer the bastion of moral authority it once was—not even in its own eyes. Communism, or a modified version of it, gained ground in a number of places around the world, most notably in Russia. Oil producing nations saw their revenues plummet and attempted to reinstate policies that brought the Middle East to the brink of war during the oil crises of the 1970s. A shrinking standard of living among the Muslim oil producing nations is a driving force behind resurgent Islamic fundamentalism. Nations like Pakistan are cracking down on moral crimes. Pakistan's code of justice demands the execution of convicted rapists within 24 hours of sentencing, for example. In Israel, it looks like the peace process is all but dead and war in the Middle East is inevitable. It seems as if things are spinning out of control.

Impending Doom, or Blessed Hope?

The good news is, nothing is spinning out of control. Instead, all the signs are pointing in exactly the opposite direction. The Bible predicted moral collapse in the last days. It predicted the rise of Muslim fundamentalism, the collapse of Russia, signs in the sun, moon and stars, and even the sense of impending doom we are discussing. The Bible predicted the controversy over Jerusalem and even the development of the European community. The Bible said all these things would begin at approximately the same point in history and would develop along parallel lines. Because that is exactly what is happening, it proves things aren't out of control, but carefully under control. Jesus told us this would happen, because He is in charge of it all. And He told us that, when we see all these things begin to come to pass, we should look up, and lift up our heads, for our redemption draws near. The feeling of impending doom is for everyone else. We have the assurance of knowing that the only way to predict an event is to be in control of it. Bible prophecy proves everything is under control and on schedule. We have nothing to fear. And we have a great hope in our immediate future.

Summary

Flooding and drought, both consequences of shifting weather patterns, are responsible for the famines that give rise to new epidemic diseases, which in turn exacerbate regional ethnic conflicts and civil war as nations fight over shrinking supplies of food, medicines, arable land and fresh water. You see, they are all related and accelerating each other.

Like birth pangs, each of the signs of the times is increasing in frequency. They are growing more intense. As I write these words, I am again staggered by the events I have been privileged to witness over my lifetime. And I am reminded of my own words from a talk show I did some months ago. The host, Warren Duffy, asked me how long until the Rapture. I told him then, "It could come even sooner than *I* think."

CHAPTER TWO

VANISHED
Into Thin Air

The Interpretation Debate

*I*n looking at the various interpretational methods used by the proponents of the different views of the timing of the Rapture of the Church, there is one thing we can all agree on. Every position has some problems. That includes the pre-Tribulational view.

But of all the different viewpoints, the one that *consistently* satisfies the majority of Scripture on the subject is the pre-Tribulational position.

It is all based on the rules of the interpretation. Literal interpretation lends itself most comfortably to a pre-Tribulational perspective. Each of the other views requires a certain amount of interpretational leeway, spiritualizing away any passages that are inconvenient.

I myself became convinced that the pre-Tribulational view was correct based on many, many elements, but the most convincing of all is the fact no other view more perfectly fits the literal interpretation of Scripture. All the rest of the positions fall short, as I will demonstrate as we progress through this book. For this reason, I remain a committed pre-Tribulationalist. The reason is simple. It answers all the hard questions. The rest don't.

Why This Book?

I decided to write this book because I see a growing confusion and anxiety developing throughout the body of Christ worldwide. This confusion and anxiety comes from an uncertainty about whether the true Church, which is composed of all true believers in Jesus regardless of denomination, will go through the Tribulation, or through the first half of the Tribulation, or will be taken out of the world by Jesus before the Tribulation begins.

In my opinion, this question is about the most important one a Christian of this generation can ask. In all probability, most of the people reading this book will live to experience the answer.

About 25 years ago this wouldn't have even been a question because most Christians didn't know much, if anything, about this issue. But since then there has been a flood of books, movies, teachers, and so forth, which have spread the message about the imminent return of the Lord Jesus Christ and the events that precede it. Teaching about these end-time prophecies has lately been met with great interest around the world.

When I set out to do the research on this book, I asked the Lord to overcome any prejudice or conditioning from the past, and to help me to be truly objective under the guidance of the Holy Spirit. My goal has not been to defend a view, but to seek the truth about when Christ is coming for His Church.

I determined that if I should find that I had been wrong on this issue, I would write a book acknowledging it.

I think it is important to bring out that as far as my own personal faith is concerned, if the Scriptures teach that the Church is to go through all or part of the Tribulation, I can certainly trust in God for His care and protection and press on. I want the truth, and I don't want to spread false hope, or to be found a liar before God. That thought is more frightening to me than the Tribulation.

But, on the other hand, if Christ's coming before the Tribulation for His Church, this great hope should be shouted from the rooftops. As our world continues to move toward greater and greater peril, this hope will have an explosive effect upon believers. According to the Scripture, it will bring greater purity of life, comfort and peace in the midst of a turbulent world and a bold witness for Christ.

In the months of study that followed, my main texts were the original languages of the Bible. However, I also read carefully the books of the major scholars representing the four different views about the time of Christ's coming for His Church. Many of these I had read before, but I wanted to make sure I had been fair with them.

A Few Terms You'll Need to Know

At this point it is necessary to introduce a few important theological terms.

The coming of Christ for the Church in which He instantly catches up all living believers to meet Him in the air and translates them into immortal bodies without experiencing physical death is called the "Rapture" (Corinthians 15:51-54; Thessalonians 4:15-18). The word *rapture* comes from a Latin translation of the Greek word ἁρπάζω in Thessalonians 4:17 which is translated in English as "caught up." It literally means "to seize" or "to snatch away." If I had my way, I would call the Rapture "the great snatch."

All who interpret the Bible in a literal sense believe in the fact of the Rapture and that it is distinct from the Second Coming of Christ. The dispute is over exactly when the Rapture occurs in relation to the Tribulation period.

Those who believe that the Church will go through the entire Tribulation and be raptured simultaneously with Jesus' return to the earth in the Second Coming are called "post-Tribulationists."

Those who believe that the Church will go through the first half of the Tribulation, and will be raptured and taken to heaven at the midpoint of the Tribulation, are called "mid-Tribulationists."

Those who believe that the Church will be raptured before the Tribulation begins, to be with Christ in heaven and to return with Him at the end of the Second Coming are called "pre-Tribulationists."

There is a very recent view that is a compromise between the mid- and post-Tribulation position. It is called the "pre-Wrath" view. It actually teaches that the Church will go through about 9/10th of the Tribulation. This view will be addressed later in the book.

I believe the following charts may help clarify the different views:

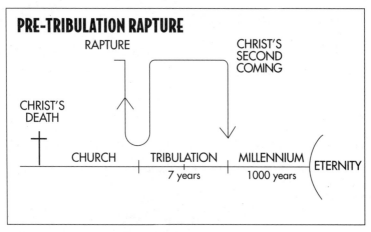

PRE-TRIBULATION RAPTURE

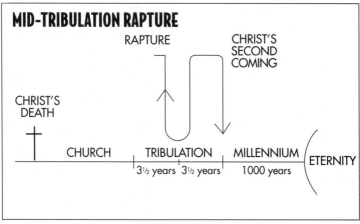

MID-TRIBULATION RAPTURE

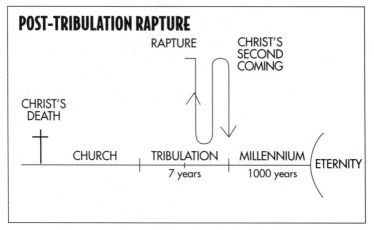

POST-TRIBULATION RAPTURE

The New Protestant Purgatory

There is a fifth view concerning the Rapture of the Church which also has recently been introduced. It is not widely taught, since it is unorthodox and at considerable variance with the Scripture. However, it is a view that could gain some following among those who are weak on knowledge of the Word of God and strong on experience and human viewpoint.

This view is in direct contradiction to one of the most central and important doctrines of all, that of salvation by grace through faith alone. It is commonly called the "Partial Rapture View."

There are some variations among its adherents, but generally it means the following: When the Lord Jesus comes to snatch away the true Church, only the spiritual believers will be taken. The carnal, or "backslidden" believers, will be left to go through the Tribulation. It's an interesting position, given the word "backslide" is an Old Testament term. A born again believer doesn't do anything to obtain his salvation, and he can't literally "backslide" to his former state. A more accurate term would be a "rebellious believer." Most adherents of this view believe that the partial Rapture will occur before the Tribulation.

This view is illustrated in the following chart:

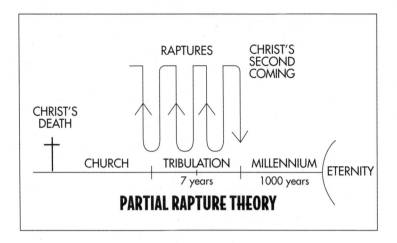

PARTIAL RAPTURE THEORY

Why So Many Views?

Many including myself have puzzled over why there are so many conflicting views concerning a doctrine that is so important. This question becomes even more mystifying when you realize the kinds of people who are involved in the disagreement.

This has been especially hard for me, because many of those with whom I disagree on this issue are people I know and respect.

Some Areas of Common Agreement

This is the crux of the problem, that all the principal scholars and exponents of pre-, post-, mid- Tribulationism, and pre-Wrath are born again, love the Lord, believe the Bible is the Word of God, desire to teach the truth, and as far as I know live godly lives.

Theologically, there is also a wide range of agreement. Almost all concerned hold to an orthodox view of the important central doctrines of the faith such as the person and work of Christ, justification by grace through faith, the inspiration of the Bible, and so forth.

In the field of prophecy (eschatology) there is general agreement that there will be a literal seven years of world Tribulation, that Jesus will return visibly and personally, that He will then set up a literal 1,000-year earthly kingdom over which He will rule, that mortals will repopulate the earth, that there will be a final judgment at "the great white throne" at the end of the 1,000 years when all unbelievers of all ages past will be finally condemned, and that eternity begins after this.

In other words, what I've described above is a Premillennial view of the Messiah's return and the Messianic kingdom. All the pre-, post-, mid-Tribulationists, and pre-Wrath are "Premillennialists." Just so you'll know what this means, on the following page I have charted three views of the millennial kingdom.

Postmillennialists, and proponents of its daughter, Reconstructionism, believes that the Church will overcome the world and bring the millennial period of peace and a perfect environment to earth on its own. Then the Messiah will come at the end of history and receive the kingdom from the Church. This view flourished in the late 19th and early 20th centuries, during a period of pseudo-optimism about the Church's missionary success and the effect of education on human nature.

But World War I seriously shook this view, and World

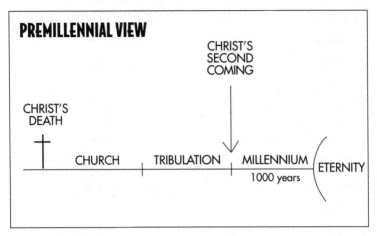

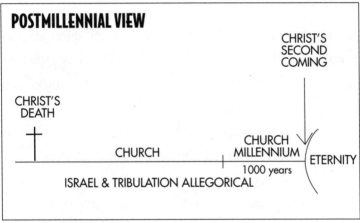

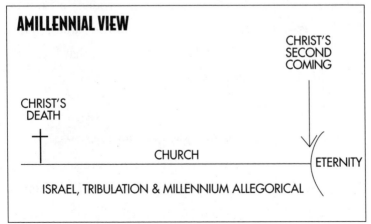

War II all but wiped it out. It should be noted that the view is founded on a gross mishandling of the prophetic Scriptures. The allegorical method of interpretation is used throughout.

The only way one can arrive at the Postmillennial view is by using an allegorical method of interpretation. This means that one assigns to words a meaning other than that normally understood and accepted at the time of writing.

No Millennium?

The term "Amillennial" means no millennium, and proponents of this view believe there will be no specific period of Tribulation, no fulfillment of Daniel's prophecy about the Seventieth Week and no millennial kingdom. Jesus will simply come at the end of history, judge all people, believers and unbelievers, and start eternity.

Much like the Postmillennialists, Amillennialists concede that if prophecy is interpreted literally (normally), grammatically, and historically it will produce a Premillennial view. The literal method allows for parable, allegory, and figures of speech, but recognizes that the context will clearly indicate when this is the case.

A Disagreement among Brothers

So it is good to remember that the pre-, post-, mid-Tribulationists and pre-Wrath apologists are all Premillennial, with all the good qualities and areas of agreement that we have just surveyed.

Such post-Tribulationists as Robert Gundry and George Ladd fit into the above category, and I have found as I have studied their books through the years that they were careful scholars. Others who believe this view, such as Pat Robertson, Walter Martin, Jim McKeever, etc., have served the Lord well.

The same is true of the mid-Tribulationists like Norman B. Harrison and J. Sidlow Baxter who are also scholars. This view became more popular with the release of books like Mary Stewart Relfe's, *When your Money Fails*. I enjoyed reading her book, with the exception of a few uncharitably critical generalizations she made about those who disagree with her.

And among the pre-Tribulation exponents, I've never found greater scholarship than that expressed by J. Dwight Pentecost, John F. Walvoord, and Charles C. Ryrie. The books of these men have dominated the scholarly side of prophetic study for decades, and they are virtually the standard in this field for our times.

I have found that almost all men who consistently proclaim a prophetic message in evangelism are pre-Tribulationists. My spiritual father, Col. Robert B. Thieme, Jr., a man who is still the best Bible teacher I have ever heard, is in this camp.

From Bouquets to Battle

You're probably saying by now, " If all these things are true, why is there disagreement about the time of the

Rapture's occurrence?" My opinion is this: Good men disagree because God deliberately made this issue difficult to settle. Only the most diligent study and comprehensive knowledge of the whole realm of Biblical prophecy can begin to answer it.

As an example, Dr. Gundry repeatedly says that pre-Tribulationism is based largely on arguments from inference and silence. This is in some measure true. But here is the big point: All of the views have to be developed to some degree on arguments from inference and silence.[4] The truth of the matter is that neither a post-, mid-, or pre-Tribulationist can point to any single verse that clearly says the Rapture will occur before, in the middle of, or after the Tribulation.

Can Anyone Offer a Sure Hope?

You may be saying, " Wow, if it's all that complicated, why bother?" I believe the first answer to that question is, "Because the Lord commanded us to seek to understand His prophetic Word." This is especially true in these last days.

Second, I believe that by comparing correlating prophecies on this issue, and by consistently adhering to the tried and proven literal method of interpretation, a sure answer to the Rapture question can be found. The most important element in this process, of course, is to consciously depend on the Holy Spirit for His guidance and illumination.

---

4 Robert H. Gundry, *The Church and the Tribulation* (Grand Rapids: Zondervan Pub. Co., 1976)

Third, as I said before, whatever the answer to the Rapture question is, we will most likely live to experience it. So how preeminently important the answer is for planning our lives for Jesus in this day and time!

I believe there is more confusion concerning the Rapture in the present day than at any time in Church history. Since I firmly believe that these are the final hours before the Tribulation begins, what *your* view of the Rapture is has enormous consequences. Whatever you believe on this imperative truth will determine how you prepare for the future, live today, and how effectively you serve the Lord.

This is *not* a trivial or unimportant subject. It just may be the most important subject you will ever settle in your mind.

CHAPTER THREE

What Is the Rapture, Exactly?

I will never forget the first time that I heard about "the Rapture." It was from a young minister in Houston, Texas, named Jack Blackwell. I was so excited that I could hardly sleep for a week.

But it wasn't long thereafter before I ran into some people who called the idea of Jesus coming for the Church before the Tribulation "a false doctrine." They even brought a minister to straighten me out on "this dangerous teaching."

The result was a real blessing because this motivated me to search the Scriptures on the issue many hours a day. In fact this was one of my first lessons in systematic study of the Bible. In the process, the whole course of my life was changed. It was during those days that I realized that I would never be happy apart from studying and teaching the Bible. All other ambitions faded into boredom in comparison to this newfound love.

There were times during this search that I experience the presence of the Holy Spirit in such power that I went into an ecstatic state. It was like lying in the ocean and feeling waves wash over me—only it was a physical experience of God's love moving over me.

During the course of these months I became completely convinced that the Lord Jesus would come for the true Christian before the Tribulation period. This conviction was not based only on what men taught me, but on a careful personal study of the Scriptures.

Now, more than 45 years later, I've rechallenged all the reasons for that hope of the Lord's pre-Tribulation Rapture. As you read the following chapters, I pray that you will also be motivated to search the Scriptures, so that you'll know *why* you believe what you believe.

"In the presence of God and of Christ Jesus, who will judge the living and the dead, and in view of his appearing and his kingdom, I give you this charge: Preach the Word; *be prepared in season and out of season***; correct, rebuke and encourage—with great patience and** *careful* **instruction"** (2 Timothy 4:1-2—emphases mine).

The most important place to start is with a careful examination of all the Biblical passages on the Rapture. They reveal that the Rapture has many unique factors.

I Love a Mystery

In 1 Corinthians, Chapter 15, the apostle Paul, under the inspiration of God's Spirit, is teaching about the certainty of every believer's resurrection from the dead. He also reveals that the resurrection body will be wonderfully changed into an eternal, immortal form that has real substance.

Paul clearly teaches that our new body will "**bear the image of the heavenly**," that is, like the Lord Jesus' resurrected body (verse 49). In this regard, he says, "**Flesh and blood cannot inherit the kingdom of God; nor does the perishable inherit the imperishable**" (verse 50).

In other words, our present body of flesh and blood, which must be sustained by elements of the earth, which are perishable, must be changed to another form. This new form has material being, but it is of a kind that is suited for the spiritual, imperishable, eternal atmosphere of heaven.

The resurrected Lord Jesus is the measure of our future existence. He could appear and disappear at will (Luke 24:31; John 20:19). He could move through solid walls (John 20:19, 26). He could be seen and felt (Matthew 28:9; Luke 24:36-42). He could eat food, though it apparently wasn't necessary (Luke 24:41-43). Though glorified, Jesus could be recognized (Luke 24:30-31). Our resurrected bodies will no longer experience death, aging, crying mourning, sorrow, or pain (Revelation 21:4)

The above are just a few of the wonders that we believers will experience in our future resurrected bodies. One thing, however, is necessary to be resurrected: We must first die! Resurrection is only for the dead. Resurrection from the dead was certainly a hope clearly taught in the Old Testament.

A New Truth

In the midst of Paul's teaching on the resurrection he says, **"Behold, I tell you a mystery; we shall not all sleep, but we shall all be changed"** (1 Corinthians 15:5). There are many important truths taught in this verse. First, Paul says he is introducing a mystery. The moment Paul uses the word "mystery," it signals that he is going to reveal a new truth not known before. The word in the original Greek (μυστήριον), as used in the New Testament, means something not previously known, but now revealed to the true believer.

So what is it that is new? In this chapter he has summed up what was known in the Old Testament: that flesh and blood cannot enter God's presence; that we must first die and then be raised in a new eternal form.

The Rapture Means No Death

The second truth in this verse, and the meaning of the mystery, is that we Christians are not all going to die! This was a totally new concept. No Old Testament believer dreamed that some future generation would enter eternity and God's presence without experiencing physical death. Death is an absolute prerequisite to entering immortality through resurrection.

There were two partial examples of the Rapture in the cases of Enoch and Elijah. They were taken directly into heaven without experiencing physical death. But even Enoch and Elijah haven't yet received their immortal bodies. As for the Old Testament believer in general, no one dared to believe that there would be a future generation of believers who would be taken en masse to God's presence.

The truly electrifying fact is that many of you who are reading this will experience this mystery. You will never know what it is to die physically. Think of it! I believe

there are people *alive today* who will never, ever, die! A
Blessed Hope, indeed!

The Rapture Includes All

The third truth in this verse is that all believers at the
time of the Rapture will escape physical death. It is not an
accident, I'm sure, that God selected the Corinthians to be
the recipients of this revelation. For of all the early churches
the New Testament records, the Corinthian church was the
most carnal.

Paul rebukes them for everything from fornication
(6:15-20) to getting drunk at communion (11:20-22). Yet
Paul says to them, **"We all will be changed."**

A famous Supreme Court decision defined the world
all as follows: "All includes everyone, and excludes no
one." That's a very apt definition for how many believers
go at the Rapture. Some will regretfully be raptured while
out of fellowship with God. This may result in a loss of
rewards for service, but not participation in the Rapture.
We base this on the same foundation upon which we base
our salvation. It is **"by grace through faith, and that not
of ourselves, it is a gift of God."** (See 1 Corinthians 3:10-
15 and Ephesians 2:8-9.) There is no Scriptural basis for
a partial Rapture. The Rapture must be based on the same
principles as salvation.

The Rapture Is a Transformation

The fourth truth revealed in the mystery of the Rapture
is that "all Christians will be changed." The Greek word

ἀλλάσσω translated "be changed" literally means "to be transformed." All Christians will be transformed in body and nature into new bodies that are suited for the eternal, spiritual, incorruptible realm in which God dwells.

All the things Paul teaches in this chapter about the resurrection body are true of the Rapture except that they are bestowed apart from death. The extent of this trans-formation is the greatest thing God could bestow upon us. He transforms us into the exact likeness of His glorified Son, the Lord Jesus Christ.

"For our citizenship is in heaven, from which also we eagerly wait for a Savior, the Lord Jesus Christ; who will transform the body of our humble state into conformity with the body of His glory, by the exertion of the power that He has even subject all things to Himself" (Philippians 3:20-21).

The Rapture Is Instantaneous

Paul says, **"In a moment, in the twinkling of an eye, at the last trumpet; for the trumpet will sound, and the dead will be raised imperishable, and we shall be changed"** (1 Corinthians 15:52). Someone said that the twinkling of an eye is about one-thousandth of a second. The Greek word is ἄτομος from which we get the word atom. It means something that cannot be divided. In other words, the Rapture will occur so quickly and suddenly that the time frame in which it occurs cannot be humanly divided.

Just think of it . . . in the flash of a second every living believer on earth will be gone! Suddenly, without warning, only unbelievers will be populating Planet Earth.

I recently watched in awe as the latest space shuttle mission blasted off into space. Within a matter of a few minutes it was out of sight and traveling at more than six times the speed of sound. What will take place for each living believer at the Rapture surpasses this by all comparison.

In another crucial passage on the Rapture, God reveals to us what will occur while we are being instantaneously transformed into immortal bodies, **"For this we say to *you by the word of the Lord,* that we who are alive, and remain until the coming of the Lord, shall not precede those who have fallen asleep. For the Lord Himself will descend from heaven with a shout, the voice of the archangel, and with the trumpet of God; and the dead in Christ shall rise first. Then we who are alive and remain shall be caught up together with them in the clouds to meet the Lord in the air, and thus we shall always be with the Lord. Therefore comfort one another with these words"** (1 Thessalonians 4:15-18).

Will We See our Loved Ones Again?

The apostle Paul wrote these words to reassure the Thessalonians who had believing loved ones who had died. They were afraid that their departed loved ones would be in some other part of God's plan. Therefore, they feared that those who were raptured would not see their dear ones again in eternity. Paul's answer is as amazing as it is comforting. For he assures them that not only will we again see Christian loved ones who have died, but that they will receive their resurrection bodies a split second before we are transformed into immortality.

The key word is " we shall be caught up." This is the translation of the Greek verb harpazo (ἁρπάζω). As I mentioned earlier, it literally means " to snatch out" or to seize." When we put together the concept of "**being caught up into the clouds to meet the Lord in the air**" together with the idea of an instantaneous transformation, the result is spine-tingling.

We will suddenly one day just blast off into space. Faster than the eye of the unbeliever can perceive, every living believer on earth will vanish. The world will probably hear a great sonic boom from all our transformed immortal bodies cracking the sound barrier. But the rest will be a mystery.

The Rapture Is a Reunion

As for us, one moment we will be going about our life here on earth; the next moment we will be hurtled into the presence of departed loved ones. And above all, we will have a face-to-face meeting with the One whose death in our place made it all happen.

Another very wonderful experience is predicted in 1 Thessalonians. The apostle Paul reveals that we will not only be reunited with all our Christian relatives and loved ones, but with all those persons who trusted in Jesus through our witness. He said of those Thessalonians to whom he had ministered, **"for who is our hope or joy or crown of exultation? Is it not even you, in the presence of our Lord Jesus at His coming?"** Paul says that these spiritual children of his will be **"his crown of exultation in the Lord's presence when He comes."** It appears that each one of us will have grouped around us those we have helped to believe in Jesus.

I don't know about you, but that excites me out of my mind! It makes me want to redouble efforts to witness for the Lord Jesus. To see even one person standing there before our Savior in a glorified body because I was available for the Holy Spirit to work through will be the most wonderful "crown" of all.

A Meeting in the Air

It is very important to note that **"We will be caught up in the clouds to meet the Lord in the air"** (1 Thessalonians 4:17). There is a major point of controversy between the pre-Tribulationists and the post-Tribulationist over what happens next.

The post-Tribulationists say that after meeting the Lord in the air we will immediately return with Him to the earth. They agree that all believers alive at the time will be instantly transformed into immortal bodies. But since this event, in their view, occurs in connection with the Second Coming, believers will meet the Lord in the air only to return immediately with Him to earth. In thoroughly examining this scenario, I find that it poses some unanswerable problems with other Scripture passages that deal with events that immediately follow the Second Coming. The pre-Wrath Rapture view has almost the same problem. All these problems will be pointed out later, but let's take up one here.

To the Father's House

Pre-Tribulationists believe that a very important personal promise of the Lord is fulfilled when we meet the Lord in the air. As Jesus taught the disciples at the Last Supper, He sought to comfort and reassure them concerning His imminent departure with this promise, **"Let not your heart be troubled; believe in God, believe also in Me. In my Father's house are many dwelling places; if it were not so, I would have told you; for I go to prepare a place for you. And if I go and prepare a place for you, I will come again and receive you to Myself; so that where I am, there you may be also"** (John 14:1-3).

Let us make several observations about this prophecy.

First, Jesus specifically makes this promise to believers in the Church. For His whole teaching at the Last Supper (which has been designated The Upper Room Discourse) emphasized the revolutionary new privileges that would come to each believer when He ascended to the Father and sent the Holy Spirit to take up permanent residence in them. It is these very privileges that make the age in which we live unique and vastly distinct from God's previous dealing with Old Testament believers in general and Israel in particular.

Second, Jesus gives a very specific location around which the whole prophecy revolves. Jesus said, **"I am going to prepare a place for you."** And that place is specifically **"His Father's house."** We know from passages like Psalm 110:1 that when Jesus left and ascended, He went to God the Father's presence and took a seat at His right hand.

Jesus continued and said that as certainly as He was going to the Father's house to prepare a place for us, that He would come again and take us to that place to be with Him.

Third, Jesus gives us the specific time that all the above will be fulfilled. It be at the time He returns for the true Church, for He says, **"I will come again, and receive you to Myself; that where I am [in the Father's house] there you may be also."**

Now if Jesus is building a dwelling place for us in the Father's house, and if we are to go there when He comes for the Church, how could He be speaking of an event that occurs simultaneously with the Second Advent? For at that time Jesus is specifically and personally coming to the earth (see Zechariah 14:4-9).

If the post-Tribulationists are right, then Jesus is engaged in a futile construction project. For when He comes to the earth in the Second Coming, He will rule out of the earthly Jerusalem for a thousand years. Since He says He is going to come in order that we may be with Him where he is, we would have to be with Him here on earth. Do you see the problem? The dwelling place in the Father's house *would be unused*. And worse by far, Jesus would be guilty of telling us a lie! For as we have seen, He is coming for the purpose of taking us to the Father's house at that time.

Post-Tribulationist Robert Gundry doesn't keep this passage in context when he says, "Jesus does not promise that upon His return He will take believers to mansions in the Father's house. Instead, He promises, 'Where I am, there you may be also.'"[5]

This makes Jesus' whole promise ridiculous. Why would He speak of preparing a place in the Father's house for us if He didn't mean that His return was to take us there? With all due respect, Gundry has violated a basic principle of interpretation here; i.e, to keep verses in context. The passage is clear to the simple folk. It takes real determination to find Gundry's interpretation in the passage.

Gundry goes on to make a truly novel allegorical interpretation of John 14:1-3.

"In order to console the disciples concerning His going away, Jesus tells them that His leaving will work to their advantage. He is going to prepare for them spiritual abodes within His own person.

5 Robert Gundry, *The Church and the Tribulation* (Grand Rapids, Mich.: Zondervan Pub. House, 1973), p. 153

Dwelling in these abiding places they will belong to God's household. This He will accomplish by going to the cross and then ascending to the Father. But He will return to receive the disciples into His immediate presence forever. Thus, the Rapture will not have the purpose of taking them to heaven. It rather follows from their being in Christ, in whom each believer already has an abode."[6]

This interpretation surprised me. Gundry usually tries to avoid the allegorical method of interpretation. I strongly disagree with him here because it takes a passage which gives every indication of being literal narrative and makes part of it allegorical.

Jesus was literally taking His physical presence away form the disciples. This is exactly why they were troubled. Jesus also literally went to take a seat at the Father's right hand. There is absolutely no indication in the context that the dwelling places He is preparing and His return to take us there are allegorical.

Later Jesus does promise that He will be with us spiritually through the indwelling Holy Spirit, and that we will experience a mystical union with Him personally. But the context is very clear that this is what is literally meant (see John 14:15-26; 16:7-25).

Once again let us remember some basic principles of interpretation. First, if the literal sense makes common sense, seek no other sense. Second, all things are intended

---

6 *Ibid.*, p. 154

to be taken literally unless the context clearly indicates otherwise.

Put It All Together

Let us briefly sum up what the Scriptures covered in this chapter have taught about the Rapture.

1. The Rapture was unknown until it was revealed to the Church by the apostles, especially Paul.

2. All believers living when the Rapture occurs will not experience physical death.

3. The Rapture will occur suddenly, without specific warning, and will be instantaneous.

4. In the Rapture, every living believer will be instantly transformed from mortal to immortal bodies that are like Jesus' glorified body.

5. Those raptured will be caught up in the air to meet the Lord and the resurrected Church-Age believers who have died.

6. At that time, we will be taken into God the Father's presence to temporary dwelling places that the Lord Jesus is presently preparing.

The post-, mid- and pre-Tribulationists would agree on all the points above except number 6 and part of number 3.

Academics aside, the really important issue is the wonder of it all! What a marvelous expectation exists for this generation! No wonder Paul taught after revealing the great hope of the Rapture, **"Therefore, my beloved** brethren be steadfast, immovable, always abounding in the work of the Lord, knowing that you toil is not in vain in the Lord" (Corinthians 15:58).

We can be steadfast and immovable in the midst of a turbulent and increasingly dangerous world, because we know that it means the Lord's coming is drawing near. Prophecy of the Rapture shines ever brighter as darkness gathers about us.

An Ancient Lesson in Hope

The earliest account of the resurrection hope in the Old Testament is recorded in the book of Job. Job actually lived before Abraham and Moses. Job took up the age-old question of resurrection when he said, **"If a man dies, will he live again? All the days of my struggle I will wait [patiently trust],** *until my change comes"* (Job 14:14—italics mine). Job responds to his own question by saying he would patiently trust until his change into a new resurrected body came.

Job states an incredible faith in his own resurrection, considering the early period of Divine revelation in which he lived, **"For I know that my redeemer liveth, and that he shall stand at the latter days upon the earth; and though after my skin worms destroy this body, yet in my flesh shall I see God, whom I shall see for myself, and mine eyes shall behold, and not another; though my heart be consumed within me"** (Job 19:25-27, KJV). This is particularly amazing because at the time this was declared, there was no known written revelation from God.

This proves, along with many other Old Testament verses that could be quoted, that resurrection was known and believed throughout man's history of redemption, which began soon after mankind's appearance upon earth. If it was true in Job's day, it is no less true today.

The following chart will help you understand the order of resurrections in relation to the Rapture.

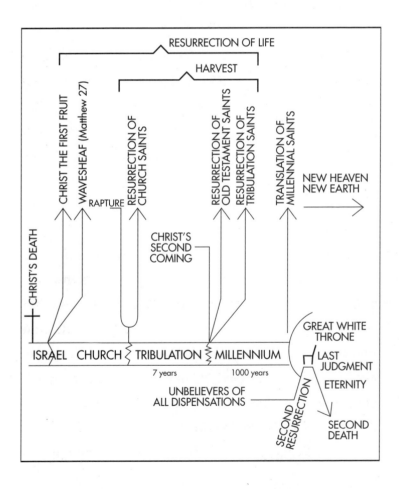

CHAPTER FOUR

Controlling the Imagination

> "About the time of the End, a body of men will be raised up who will turn their attention to the prophecies, and insist on their literal interpretation in the midst of much clamor and opposition."
>
> —Sir Isaac Newton (AD 1643-1727)

*A*s I have already mentioned, the most critical factor in determining the meaning of prophecy in general and the pre-Tribulation Rapture position specifically is literal interpretation.

There are two basic ways of interpreting Scripture. One is to draw the meaning *from* the text itself. The other is to read a meaning *into* the text that is foreign to the normal sense of the words, grammar, and context.

The first method is commonly called *exegesis*. It is formed from two Greek words: ἐκ, out of; and ἡγέομα, to lead. The literal meaning is "to lead out." The goal of this method is to allow the normal meaning of the words, grammar, and context to speak for itself.

The second method might best be described as *eisegesis*, which means to read into the text an allegorical or mythical meaning that is different from the natural meaning of the passage. This would best describe the method used by the Amillennialists, Postmillennialists and their recent offspring Dominionists or Reconstructionists.

In varying degrees this method is also used by the mid-Tribulationists, pre-Wrath Rapture proponents and post-Tribulationists.

A Cardinal Maxim

It gets back to one of the cardinal maxims of interpretation: every passage has one basic meaning but many applications. You must first find the meaning of a passage before applying it, not start with your conclusion and find a Biblical illustration to support it.

The most common criticism leveled against me by my adversaries is that I see "Cobra helicopters" as possibly being described in Revelation 9:5-10. This was presented as an opinion in my book *The Apocalypse Code*,[7] in which I gave a detailed explanation for it. Whatever this passage means, it is a composite description from many different things that is obviously intended to be symbolic. There is no insect, beast, or man in nature that fits what is described. Ample evidence can be found within the Book of Revelation to establish that John wrote about things he *saw* and *heard* while projected into the future. I believe John actually saw and heard things by direct Divine revelation that were centuries future to his own time and still future to us. He was then commanded to write about what he had seen. He therefore had to describe very advanced scientific creations of a much later time in terms of his first-century knowledge and experience. This is my

7 Lindsey, Hal. *The Apocalypse Code,* Western Front Ltd. (1998)

opinion, and I believe it makes good sense. If you don't buy that, it's okay with me; show me something better.

How to Avoid Error

The most important single principle in determining the true meaning of any doctrine of our faith is that we start with the clear statements of the Scriptures that specifically apply to it, and use those to interpret the parables, allegories, and obscure passages. This allows Scripture to interpret Scripture. The Reconstructionists in particular frequently reverse this order, seeking to interpret the clear passages by obscure passages, parables, and allegories.

The second most important principle is to consistently interpret by the literal, grammatical, historical method. This means the following:

- each word should be interpreted in the light of its normal, ordinary usage that was accepted in the times in which it was written;
- each sentence should be interpreted according to the rules of grammar and syntax normally accepted when the document was written;
- each passage should also be interpreted in the light of its historical and cultural environment.

Most false doctrine and heresy of Church history can be traced to a failure to adhere to these principles. Church history is filled with examples of disasters and wrecked lives wrought by men failing to base their doctrine, faith, and practice upon these two principles.

The Reformation, more than anything else, was caused by an embracing of the literal, grammatical, and historical method of interpretation, and a discarding of the allegorical method. The allegorical system veiled the Church's understanding of many vital truths for nearly a thousand years.

Alexandria, the Beginning of Darkness

As briefly mentioned previously, darkness began to envelop the Church from the time the theological school of Alexandria began to rise to prominence. Dr. J. Dwight Pentecost, in his book *Things to Come*, which is a classic in scholarly interpretation of prophecy, quotes F. W. Farrar concerning the impact of the Alexandrian school:

"It was in the great catechetical school of Alexandria, founded (according to tradition) by St. Mark, that there sprang up the chief school of Christian Exegesis. Its object, like that of Philo [a Jewish allegorist who loved Greek philosophy], was to unite philosophy with revelation, and thus to use the borrowed 'jewels of Egypt' to adorn the sanctuary of God. Hence, CLEMENT of Alexandria and ORIGEN furnishes the direct antithesis of TERTULLIAN and IRENAEUS. The first teacher of the school who rose to fame was the venerable Pantaenus, a converted Stoic, of whose writings only a few fragments remain. He was succeeded by Clement of Alexandria, who, believing in the divine origin of Greek philosophy, openly propounded the principle that all Scripture must be allegorically understood."[8]

One of the main reasons, then, for the initial raise of the allegorical method of interpretation within the Church was to facilitate the integration of Greek philosophy with the inspired Scriptures.

Premier Church historian Philip Schaff, who was not a Premillennialist, gave an unbiased assessment of Origen's method of interpretation that was passed on to the Church at large.

"Origen was the first to lay down, in connection with the allegorical method of the Jewish Platonist, Philo, a formal theory of interpretation, which he carried out in a long series of exegetical works remarkable for industry and ingenuity, but meager in solid results. He considered the Bible a living organism, consisting of three elements that answer to the body, soul, and spirit of man, after the Platonic psychology. Accordingly he attributed to the Scriptures a threefold sense: (1) a somatic [body], literal, or historical sense, furnished immediately by the meaning of the words, but only serving as a veil for a higher idea; (2) a psyche [soul] or moral sense, animating the first, and serving for general edification; (3) a

8 F. W. Farrar, quoted by J. Dwight Pentecost *Things to Come* (Finley, OH: Dunham Publishing Co., 1958) p. 22

pneumatic [spirit] or mystic and ideal sense, for those who stand on the high ground of philosophical knowledge, In the application of this theory he shows the same tendency as Philo, to spiritualize away the letter of Scripture . . . and instead of simply bringing out the sense of the Bible, HE PUTS INTO IT ALL SORTS OF FOREIGN IDEAS AND IRRELEVANT FANCIES"9 (emphasis mine).

The Blessing and Curse of Augustine

Pentecost accurately points out the reason for the rapid adoption by the Church of Origen's views: "It was the rise of ecclesiasticism and the recognition of the authority of the church in all doctrinal matters that gave great impetus to the adoption of the allegorical method. Augustine, according to Farrar, was one of the first to make Scripture conform to the interpretation of the church."10 Pentecost then quotes Farrar:

"The exegesis of St. Augustine is marked by the most glaring defects. . . . He laid down the rule that the Bible must be interpreted with reference to Church Orthodoxy, and that no Scriptural expression can be out of accordance with any other. . . . Snatching up the old Philonian and Rabinic rule

---

9 Shaff, Philip, *Ante-Nicene Christianity: AD 100-325,* Vol. 2 of *A History of the Christian Church* (Grand Rapids, MI: Wm. B. Eerdmans Publishing Co., 1958) p. 521

10 Pentecost, op. cit., p. 23

which has been repeated for so many generations, that everything in Scripture which appeared to be unorthodox or immoral must be interpreted mystically, he introduced confusion into his dogma of supernatural inspiration by admitting that there are many passages 'written by the Holy Ghost,' which are objectionable when taken in their obvious sense. He also opened the door to arbitrary fancy. . . . When once the principle of allegory is admitted, when once we start with the rule that whole passages and books of the Scripture say one thing when they mean another, the reader is delivered bound and hand and foot to the caprice of the interpreter. He can be sure of absolutely nothing except what is dictated to him by the Church, and in all ages the authority of the Church has been falsely claimed for the presumptuous tyranny of false prevalent opinions."[11]

The record of Church history shows that the Alexandrian school's system of allegorical interpretation of the Bible did not arise out of a pursuit of a better understanding of God's message, but rather out of the desire to integrate Greek philosophy with the Scriptures. It grew out of the erroneous assumption that these philosophies were equal in Divine inspiration with the Word of God.

Augustine not only accepted this cursed allegorical method, but added another equally dangerous principle—

---

11 quoted by Pentecost, *ibid.* p. 23

that the Church has authority superior to the Scriptures. The Roman Popes later grabbed hold of this error and developed two even greater errors—Papal infallibility and the exclusive authority of the priests to interpret the Bible. This resulted in the greatest curse of all; the Bible was removed from the common man's hands. This was the greatest single cause of the "Dark Ages."

Augustine was both a blessing and a curse. He was a blessing in that he used a more literal method of interpretation in establishing the doctrine of justification by faith, which was orthodox.

He was a curse in that he so powerfully injected the allegorical method of interpretation into the bloodstream of the Church that it prevailed for over 1,000 years. Virtually all Bible prophecy was viewed as allegory. Ironically, the Church later used his teaching concerning its superior authority over the Scriptures and the allegorical method of interpretation to explain away Augustine's orthodox view of justification by faith alone.

The late David Chilton, a prominent Reconstruction teacher, helped me to understand where he got his method of interpretation when he said, as he was teaching a series on the Book of Revelation, "Believe me, this is not brainy David Chilton coming up with a bunch of new ideas. You know what I did? I went back to the Church Fathers and I read Saint Athenasius. I read Saint AUGUSTINE and saw what he had to say about the mark of the beast. He says some very profound things. I saw what the Church Fathers said about this stuff, and the kind of EXEGESIS they did. . . ."[12]

Chilton got his system of interpretation from studying the Church Fathers who had all swallowed Origen's allegorical system. In essence, he ignored the example of the Apostolic Fathers (who were virtually all literalists), leapfrogged right over the lessons of the post-Reformation, and plunged headlong into the allegorical method of interpretation that gave us the Dark Ages. (R.I.P.)

The Impact of the Reformation on Interpretation

The courageous Bible scholar William Tyndale (1494-1536) was one of the important spiritual lamps who showed the way to the Reformation. He said concerning Bible interpretation, "Thou shalt understand, therefore, that the Scripture hath but one sense, which is the literal sense. And that literal sense is the root and ground of all, and the anchor that never faileth, whereunto if thou cleave, thou canst never err or go out of the way. And if thou leave the literal sense, thou canst not but to go out of the way."[13]

Tyndale was tried and convicted of heresy by the Catholic Church for the terrible crime of translating the Bible into the common language of the people. For his "heinous act" he was burned at the stake. *Foxe's Book of Martyrs* records that he was burned in a fire kindled with

---

12 Tape #4 of a series by David Chilton at Reformation Covenant Church, August 8, 1987
13 William Tyndale, quoted by Pentecost op. cit., p. 27

the pages of his own Bibles. But thank God his work was not in vain. His martyrdom ignited the flames of reformation that spread to the Continent and Martin Luther. His translation work later became the basis of the King James Bible.

When Luther turned to the literal, grammatical, historical method of interpretation, the Reformation was born. Luther said, "Every word should be allowed to stand in its natural meaning and that should not be abandoned unless faith forces us to it. . . ."[14] Unfortunately, he applied this method to all Scriptures except to the interpretation of prophecy. There he continued in the tradition of Augustine.

Luther, nevertheless, was used in an extraordinary way to recover the doctrines of salvation. To stand on the edge of a theological precipice staring back into a thousand years of institutionalized spiritual darkness, and then, in spite of all of the consequences, to choose to stand on the literal, naked statements of the Word of God, was a remarkable demonstration of faith.

John Calvin was one of the first of the reformers to truly systematize and apply the literal grammatical method of interpretation. But there was one major problem. The reformers were not concerned with prophecy per se. They were primarily concerned with the doctrine of salvation.

---

14 Martin Luther, quoted by Pentecost ibid., op. cit., p. 27

The Forerunners of Serious Prophetic Studies

In the 17th century, a few scholars began to apply the light of the reformer's interpretive methods to the study of prophecy. The great scientist Sir Isaac Newton (AD 1643-1727) was one of those men who began to study prophecy as something other than just a collection of allegories, symbols, poems, and meaningless metaphors that had already been fulfilled in past history. After a lifetime of studying Bible prophecy, Newton acted as an unwitting prophet when he predicted the following: "About the time of the End a body of men will be raised up who will turn their attention to the prophecies, and insist upon their literal interpretation in the midst of much clamor and opposition."[15] All I can say is, "Amen."

The Bible scholar Bishop Richard Hooker (1553-1600) was also a trailblazer for the literal interpretation of prophecy. He said the following about those who had followed in the tradition of Origen and Augustine: "I hold it for a most infallible rule, that where a literal construction will stand, the farthest from the letter is commonly the worst. Nothing is more dangerous than this licentious deluding art which changes the meaning of words as Alchemy does, or would do, the substance of metals, makes of anything what it lists, and brings in the end all truth to nothing."[16]

---

15 Sir Isaac Newton, quoted by Nathaniel West D.D., *The Thousand Years in Both Testaments* (New York: Fleming H Revel, 1880) p. 462
16 Bishop Richard Hooker, quoted by Nathaniel West *ibid*

LITERAL, GRAMMATICAL, AND HISTORICAL INTERPRETATION DEFINED

To interpret literally does not mean that there is no recognition of allegories, parables, or figures of speech in the Scriptures. Once again, it means to take each word and passage in its plain, common, normal, literal sense unless the context clearly demands otherwise. Dr. David L. Cooper, Hebrew scholar and missionary to Israel, gave the golden rule of Biblical interpretation: "When the plain sense of Scripture makes common sense, seek no other sense; therefore, take every word at its primary, ordinary, usual literal meaning unless the facts of the immediate context, studied in the light of related passages and axiomatic and fundamental truths, indicate clearly otherwise."[17]

Cooper succinctly states the whole issue. All interpreters should follow this rule. When the Bible uses all allegory or figure of speech, it is usually obvious. But when an interpreter arbitrarily takes a passage that is obviously intended to be a literal statement of fact, and treats it as allegory, he is twisting the Word of God and knowingly perverting its meaning.

The following are some examples of how the Lord Jesus, the ultimate Exegete, interpreted the Old Testament.

Example #1, Jesus Interpreted Literally

The Lord Jesus left us some supreme examples of how

---

17 David L. Cooper, *The God Of Israel* (Los Angeles: Biblical Research Society, 1945), front page

to interpret the Word of God. Jesus *literally* interpreted a prophecy about Himself in a debate with the Pharisees concerning what kind of person the Messiah would truly be.

Late in the Lord's ministry, the Pharisees engaged Him in a debate in order to trap Him in a statement they could use to convict Him of blasphemy. After a few questions, the Lord Jesus fired one question that immediately silenced them for the rest of His ministry. Here is the question that left them on the horns of a dilemma:

> **"Now while the Pharisees were gathered together, Jesus asked them a question, saying, 'What do you think about the Messiah, whose son is He?' They said to Him, 'The son of David.' He said to them, 'Then why does David in the Spirit call Him "LORD," saying, "The LORD said to MY LORD, 'Sit at My right hand, until I put Thine enemies beneath Thy feet'"? If David then calls Him "LORD," how is He his son?' And no one was able to answer Him a word, nor did anyone dare from that day on to ask Him another question"** (Matthew 22:41-46, NASB).

The Lord Jesus baited a logical trap for the Pharisees. He knew what their answer would be, that the Messiah is the son of David. He then set the trap by reminding them that David was under the inspiration of the Spirit of God when wrote Psalm 110. The Pharisees vigorously professed to believe this. Jesus then forced them to see the logical inconsistency of their interpretation of this prophecy. Jesus pointed out that David himself recognized his future descendant not only to be the Messiah, but **his Lord**. David applied to his son a title reserved only for Deity. Jesus drove home the fact that there were two persons called **LORD** in this prophecy, and the second person David called **"his LORD."**

The dilemma was this, "How could David's own son also be his Lord?"

If the Messiah was only to be the physical descendant of David, then why did David, under the inspiration of the Holy Spirit, call Him by the title of Deity?

The only answer was *the Messiah had to be not only a true man, but also God.* No wonder the Pharisees kept quiet. They either had to completely change their theology and admit that Jesus' claim to be the Messiah and equal with God was consistent with Messianic prophecy, or say that the Scriptures were in error. They couldn't consistently deny either one of these propositions, so they kept quiet. A short time later they crucified Jesus for claiming to be God's own unique Son, the very thing prophecy said He had to be.

Now, this whole argument revolved around taking the clause **"The LORD said to my LORD"** literally. The Pharisees refused to do so because it didn't fit their preconceived theology. They held it impossible for God to become a man.

I believe all those who use allegorical interpretation are making the same sort of error today.

An example is the Reconstructionists' teaching that there will be no personal Antichrist, yet 2 Thessalonians 2:1-12 clearly predicts such a person. But the Reconstructionists' doctrine of "optimism" hinders them from being objective with the passage. They cannot accept the clear teaching of this passage which says that the Man of Lawlessness will not only declare himself to be God, but personally oppose the Lord Jesus Christ at His Second Coming. The reason is because the Reconstructionists would have to admit that this present age will end in a great cataclysm and not with the Church conquering the world and establishing the Kingdom of God.

Example #2, Jesus Interpreted Grammatically

On another occasion, Jesus debated the Sadducees concerning the resurrection of the dead (which they didn't believe). His whole argument turned upon the Hebrew grammatical construction that described God as *perpetually being* the God of Abraham, Isaac, and Jacob. Jesus taught, **"But regarding the resurrection of the dead, have you not read that which was spoken to you by God, saying, 'I AM the God of Abraham, and the God of Isaac, and the God of Jacob'? He is not the God of the dead but of the living"** (Matthew 22:31-32, NASB).

Jesus quoted this from Exodus 3:6 and took it at literal face value. He testified that this is what God had said, and to Him it was the ultimate authority. His argument was based on a minute point of grammar. If the Scripture had said, **"I WAS the God of Abraham, Isaac, and Jacob,"** then God would have indeed been the God of the dead. But since God used a grammatical construction in Hebrew that means continuous being, it revealed that Abraham, Isaac, and Jacob were alive before Him, and would continue to be alive, which demanded a resurrection.

Example #3, Jesus Recognized Double Reference in Prophecy

One of the most instructive examples of the Lord Jesus' interpretations of prophecy is recorded in Luke 4:14-21:

"Jesus returned to Galilee IN THE POWER OF THE SPIRIT, and news about him spread through the whole countryside. He taught in their synagogues and everyone praised him.

"He went to Nazareth, where he had been brought up, and on the Sabbath day he went into the synagogue, as was his custom. And He stood up to read. The scroll of the Prophet Isaiah was handed to him. Unrolling it, he found the place where it is written:

"'The SPIRIT OF THE LORD IS ON ME, because he had anointed me to preach good news to the poor. He has sent me to proclaim freedom for the prisoners and recovery of sight for the blind, to release the oppressed, to proclaim the year of the LORD's favor. . . . [Jesus read to this point, then quit right in the middle of a sentence. See Isaiah 61:1-2 from which He was quoting.]

"Then he rolled up the scroll, gave it back to the attendant and sat down. The eyes of everyone in the synagogue were fastened on him, and he began by saying to them. 'TODAY THIS SCRIPTURE IS FULFILLED IN YOUR HEARING'" (emphases mine).

Everyone in the synagogue was startled by Jesus' strange behavior. It was not customary to read only a short passage of Scripture. And it was absolutely unprecedented for a reader in the synagogue to quit in the middle of a sentence without completing it, especially when it dealt with this subject. But the statement that should have immediately brought the house down on its knees was, **"Today this Scripture is fulfilled in your hearing."** It was such an enormous claim that its full meaning didn't hit them immediately. When a person makes a claim like this, from a passage that all recognized as predicting the Messiah, one either falls on his face and worships him, or stones him for blasphemy.

But another imperative lesson Jesus taught relates to His method of interpreting the prophecy of Isaiah Chapter 61. Jesus demonstrates for us how to lead forth from the text the meaning of these vital and sometimes difficult prophecies.

As noted in the quote above, Jesus stopped in the middle of a sentence and rolled up the scroll. The very next phrase of that sentence says, **". . . and the day of vengeance of our God . . ."** (Isaiah 61:2b). A careful study of the context, beginning with this phrase, reveals that it is a prophecy of the events connected with the Second Coming of Christ. Had Jesus continued, He could not have said, **"Today this Scripture is fulfilled in your hearing."** Associated with **"the day of vengeance of our God"** are such things as: (1) comforting and restoring the believing remnant of Israel to the land; (2) rebuilding Jerusalem and the other devastated cities of Israel; (3) making Israel's remnant into priests of the LORD; (4) the Messiah personally bringing devastating judgment on the nations of the world which have afflicted Israel.

Reconstructionists believe the passages like this one apply to the destruction of Jerusalem. But there is no way that this passage can be applied to the judgment against Israel in AD 70 without twisting it beyond recognition. Nor can this be applied to the Church without allegorizing the meaning of the words into nonsense.

This is a classic case to demonstrate that two prophecies whose fulfillment may be separated by centuries may be separated only by a comma in the Scriptures.

The most important point of interpretation is that Isaiah predicted events of the First and Second Coming within one sentence without any obvious initial indication that this was the case. Those who looked for the coming of the Messiah before His First Coming were perplexed as to just how such different themes of prophecy could both be true of the same person.

This is why some rabbis before Jesus developed a theory that there would be two Messiahs. One would be a

Conquering King who would come at a time of global disaster and save Israel. This one they identified as the son of David. The other Messiah would be a Suffering Servant who would come in lowly humility and give Himself for the sins of the people. He was identified as a son of Joseph. They did not realize that there would be only one Messiah who would come at two separate times in two different roles.

We can learn a very important lesson about interpreting prophecy by raising the question, "Why did God arrange Old Testament prophecy in this way?"

I believe that God did this to force men to take prophecy literally be faith, even though at the time it might not seem reasonable. A person of that era who realized that he was a sinner in need of a Savior would be open to the claims Jesus made. He would be enlightened to understand that the "Suffering Messiah" came to give His life a ransom for his sins.

But the self-righteous person who was convinced that his law-keeping had purchased him salvation would not see a need for a humble Suffering Messiah to die for his sins. His religious views blinded him to those prophecies that predicted such a Messiah. He would look to the portrait of a King-Messiah, who would deliver Israel from the oppression of Rome and establish it as ruler over the nations because this appealed to the flesh.

For this reason, the fanatically zealous religious groups, known as the Pharisees and the Sadducees, could not be objective when the Lord Jesus presented evidence that He was the Suffering Messiah who had to save them from their sins. Their very religious zeal and self-righteousness blinded them to the clear, literal predictions of passages like Isaiah 53:1-12 and 49:1-6. In fact, most of their descendants still have a veil over their hearts.

A Lesson *and* a Warning

This should serve as a lesson and a warning to us today. All who believe in prophecy today interpret it both literally and allegorically. *The issue is to let the text dictate when to interpret allegorically or literally.*

We must come to the Word of God with a humble dependence upon the Holy Spirit as our teacher, and take each Scripture at face value. We must not allegorize a Scripture that is clearly intended to be normal and literal simply because it doesn't fit our presuppositions and peculiar doctrinal system.

Are You the One Who Was to Come, or Should We Expect Someone Else?

Another case history that illustrates how Jesus interpreted prophecies with double reference occurred when John the Baptist was thrown into jail. Even John was apparently confused as to just how the strange turn of recent events fit into the prophecies. While he was in jail, with opposition against the Lord Jesus growing daily, these prophecies must have been baffling. John's faith didn't waver, but he did want and need some clarifications as to just how these events fit into the predicted pattern of events.

John sent some of his disciples to ask Jesus, **"Are you the one who was to come, or should we expect someone else?"** (Matthew 11:3). It is obvious that even the great John the Baptizer was confused. John had an excellent overall knowledge of the Messianic predictions, but he could not reconcile the idea that Jesus could be both a humble submissive servant as well as a great conquering deliverer. This was not an academic question to John. He could see that the opposition to Jesus by both the religious and political leaders was rapidly growing. And Jesus was still teaching about "turning the other cheek."

A key to John's confusion can be found in the very prophecy that spoke of his mission and purpose. When John was officially interrogated by an inquisition board from the High Priest as to who he was, and to the ground of authority for his message, he answered, **"I am the voice of one crying in the wilderness: 'Make straight the way of the Lord,' as the prophet Isaiah said"** (John 1:23, NKJV). John's answer meant: I am the prophetic Voice predicted by Isaiah; my mission is to prepare the way for the LORD God of Israel to appear on earth; my authority is from God Himself.

But it must be carefully noted that the context of Isaiah chapter 40, from which John quoted, primarily speaks of events associated with the Messiah's role in the Second Coming as Israel's Liberator and Conquering King. John must have thought, "This doesn't match Jesus' present message and action." However, the part of Isaiah chapter 40 that John actually quoted was fulfilled in the First Coming. The rest of the context can only be fulfilled in the Messiah's Second Coming.

Jesus reassured John the Baptist by sending back to him the following message: **"Go back and report to John what you hear and see: the blind receive sight, the lame walk, those who have leprosy are cured, the deaf hear, the dead are raised, and the good news is preached to the poor. Blessed is the man who does not fall away on account of Me"** (Matthew 11:4-5).

The fascinating thing about Jesus' message of reassurance is that He quotes from another prophecy (Isaiah 35:5-6a) that had only a partial fulfillment in His First Advent. The whole context is couched in events that will be connected with the Second Advent. But Jesus appealed to John's faith and in essence said to him, "Though you don't understand it all now, John, these miracles predicted by Isaiah are My credentials. So just trust Me! Don't stumble over Me because you're having trouble understanding how all the prophecies fit together."

The Mystery of Elijah's Coming

Another example of how Jesus interpreted a double reference prophecy also has to do with John the Baptist. This time the disciples were confused about the relationship of John the Baptist to Elijah. They asked Jesus, **"'Why then do the teachers of the law say that Elijah must come first?' Jesus replied, 'To be sure, Elijah COMES [literally is** going to come] and WILL RESTORE all things, but I tell you, Elijah has already come, and they did not recognize him, but have done to him everything they wished' ... Then the disciples understood that he was talking to them about John the Baptist" (Matthew 17:10-13).

Note carefully how Jesus clearly said, **"To be sure, Elijah is going to come and will restore all things."** So Jesus emphatically promises that the real Elijah will yet come and prepare the way for the Second Advent. The following prophecies clearly apply to Elijah and the events connected with the Second Coming:

> **"'See, I will send my messenger, who will prepare the way before me. Then suddenly the Lord you are seeking will come to his temple; the messenger of the covenant, whom you desire, will come.' Says the LORD Almighty. But who can endure the day of his coming? Who can stand when he appears? For he will be like a refiner's fire or a launderer's soap. He will sit as a refiner and purifier of silver; he will purify the LEVITES and refine them like gold and silver. Then the Lord will have men who will bring offerings in righteousness, and the offerings of JUDAH and JERUSALEM will be acceptable to the LORD, as in days gone by, as in former years"** (Malachi 4:5-6).

The prophecy in Isaiah chapter 40 that spoke of John the Baptist's ministry as forerunner of the Lord carefully calls him simply, **"The VOICE of one crying in the wilderness."** God always knew that Israel would reject the Messiah in His First Coming, so He sent a bona fide substitute in the spirit and power of Elijah. As Jesus said, **" And IF you are willing to accept it, this is Elijah who was to come"** (Matthew 11:14). The majority of Israel was not willing to accept it, so Elijah must yet come to restore their hearts to the faith of their fathers and make the offerings of Judah and Jerusalem acceptable.

The lesson is this: Part of the predictions of Isaiah and Malachi were fulfilled in John the Baptist. But the full scope of these prophecies can only be fulfilled in the time of the Second Advent when the real Elijah will return. Nowhere is the beauty of God's foreknowledge more resplendent than in this kind of double reference prophecy.

The Dominionists flatly deny the possibility of double-reference prophecy. This factor is critical to their novel interpretation of passages like Matthew Chapters 24 and 25, as we will see.

THE APOSTLES INTERPRETED LITERALLY

There are examples of how the apostles interpreted the Old Testament throughout the Book of Acts and the Epistles. Paul built his whole case for justification through faith from the Old Testament. In witness of this he wrote, **"But now a righteousness from God, apart from law, has been made known, to which the Law and the Prophets testify"** (Romans 3:21).

Paul's summation argument on the guilt of all men before God is made from direct quotes from the Psalms and Isaiah. Each quote is taken in its normal, literal sense. (See Romans 3:10-20 and 4:1-8.)

Paul's argument for salvation by faith alone is based not only on literal interpretation, but also on a careful analysis of Biblical history. When Abraham was about 77 years old, he became discouraged because God had not yet fulfilled His promise that he would have a son through whom he would become a great nation and bless the world. So God spoke to Abraham in a vision and reassured him, and added this promise: "'**Look now toward heaven, and count the stars if you are able to number them.' And He said to him, 'So shall your descendants be.'**" Abraham's response was, **"And he believed in the LORD, and He accounted it to him for righteousness"** (Genesis 15:5-6, NKJV).

After this, Abraham got impatient again and decided that God needed His help to fulfill the promise. The whole episode was the result of unbelief. Since his wife Sarah seemed to be barren, he took her handmaid, as was the practice of the world of that time, and got her pregnant. God was very displeased with Abraham because he not only was trying to help Him fulfill His promise by human means, but also committed the sin following the world's standards of morality rather than God's. Israel is still paying for this lapse of faith because the resulting illegitimate son, Ishmael, became the father of the Arabs. The original enmity that existed between Ishmael and Isaac has been perpetuated by their descendants to this present day.

Because of Abraham's lapse of faith, God delayed fulfilling His promise until he was 99 years old (Genesis 17:1). It was at that time that God gave the covenant of circumcision to Abraham. So Abraham was saved at age 77. He was circumcised at age 99.

Paul draws upon these literal facts in Romans 4:9-14, where he shows that God declared Abraham righteous in His sight on the basis of faith alone, apart from works or rituals.

Again, my main point is that Paul interpreted the events as *literal history*.

Peter Interprets a Prophecy with Double Reference

When Peter stood up to preach the Gospel on the Day of Pentecost, he had to explain the miraculous phenomenon of the 120 Jewish believers speaking in various new languages. He also had to demonstrate from the Old Testament that this very thing had been predicted and was proof of certain imperative things to Israel. First, it was evidence that the general time known as **"the last days"** had begun. Second, it was evidence that the Holy Spirit had been poured out upon the true believers. Third, it was evidence that special grace was available for all those who would in faith call upon the name of the LORD to be saved. (See Acts 2:14-21.)

Peter drew upon and developed only these three points in his message. But when we put Peter's quote from Joel

2:28-32 back into its entire original context, it becomes
clear why other prophetic aspects of this quote were not
developed. Joel's prophecy also predicts,

**"I will show wonders in the heavens and on
the earth, blood and fire and billows of smoke.
The sun will be turned to darkness and the
moon to blood BEFORE THE COMING OF
THE GREAT AND DREADFUL DAY OF THE
LORD. And everyone who calls on the name of
the LORD will be saved; for on Mount Zion
and in Jerusalem there will be deliverance, as
the LORD has said, among the SURVIVORS
whom the LORD calls. IN THOSE DAYS AND
AT THAT TIME, when I restore the fortunes of
Judah and Jerusalem, I WILL GATHER ALL
NATIONS and bring them down to the Valley
of Jehoshaphat. There I WILL ENTER JUDG-
MENT AGAINST THEM CONCERNING my
inheritance, MY PEOPLE ISRAEL, for they
scattered my people among the nations and
divided up my land. They cast lots for my
people and traded boys for prostitutes; they
sold girls for wine that they may drink"** (Joel
2:30—3:3, NIV).

**[And again in the same context] "Proclaim
this among the nations: Prepare for war! Rouse
the warriors! Let all the fighting men draw near
and attack. Beat your plowshares into swords**

and your pruning hooks into spears. Let the weakling say, 'I am strong!' Come quickly, all you nations from every side, and assemble there. Bring down your warriors, O LORD!

"Let the nations be roused; let them advance into the Valley of Jehoshaphat for there I WILL SIT TO JUDGE ALL THE NATIONS ON EVERY SIDE. [This refers to the same judgment as Matthew 25:31-46.]

"Swing the sickle, for the harvest is ripe. Come, trample the grapes, for the winepress is full and the vats overflow—so great is their wickedness! [This is also predicted in Revelation 14:14-20.]

"Multitudes, multitudes in the valley of decision! For THE DAY OF THE LORD IS NEAR IN THE VALLEY OF DECISION. The sun and moon will be darkened, and the stars no longer shine. The LORD will roar from Zion and thunder from Jerusalem; the earth and the sky will tremble. But the LORD will be a refuge for HIS PEOPLE, a stronghold for THE PEOPLE OF ISRAEL.

"THEN you will know that I, the LORD your God, dwell in Zion, my holy hill. Jerusalem will be holy; never again WILL FOREIGNERS INVADE HER. [Jerusalem has seen multiple invasions since AD 70.]

"IN THAT DAY the mountains will drip new wine, and the hills will flow with milk; all the ravines of Judah will run with water. A fountain will flow out of the LORD's house and will water the valley of acacias [i.e., the Wadi al Arabah that extends from the Dead Sea to the Gulf of Aqabah] [This is also predicted in Zechariah 14:8] . . .

"Judah will be inhabited forever and Jerusalem through all generations. THEIR BLOOD GUILT, WHICH I HAVE NOT PARDONED, I WILL PARDON. [This includes their guilt for rejecting the Messiah.] **The LORD dwells in Zion!"** (Joel 3:9-21—emphases mine).

I quoted this lengthy passage because it is imperative to see in context all of the events that are necessary for its greater fulfillment. Reconstructionists teach that this was fulfilled partly on the day of Pentecost and partly in AD 70.

There is simply no way to be honest with the normal, literal meaning of the passage and say that it was ALL fulfilled on the Day of Pentecost, or in the destruction of Jerusalem in AD 70. This *has* to be another case of a prophecy with a double reference for some of the following reasons:

First, God did not darken the sun and turn the moon to the appearance of blood on the Day of Pentecost. Nor did He show astrological wonders in the heavens. There was no blood, fire, and billows of smoke.

All of these things are consistently associated with the great war of Divine judgment upon the NATIONS, which is stated in this prophetic context (Joel 3:2, 9-16), and in numerous other prophecies about this same event. Chilton writes that these things occurred during the destruction of Jerusalem in AD 70.[18] If this is so, then they occurred 37 years after Peter said on the Day of Pentecost, **"This is what was spoken by the prophet Joel."**

The Double-Reference Dilemma

Reconstructionists teach that this is a prophecy with a double reference, which on other occasions they try to deny exists. Chilton writes, "Contrary to some modern exposi-tions of this text, Peter did not say that the miracles of Pente-cost were like what Joel prophesied, or that they were some sort of 'pro-fulfillments' of Joel's prophecy; he said that this was the fulfillment: 'This is that which was spoken of through the prophet Joel.' The last days were here: the Spirit had been poured out, God's people were prophesying and speaking in tongues, and Jerusalem *would be* destroyed with fire."[19] (Note the shift to future tense when he refers to the destruction of Jerusalem, thus admitting double reference.)

The difference is that Premillennialists say that the gap between the partial fulfillment on the Day of Pentecost and its ultimate fulfillment on **the great and dreadful day of the LORD** is much longer than 37 years.

18 David Chilton, *Paradise Restored* (Tyler, TX: Dominion Press, 1986), pp. 100-101
19 *ibid.,* p. 117

Second, God did not restore the fortunes of Judah and Jerusalem in AD 70. He removed them. This prophecy clearly has to do with the fulfillment of the unconditional Palestinian Covenant to Israel's believing remnant at the Second Advent.

Third, God did not bring all the nations to **the Valley of Jehoshaphat** (between Jerusalem and the Mount of Olives) and judge them for afflicting and scattering His people Israel. Chilton's contention (which is typical for Amillennialists, Postmillennialists and Reconstructionists) that the prophecy of Joel was ultimately fulfilled in the AD 70 destruction of Jerusalem is impossible to fit into this context.

Such an interpretation is ludicrous. The very opposite of what they contend actually happened in AD 70. This prophecy predicts the nations will be judged for what they did to Jerusalem and for scattering Israel among the nations. The Romans destroyed Jerusalem and scattered the survivors throughout the nations until our times. What they did in AD 70 is the very thing for which this prophecy declares the nations will be judged. In Joel's prophecy it is the GENTILE NATIONS that are going to be judged, not Israel.

Context Tells the Story

This is just one of many cases in which Chilton and all the allegorists disregard the original context of a prophecy quoted in the New Testament. They have to do this in order to superimpose their preconceived system upon it.

Fourth, Joel predicts that **"in those days and at that time"** God will *restore* the fortunes of Judah and Jerusalem, not take them away and give them to the Church as the allegorical interpreters claim.

Chilton says about the significance of the AD 70 holocaust:

"The divinely ordained cataclysm of AD 70 revealed that Christ had taken the Kingdom from Israel and given it to the Church; the desolation of the old Temple was the FINAL SIGN that God had deserted it and was now dwelling in a new Temple, the Church. These were all aspects of the First Advent of Christ, crucial parts of the work He came to accomplish by His death, resurrection, and ascension to the throne. This is why the Bible speaks of the outpouring of the Holy Spirit upon the Church and the destruction of Israel as being the same event, for they were intimately connected theologically. The prophet Joel foretold both the Day of Pentecost and the destruction of Jerusalem in one breath . . . Peter's inspired interpretation of this text in Acts 2 determines the fact that Joel is speaking of the period from the initial outpouring of the Spirit to the destruction of Jerusalem, from Pentecost to Holocaust."[20]

If in fact Chilton's interpretation is correct, God is a liar. This prophecy not only explicitly anticipated the destruction of Israel and the dispersion of its people, but predicted their restoration in the last days (Joel 3:1, 17-20), their forgiveness for blood guilt (3:21), and the destruction of the nations who mistreated them (3:2-3, 9-16).

This prophecy was fulfilled only in part on the day of Pentecost. It will be completely fulfilled at the Second Coming of Jesus, the Messiah. So often in the Bible, prophecy is made in this way. The partial fulfillment actually becomes an illustration of the future greater fulfillment and helps to illuminate its ultimate fulfillment.

The Dominionists, Postmillennialists, and Amillennialists have made havoc of Bible prophecy by refusing to interpret passages like this literally and in context.

In the next chapter, I will show how the truth of the pre-Tribulation Rapture was discovered through the consistent application of the literal interpretation method.

---

20 *ibid.* pp. 100-101

CHAPTER FIVE

How Rapture Truth Was Rediscovered

*A*s noted in the last chapter, one of the most important results of the Reformation was the recovery of the literal method of interpretation. It took about two centuries before this method was applied to the field of Bible prophecy (eschatology).

It wasn't until the 18th century that we find evidence of a systematic study of Bible prophecy using literal interpretation. During the 18th and 19th centuries there was a growing enthusiasm about the field of prophecy and many works began to appear on the subject. Premillennialism reappeared on the scene quickly after literal interpretation was used.

In the early 19th century, Bible conferences and camp meetings featuring prophecy became increasingly popular in England, Scotland and Ireland. The man best known for popularizing prophecy at that time was John Darby. This movement influenced even members of Parliament. In fact, it was the powerful teaching of Premillennial, pre-Tribulation truth that influenced a number of the members of Parliament to draft and pass the Balfour Declaration.

Darby wrote that it was while conducting a systematic study of the New Testament on the doctrine of the Church that he discovered what to him was a new truth. He saw that God's purposes for Israel and the Church were very different; that they both could not be conducted at the same time; and that the Church had to removed for God to deal again with Israel as a distinct people and nation. He had already discovered that Israel must be reborn as a nation and that God had a future for them as a distinct people and nation.

As he pondered this problem, he began to study critically the passages that described the future return of Christ. He found that there were some amazing distinctions between the descriptions of Christ coming for the Church and Christ coming to earth to judge and set up the promised 1,000 year Kingdom to Israel.

This chart contrasts some of the distinctions ascribed to each event.

THE RAPTURE

1. Translation of believers into immortality
2. Saints go to Heaven
3. Only believers judged for rewards
4. Earth not judged
5. Can occur at any moment without signs
6. Not predicted by O.T.
7. Affects believers only
8. *Before* the Day of Wrath
9. No reference to Satan
10. Christ comes *for* His own
11. He comes in the air
12. He claims His bride
13. *Only* the elect see Him
14. Tribulation begins

THE SECOND COMING OF CHRIST

1. Believers must remain mortals
2. Saints remain on earth
3. Believers and unbelievers judged on earth
4. Earth judged
5. Date can be calculated *[2,520 days days after Antichrist treaty with Israel]*
6. Predicted by O.T.
7. Affects all men
8. *Concludes* the Day of Wrath
9. Satan bound for 1,000 years
10. Christ comes *with* His own
11. His foot splits the Mount of Olives
12. He comes with His bride
13. *Every eye* shall see Him
14. Millennial Kingdom begins

This chart clearly reveals that these two events could not be the same, nor could they occur in close proximity to each other. The great debate is basically over how much time separates the Rapture from the Second Coming of Christ.

It was the discovery of the following doctrines through a literal study of prophecy that brought about the belief in the pre-Tribulation Rapture:

- The above distinctions between the Rapture and the Second Coming;
- The uniqueness of the Church;
- God's distinct and unmixable purposes for the Church and Israel;
- God's future plan for restored Israel.

All of these factors will be elaborated on later.

Unsealing the Apocalypse Code

"But as for you, Daniel, conceal these words and seal up the book until the end time; many will go back and forth, and knowledge will increase. . . . As for me, I heard but could not understand; so I said, 'My lord, what will be the outcome of these events?' And he said, 'Go your way Daniel, for these words are concealed and sealed up until the end time. Many will be purged, purified and refined; but the wicked will act wickedly, and none of the wicked will understand, but those who have insight [who are wise] will understand'" (Daniel 12:4, 8-10).

Frankly, I have become a bit bored with those nouveau post-Tribulationists who give the impression that if you were truly an intellectual and macho Christian, you would charge headlong with them into the Tribulation. This issue cannot be settled on the basis of human machismo or positive thinking. And I am amazed that some of the older post-Tribulationists like Alexander Reese, George Ladd, and Robert Gundry spend an inordinate amount of time and energy trying to prove the recent origins of the pre-Tribulation view. Ladd devotes almost a third of his book to this point.[21]

Some never tire of trying to trace the whole original concept of the pre-Tribulation Rapture back to 1830 and to a young Scottish girl named Margaret MacDonald, to a Scotsman named Edward Irving, and to an Englishman named John Darby.

More will be said about this in a moment, but my main point here is that even if this could all be proven (and it can't be), so what?

The Roman Catholic Church used this same method of reasoning against Martin Luther, John Calvin and the other theologians of the Reformation. They brought up more than a thousand years of Church tradition and institutionalized Bible interpretation against the reformers' new doctrine of *justification by faith alone*. Just as now, the major denominational leaders quoted from a large number of the earlier Church fathers of the second

---

21 George Eldon Ladd, *The Blessed Hope*

through the fifth centuries who believed in salvation by faith plus works. But did that disprove what the Scriptures said? Didn't this rather show that traditional allegorical interpretation could sometimes miss a truth that is nevertheless contained in the Scriptures?

Mine Are Better Than Yours?

Another surprising method of attack used by many post-Tribulationists against the pre-Tribulation position is to list a number of impressive theologians who hold the post-Tribulation view. There is no question that there have been and still are godly, scholarly and effective men of God who hold this view. But does that really prove anything? Pre-Tribulationists can make their own list of adherents which is just as impressive. What are we going to say: My godly scholars are more godly and scholarly than yours? Such arguments prove nothing.

The real issue of eschatology (prophecy of last days) is that God through Daniel clearly forewarned that the book of prophecy would be "**concealed and sealed**" until the time of fulfillment began to draw near. So what in fact has happened in the historical development of theology should be no surprise. Although every other doctrine of the Bible was progressively and systematically defined, eschatology was the last.

A Short History of Prophetic Interpretation

The first century Church held an undefined faith in the "any moment" possibility of Christ's return, called the doctrine of *imminence*. It also believed in a literal thousand-year reign of Christ on earth after the Second Advent, called *Premillennialism.*

Prophecy's Dark Ages

The influential early church leader, Augustine (AD 354-430), dealt the doctrine of prophecy the most damaging blow of anyone in history. He plunged the study of prophecy into darkness for almost 1,400 years by systematically teaching that prophecy could not be interpreted literally. Remember Daniel was told that the words were **"sealed up until the time of the end"** (Daniel 12:9). We are, therefore, eyewitnesses to the fulfillment of this 2,500 year old prophecy in our lifetime.

Augustine held a literal, grammatical and historical interpretation of every other field of Bible doctrine, but taught that prophecy must be interpreted allegorically. He did this in order to be able to sustain his views of the Church, which he set forth in a profound book called *The City of God.* This book dominated the thinking of the Church for hundreds of years afterward.

The Curse of Replacement Theology

Augustine taught that the Church had taken Israel's place, and had been given the promises and covenants which (in this view) Israel had forfeited by rejecting Christ. He taught that the Church is the Kingdom of God in an allegorical sense and that there would be no literal future 1,000-year earthly kingdom over which Christ would reign. He taught that the Church should rule the world even in a political sense (as the Millennial Kingdom will rule in the future).

Augustine's Influence

Augustine's views became the foundation upon which the Roman Catholic Church was built. It still holds most of his views.

Augustine's teachings also became the philosophical basis for "Christian" anti-Semitism. He taught that Jews had no more purpose in God's plan; that they would never be reborn as a nation; that the covenants were no longer valid to them; that they were spiritual castaways with no future hope, *Christ-killers* who had no more place in God's plan and imposters. (All this, as strange as it may sound, was the result of a method of interpreting prophetic passages in an allegorical sense. Let me emphasize again, no one who interprets prophecy literally, as Jesus Himself and the apostles interpreted Old Testament prophecies in the New Testament, could ever fall into Satan's anti-Semitic trap.)

Early Church Was Pre-Tribulational

The argument that the pre-Tribulation Rapture is a recent doctrine is a convincing argument, provided you only consider the evidences offered by the pre-Tribulation opposition. But if you look a little deeper into the past, it is evident that the early church didn't have such a wide menu of doctrinal choices. The earliest Christians knew, based on the clear, unpolluted teaching of the earliest

Church fathers, that the Rapture occurs *before* the revelation of the antichrist and his rise onto the global stage.

Don't Take My Word for It, Let's Ask Ephraem!

In early 1997, Canadian prophecy scholar Grant Jeffrey made a discovery of historic proportions. He located an ancient epistle, or *letter*, written more than a thousand years before Margaret MacDonald, Darby or any supposed "evidence" of the late origins of pre-Tribulationism.

Grant's discovery turned pre-Tribulation scholarship on its ear! The discovery is called *Pseudo-Ephraem.*

"Pseudo-Ephraem claims that his sermon was written by Ephraem of Nisibis (306-73), considered to be the greatest figure in the history of the Syrian church. He was well-known for his poetics, rejection of rationalism, and confrontations with the heresies of Marcion, Mani, and the Arians. As a poet, exegete, and theologian, his style was similar to that of the Jewish midrashic and targumic traditions and he favored a contemplative approach to spirituality. So popular were his works that in the fifth and sixth centuries he was adopted by several Christian communities as a spiritual father and role model. His many works, some of doubtful authenticity, were soon translated from Syriac into Greek, Armenian, and Latin."[22]

---

22 Examining an Ancient Pre-Tribulation Rapture Statement—Thomas Ice—*The Pre-Tribulation Research Center.*

The Ephraem Document, as translated, is reproduced below. Note the underlined sections. It is important to understand several points as you read through it. First, the Ephraem Document is a *sermon*, not Scripture. And it is not necessarily true that it was authored by Ephraem of Nisibis. It could have been authored as late as the eighth century. The only dating the scholars agree to accept is that the document was undoubtedly written before the advent of Islam.

What *is* important is this. The opponents of pre-Tribulationism claim the early Church did not believe in a pre-Tribulation Rapture. The only support they have for this contention is the *absence* of documentation to the contrary from early Church history. Ephraem's sermon, entitled *"On the Last Times, the Antichrist, and the End of the World,"* leaves little doubt before the world ever heard of Mohammed the Prophet, Allah, or the Dome of the Rock, the Church *already* believed that the antichrist would not appear on the world's stage until *after* the Church has been evacuated.

On the Last Times, the Antichrist, and the End of the World

Section 1

Dearly beloved brothers, believe the Holy Spirit who speaks in us. We have already told you that the end of the world is near, the consummation remains. Has not faith withered away among mankind? How many foolish things are seen among youths, how many crimes among prelates, how many lies among priests, how many perjuries among deacons! There are evil deeds among the ministers, adulteries in the aged, wantonness in the youths—in mature women false faces, in virgins dangerous traces! In the midst of all this there are the wars with the Persians, and we see struggles with diverse nations threatening and "kingdom rising against kingdom" (Matthew 24:7). When the Roman empire begins to be consumed by the sword, the coming of the Evil One is at hand. It is necessary that the world come to an end at the completion of the Roman empire.

In those days two brothers will come to the Roman empire who will rule with one mind; but because one will surpass the other, there will be a schism between them. And so the Adversary will be loosed and will stir up hatred between the Persian and Roman empires. In those days many will rise up against Rome; the Jewish people will be her adversaries. There will be stirrings of nations and evil reports, pestilences, famines, and earthquakes in various places. All nations will receive captives; there will be wars and rumors of wars. From the rising to the setting of the sun the sword will devour much. The times will be so dangerous that in fear and trembling they will not permit thought of better things, because many will be the oppressions and desolations of regions that are to come.

Section 2

We ought to understand thoroughly therefore, my brothers, <u>what is imminent or overhanging.</u> Already there have been hunger and plagues, violent movements of nations and signs, which have been predicted by the Lord, they have already been fulfilled (consummated), and there is not other which remains, except the advent of the wicked one in the completion of the Roman kingdom. Why therefore are we occupied with worldly business, and why is our mind held fixed on the lusts of the world or on the anxieties of the ages? Why therefore do we not reject every care of earthly actions and prepare ourselves for the meeting of the Lord Christ, so that he may draw us from the confusion, which overwhelms all the world? Believe you me, dearest brother, because the coming (advent) of the Lord is nigh, believe you me, because the end of the world is at hand, believe me, because it is the very last time. Or do you not believe unless you see with your eyes? See to it that this sentence be not fulfilled among you of the prophet who declares: *"Woe to those who desire to see the day of the Lord!"* <u>For all the saints and elect of God are gathered</u>, [gathered to where—H.L.] **prior to the tribulation that is to come**, <u>and are taken to the Lord</u> **lest they see the confusion that is to overwhelm the world because of our sins.** And so, brothers most dear to me, it is the eleventh hour, and the end of the world comes to the harvest, and angels, armed and prepared, hold sickles in their hands, awaiting the empire of the Lord. And we think that the earth exists with blind infidelity, arriving at its downfall early. Commotions are brought forth, wars of diverse peoples and battles and incursions of the barbarians threaten, and our regions shall be desolated, and we neither become very much afraid of the report nor of the appearance, in order that we may at least do penance; because they hurl fear at us, and we do not wish to be changed, although we at least stand in need of penance for our actions!

Section 3

When therefore the end of the world comes, there arise diverse wars, commotions on all sides, horrible earthquakes, perturbations of nations, tempests throughout the lands, plagues, famine, drought throughout the thoroughfares, great danger throughout the sea and dry land, constant persecutions, slaughters and massacres everywhere, fear in the homes, panic in the cities, quaking in the thoroughfares, suspicions in the male, anxiety in the streets. In the desert people become senseless, spirits melt in the cities. A friend will not be grieved over a friend, neither a brother for a brother, nor parents for their children, nor a faithful servant for his master, but one inevitability shall overwhelm them all; neither is anyone able to be recovered in that time, who has not been made completely aware of the coming danger, but all people, who have been constricted by fear, are consumed because of the overhanging evils.

Section 4

Whenever therefore the earth is agitated by the nations, people will hide themselves from the wars in the mountains and rocks, by caves and caverns of the earth, by graves and memorials of the dead, and there, as they waste away gradually by fear, they draw breath, because there is not any place at all to flee, but there will be concession and intolerable pressure. And those who are in the east will flee to the west, and moreover, those who are in the west shall flee to the east, and there is not a safer place anywhere, because the world shall be overwhelmed by worthless nations, whose aspect appears to be of wild animals more than that of men. Because those very much horrible nations, most profane and most defiled, who do not spare lives, and shall destroy the living from the dead, shall consume the dead, they eat dead flesh, they drink the blood of beasts, they pollute the world, contaminate all things, and the one who is able to resist them is not there. In those days people shall not be buried, neither Christian, nor heretic, neither Jew, nor pagan, because of fear and dread there is not one who buries them; because all people, while they are fleeing, ignore them.

Section 5

Whenever the days of the times of those nations have been fulfilled, after they have destroyed the earth, it shall rest; and now the kingdom of the Romans is removed from everyday life, and the empire of the Christians is handed down by God and Peter; and then the consummation comes, when the kingdom of the Romans begins to be fulfilled, and all dominions and powers have been fulfilled. Then that worthless and abominable dragon shall appear, he, whom Moses named in Deuteronomy, saying:-Dan is a young lion, reclining and leaping from Basan. Because he reclines in order that he may seize and destroy and slay. Indeed (he is) a young whelp of a lion not as the lion of the tribe of Judah, but roaring because of his wrath, that he may devour. "And he leaps out from Basan." "Basan" certainly is interpreted "confusion." He shall rise up from the confusion of his iniquity. The one who gathers together to himself the children of confusion, also shall call them, whom he has not brought forth, just as Jeremiah the prophet says. Also in the last day they shall relinquish him just as confused.

Section 6

When therefore the end of the world comes, that abominable, lying and murderous one is born from the tribe of Dan. He is conceived from the seed of a man and from an unclean or most vile virgin, mixed with an evil or worthless spirit. But that abominable corrupter, more of spirits than of bodies, while a youth, the crafty dragon appears under the appearance of righteousness, before he takes the kingdom. Because he will be craftily gentle to all people, not receiving gifts, not placed before another person, loving to all people, quiet to everyone, not desiring gifts, appearing friendly among close friends, so that men may bless him, saying;-he is a just man, not knowing that a wolf lies concealed under the appearance of a lamb, and that a greedy man is inside under the skin of a sheep.

Section 7

But when the time of the abomination of his desolation begins to approach, having been made legal, he takes the empire, and, just as it is said in the Psalms:-They have been made for the undertaking for the sons of Loth, the Moabites and the Ammanites shall meet him first as their king. Therefore, when he receives the kingdom, he orders the temple of God to be rebuilt for himself, which is in Jerusalem; who, after coming into it, he shall sit as God and order that he be adored by all nations, since he is carnal and filthy and mixed with worthless spirit and flesh. Then that eloquence shall be fulfilled of Daniel the prophet:- And he shall not know the God of their fathers, and he shall not know the desires of women.

Because the very wicked serpent shall direct every worship to himself. Because he shall put forth an edict so that people may be circumcised according to the rite of the old law. Then the Jews shall congratulate him, because he gave them again the practice of the first covenant; then all people from everywhere shall flock together to him at the city of Jerusalem, and the holy city shall be trampled on by the nations for 42 months, just as the holy apostle says in the Apocalypse, which become three and a half years, 1,260 days.

Section 8

In these three years and a half the heaven shall suspend its dew; because there will be no rain upon the earth, and the clouds shall cease to pass through the air, and the stars shall be seen with difficulty in the sky because of the excessive dryness, which happens in the time of the very fierce dragon. Because all great rivers and very powerful fountains that overflow with themselves shall be dried up, torrents shall dry up their water-courses because of the intolerable age, and there will be a great tribulation, as there has not been, since people began to be upon the earth, and there will be famine and an insufferable thirst. And children shall waste away in the bosom of their mothers, and wives upon the knees of their husbands, by not having victuals to eat. Because there will be in those days lack of bread and water, and no one is able to sell or to buy of the grain of the fall harvest, unless he is one who has the serpentine sign on the forehead or on the hand. Then gold and silver and precious clothing or precious stones shall lie along the streets, and also even every type of pearls along the thoroughfares and streets of the cities, but there is not one who may extend the hand and take or desire them, but they consider all things as good as nothing because of the extreme lack and famine of bread, because the earth is not protected by the rains of heaven, and there will be neither dew nor moisture of the air upon the earth. But those who wander through the deserts, fleeing from the face of the serpent, bend their knees to God, just as lambs to the udders of their mothers, being sustained by the salvation of the Lord, and while wandering in states of desertion, they eat herbs.

Section 9

Then, when this inevitability has overwhelmed all people, just and unjust, the just, so that they may be found good by their Lord; and indeed the unjust, so that they may be damned forever with their author the Devil, and, as God beholds the human race in danger and being tossed about by the breath of the horrible dragon, he sends to them consolatory proclamation by his attendants, the prophets Enoch and Elijah, who, while not yet tasting death, are the servants for the heralding of the Second Coming of Christ, and in order to accuse the enemy. And when those just ones have appeared, they confuse indeed the antagonistic serpent with his cleverness and they call back the faithful witnesses to God, in order to (free them) from his seduction . . . .

Section 10

And when the three and a half years have been completed, the time of the Antichrist, through which he will have seduced the world, after the resurrection of the two prophets, in the hour which the world does not know, and on the day which the enemy of son of perdition does not know, will come the sign of the Son of Man, and coming forward the Lord shall appear with great power and much majesty, with the sign of the word of salvation going before him, and also even with all the powers of the heavens with the whole chorus of the saints, with those who bear the sign of the holy cross upon their shoulders, as the angelic trumpet precedes him, which shall sound and declare: Arise, O sleeping ones, arise, meet Christ, because his hour of judgment has come! Then Christ shall come and the enemy shall be thrown into confusion, and the Lord shall destroy him by the spirit of his mouth. And he shall be bound and shall be plunged into the abyss of everlasting fire alive with his father Satan;

and all people, who do his wishes, shall perish with him forever; but the righteous ones shall inherit everlasting life with the Lord forever and ever.

The Essence of Pseudo-Ephraem

No matter what else the writer of this sermon believed, the fact Pseudo-Ephraem taught a pre-tribulational Rapture is undeniable. That utterly destroys the commonly-offered conventional wisdom that there was no one prior to 1830 who believed in a pre-Tribulational Rapture. They are off by at least a thousand years, maybe by 1600 years or more. As I said earlier, Ephraem is *not* Bible, it is a *sermon*. Therefore, we cannot accept Ephraem as *proof* of the pre-Tribulation position. Only the Bible can *prove* doctrine, and it proves the pre-Tribulation position conclusively. What the Ephraem sermon does *prove* is that the doctrine of a pre-Tribulational Rapture had been exegeted, interpreted, preached and taught a thousand years earlier than had been previously accepted by most Bible scholars.

The Period of Prophetic Ferment

When the Reformers broke away from the Roman Church in the early 16th century, they unfortunately retained Augustine's allegorical, Amillennial view of prophecy.

Over the next 250 years, reformed theologians began to reexamine all areas of systematic theology. It was during this period, when Protestants were dividing into many denominations with divergent views about amillennialism, that a new view, Postmillennialism, emerged.

This view taught that the Church would eventually convert the whole world through the preaching of the Gospel. This would usher in the golden age promised for the Millennial Kingdom. They believed the Church would rule the world for a thousand years. Christ would then return and take the Church into eternity. Liberals at this time even accepted Darwin's theory of evolution, with all its optimism, as God's method of ushering in the "golden age." More conservative post- and amillennial theologians recognized this as a departure from the faith and attempted to combat the theory. This was one of the reasons for the rise of the many prophetic conferences of the last century. Augustine's nonliteral interpretation of prophecy was called into question. Premillennialism emerged, claiming to return to the early Church's prophetic view and method of prophetic interpretation.[23]

From the time of Augustine until the early 19th century, the traditional church's interpretation of prophecy did not allow for the possibility of a literal 1,000-year Kingdom, a literal Tribulation, or a Rapture that was distinguished from the Second Advent. In their view, the Church was already in the "Tribulation," so it stands to reason that they would hold to the post-Tribulation coming of Christ.

The return to a literal, grammatical, historical interpretation of prophecy during the early 19th century called for a thorough redefining of systematic eschatology for the first time in history. It was in this larger historical context that the whole controversy concerning the Rapture

---

23 Walvoord, *The Blessed Hope and the Tribulation,* pp. 14, 15

began. To say that the controversy started with the single vision of a 15-year-old Scottish girl is patently ridiculous.

Because there has been so much made of this girl's vision, I am going to quote it in its entirety. The following is Margaret MacDonald's account of her vision that was received in 1830. This is taken from Robert Norton's publication, *Memoirs of James and George MacDonald, of Port-Glasgow* (1840):

"It was first the awful state of the land that was pressed upon me. I saw the blindness and infatuation of the people to be very great. I felt the cry of Liberty just to be the hiss of the serpent, to drown them in perdition. It was just 'no God.' I repeated the words, Now there is distress of nations, with perplexity, the seas and the waves roaring, men's hearts failing them for fear—now look out for the sign of the Son of man. Here I was made to stop and cry out, O it is not known what the sign of the Son of man is; the people of God think they are waiting, but they know not what it is. I felt this needed to be revealed, and that there was great darkness and error about it; but suddenly what it was burst upon me with a glorious light. I saw it was just the Lord himself descending from Heaven with a shout, just the glorified man, even Jesus; but that all must, as Stephen was, be filled with the Holy Ghost, that they might look up, and see the brightness of the Father's glory. I saw the error to be, that men think that it will be something seen by the natural eye; but 'tis spiritual discernment that is needed, the eye of God in his people. Many passages were revealed, in a light in which I had not before seen them. I repeated, 'Now is the kingdom of Heaven like unto ten virgins, who went forth to meet the Bridegroom, five wise and five foolish; they that were foolish took their lamps, but took no oil with them, but they that were wise took oil in their vessels with their lamps.' 'But be ye not unwise, but understanding what the will of the Lord is; and be not drunk with wine wherein is excess, but be filled with the Spirit.' This was the oil the wise virgins took in their vessels—this is the light to be kept burning—the light of God—that we may discern that which cometh not with observation to the natural eye. Only those who have the light of God within them will see the sign of his appearance. No need to follow them who say, see here, or see there, for his day shall be as the lightning to those in whom the living Christ is. 'Tis Christ in us that will lift us up—he is the light—'tis only those that are alive in him that will be caught up to meet him in the air. I saw that we must be in the Spirit, that we might see spiritual things. John was in the Spirit, when he saw a throne set in Heaven. But I saw that the glory of the ministration of the Spirit had not been known. I repeated frequently, but the spiritual temple must and shall be reared, and the fulness of Christ be poured into his body, and then shall we be caught up to meet him. Oh none will be counted worthy of this calling but his body, which is the church, and which must be a candlestick all of gold. I often said, Oh the glorious inbreaking of God which is now about to burst on this earth; Oh the glorious temple which is now about to be reared, the bride adorned for her husband; and Oh what a holy, holy bride she must be, to be prepared for such a glorious bridegroom. I said, Now shall the people of God have to do with realities—now shall the glorious mystery of God in our nature be known—now shall it be known what it is for man to be glorified. I felt the revelation of Jesus Christ had yet to be opened up—it is not knowledge about God that it contains, but it is an entering into God—I saw that there was a glorious breaking in of God to be. I felt as Elijah, surrounded with chariots of fire. I saw as it were, the spiritual temple reared, and the Head Stone brought forth with shoutings of grace, grace, unto it. It was a glorious light above the brightness of the sun, that shown round about me. I felt that those who were filled with the Spirit could see spiritual things, and feel walking in the midst of them, while those who had not the Spirit could see nothing—so that two shall be in one bed, the one taken and the other left, because the one has the light of God within while the other cannot see the Kingdom of Heaven. I saw the people of God in an awfully dangerous situation, surrounded by nets and entanglements, about to be tried, and many about to be deceived and fall. Now will the wicked be revealed, with all power and signs and lying wonders, so that if it were possible the very elect will be deceived. This is the fiery trial which is to try us. It will be for the purging and purifying of the real members of the body of Jesus; but Oh it will be a fiery trial. Every soul will be shaken to the very centre. The enemy will try to shake everything we have believed—but the trial of real faith will be found to honour and praise and glory. Nothing but what is of God will stand. The stony-ground hearers will be made manifest—the love of many will wax cold. I frequently said that night, and often since, now shall the awful sight of the false Christ be seen on earth, and nothing but the living Christ in us can detect this awful attempt of the enemy to deceive—for it is with all deceivableness of unrighteousness he will work—he will have a counterpart for every part of God's truth, and an imitation for every work of the Spirit. The Spirit must and will be poured out on the Church, that she may be purified and filled with God—and

just in proportion as the Spirit of God works, so
will he when our Lord anoints men with power, so
will he. This is particularly the nature of the trial,
through which those are to pass who will be
counted worthy to stand before the Son of Man.
There will be outward trial too, but 'tis principally
temptation. It is brought on by the outpouring of
the Spirit, and will just increase in proportion as
the Spirit is poured out. The trial of the Church is
from Antichrist. It is by being filled with the Spirit
that we shall be kept. I frequently said, Oh be
filled with the Spirit—have the light of God in
you, that you may detect Satan—be full of eyes
within—be clay in the hands of the potter—
submit to be filled, filled with God. This will build
the temple. It in not by might nor by power, but by
my Spirit, saith the Lord. This will fit us to enter
into the marriage supper of the Lamb. I saw it to
be the will of God that all should be filled. But
what hindered the real life of God from being
received by his people, was their turning from
Jesus, who is the way of the Father. They were not
entering in by the door. For he is faithful who hath
said, by me if any man enter in he shall find pas-
ture. They were passing the cross, through which
every drop of the Spirit of God flows to us. All
power that comes not through the blood of Christ
is not of God. When I say, they are looking from

the cross, I feel that there is much in it—they turn from the blood of the Lamb, by which we overcome, and in which our robes are washed and made white. There are low views of God's holiness, and a ceasing to condemn sin in the flesh, and a looking from him who humbled himself, and made himself of no reputation. Oh! It is needed, much needed at present, a leading back to the cross. I saw that night, and often since, that there will be an outpouring of the Spirit on the body, such as has not been, a baptism of fire, that all the dross may be put away. Oh there must and will be such an indwelling of the living God as has not been—the servants of God sealed in their foreheads—great conformity to Jesus—just the bride made comely, by his comeliness put upon her. This is what we are at present made to pray much for, that speedily we may all be made ready to meet our Lord in the air—and it will be. Jesus wants his bride. His desire is toward us. He that shall come, will come, and will not tarry. Amen and Amen. Even so come Lord Jesus."

Some Observations

How anyone with a straight face can say that this vision is the origin of the whole pre-Tribulation Rapture view is beyond me. Here are a few simple observations on what this vision teaches:

- She definitely teaches a *partial Rapture*. The spiritual Christians are to be removed and the unspiritual remain to go through fiery trials.

- She taught that even the spiritual ones would be on earth during the Antichrist's (The Wicked One) period of terrible deceptions. This means that the "spiritual Christians" would at least go through half of the Tribulation.

- She equates **"the sign of the Son of man"** from Matthew 24:30—which can only refer to the Second Advent—with the Rapture statement of 1 Thessalonians 4:16, **"The Lord Himself will descend from heaven with a shout."**

She says they occur at the same time. Even Dave MacPherson acknowledges this.[24] In spite of what anyone may say, this makes her vision teach both a post-Tribulational and partial rapture.

The Snow Job

The chief exponent of the Margaret MacDonald Rapture theory is Dave MacPherson. He has tried to couch his arguments in the form of accusations of conspiracies, deliberate deceptions, and deliberate cover-ups. His unchristian attitude is exceeded only by his lack of evidence. The sad thing is that, even if any of it could be proven, so what? MacPherson and others have sought to disprove pre-Tribulationism by tracing it to this vision. But

---

24 *The Incredible Cover Up* by Omega Publications, p. 154

the very evidence MacPherson and company quote as proof, proves the very opposite of what they claim.

Furthermore, to say that John Darby, who was adamantly against the charismatic gifts, got his insight into prophecy from Margaret MacDonald is incredible and unprovable. Margaret MacDonald herself doesn't seem to have made much of her vision. In fact, there's very little recorded about it.[25]

It is possible that Darby was not aware of it, for he never mentions it, though he does write concerning her.[26] But even if he had been aware of it, it really makes no difference, for her views are not only different but contradictory to what Darby believed. To portray Darby as a plagiarist, eager to take all the glory, is to slander a brother in the Lord with no evidence. There's just no reason to believe that a careful scholar like Darby would allow himself to be influenced by the vision of a young, unschooled girl. Darby, at the very least, thought the source of her vision was questionable.

From all we can gather of the times, John Darby was a Biblical scholar who was simply a part of the wave of new interest in prophecy. The return to literal interpretation of prophecy led him and others to begin to redefine prophecy, and to arrange it into a cohesive system.

---

25 Although I don't agree with the authenticity of her vision, records show her to be a beautiful sister in the Lord, filled with love and compassion for others.
26 In Darby's book, *The Irrationalism of Infidelity* (1853), he speaks of Margaret MacDonald and her two brothers, disputing the authenticity of their gift of tongues.

Another Blast from the Past

Even before Darby, a pre-Tribulation Rapture was not unheard of. Morgan Edwards was born May 9, 1722, in Trevethin parish, Wales, and after education at Bristol College, began preaching in 1738. He served several small Baptist congregations in England for seven years, before moving to Cork, Ireland, where he pastored for nine years. Edwards emigrated to America, and in May 1761, became pastor of the Baptist Church in Philadelphia. After the Revolutionary War (he was the only known Baptist clergy of Tory persuasion), Edwards became an educator and the premier Baptist historian of his day.

Edwards taught a form of pre-Tribulationalism that, although not as completely developed as the modern doctrinal view, certainly left no doubt that there will be a Great Evacuation of believers from the earth.

"The distance between the first and second resurrection will be somewhat more than a thousand years. I say, somewhat more; because the dead saints will be raised, and the living changed at Christ's 'appearing in the air' (1 Thessalonians iv. 17); and **this will be about three years and a half before the millennium,** as we shall see hereafter: but will he and they abide in the air all that time? No: they will ascend to paradise, or to some one of those many 'mansions in the father's house' (John xiv. 2), and **so disappear during the foresaid**

period of time. The design of this retreat and disappearing will be to judge the risen and changed saints; for 'now the time is come that judgment must begin,' and that will be 'at the house of God' (1 Peter iv. 17) . . . "

Although Edwards sees the event happening at the three and one half year point, it is significant to note that as early as 1788, the Rapture was an established doctrine.

So What?

The most important factor in this whole controversy is, "What does the Bible say?" I totally agree with Ladd when he said, "Let it be at once emphasized that we are not turning to the church fathers to find authority for either pre- or post-Tribulationism. The one authority is the Word of God, and we are not confined in the straitjacket of tradition." All I can say is "amen" to that statement.

As I stated at the beginning of this study, my purpose for writing this book was not to cling blindly to a system of prophetic interpretation, but rather to objectively and honestly investigate what the whole Bible says.

In closing this chapter, I can say in all good conscience that I believe the Scriptures teach a pre-Tribulational coming of the Lord Jesus Christ for His Church. So have many who have gone before, going as far back as Ephraem of Syria in the fourth century.

No matter which view one holds on the Rapture questions, there are some difficult problems that have to be reconciled within the system. I believe that the pre-Tribulation system answers all the Scriptures on the subject in the most consistent and harmonious way.

On the other hand, the post-Tribulation system has to allegorize some major portions of the Scripture, such as Matthew 25:31-46, and the question of who will populate the Kingdom, in order to make their system work.

Second, the major assumption of many of the post-Tributationists' arguments is that, if they can punch holes in the pre-Tribulation system, it somehow establishes their own.

What is said about the post-Tribulationists also applies to the mid-Tribulation view.

CHAPTER SIX

So Many Views, So Little Space

*T*here are basically six major theological views about the Rapture of the Church. They are the pre-, mid-, post-, and pre-Wrath Tribulation views. There is also the Preterist view. This teaches that virtually all prophecy has already been fulfilled. The Reconstructionists or Dominionists are in this latter camp. There is also the Partial Rapture view, which believes that only the spiritual Christians go in the Rapture.

How can there be so many different perspectives when there is only one Bible? There is a principle of Biblical interpretation called *Dispensationalism.* Dispensational-ists believe that God dealt in different ways at different times with different cultures, according to a Divine Plan. We get our English word "dispensationalism" from the Latin word *dispensatio.* That word was translated in the Latin Vulgate from the Greek word *oikonomia.* The Latin word means "to weigh out, or dispense." The word con-veys three principal ideas that carry over to the English meaning:

1. the action of dealing out, or distributing;
2. the action of administrating, ordering or managing the system by which things are administered, and
3. the action of dispensing with some requirement.[28]

The *American Heritage Dictionary* defines a dispen-sation this way:

---

28 *Dictionary of Premillennial Theology* Couch, p. 93, Kregel Publications, Grand Rapids, MI

"The divine ordering of worldly affairs. **b.** A religious system or code of commands considered to have been divinely revealed or appointed."[29]

According to the *Oxford English Dictionary* a dispensation is "a stage in a progressive revelation, expressly adapted to the needs of a particular nation or period of time. . . Also, the age or period during which a system has prevailed."

The Greek verb oikonomia (οἰκονομία) is even more precise. The word itself is a compound whose parts literally mean "to divide, apportion, administer or manage the affairs of an inhabited house. The person, or officer, oikonomos (οἰκονόμος), who oversaw a household dispensation was a steward, estate manager or treasurer. Dispensational theologians use the word "dispensation" in the context of overseeing a household for its Owner. We'll explore this concept in some detail.

Some Divine Distinctions

Dispensationalism not only helps answer the Rapture question, but it also helps harmonize many Scripture passages that on first observation seem to be contradictory. Here are a few examples: First, Jesus taught in the Sermon on the Mount, **"Do not think that I came to abolish the Law and the Prophets, I did not come to abolish, but to fulfill, For truly I say to you, until heaven and earth pass away, not the smallest letter or stroke shall pass**

---

29 *The American Heritage® Dictionary of the English Language, Third Edition,* copyright © 1992 by Houghton Mifflin Company. Electronic version licensed from INSO Corporation. All rights reserved

away form the Law, until all is accomplished" (Matthew 5:17-18).

But Paul said in Galatians, **"Nevertheless knowing that a man is not justified by the works of the Law but through faith in Christ Jesus, even we [Jews] have believed in Christ Jesus, that we may be justified by faith in Christ, and not by the works of the Law; since by the works of the Law shall not flesh be justified"** (Galatians 2:16).

Trying to reconcile those two statements as a new Christian was practically impossible. In fact it troubled me. It was obvious that something radical must have happened between the Sermon on the Mount and the ministry of the apostle Paul.

Second, later in Jesus' ministry, He made another statement that confused me, **"these twelve Jesus sent out after instructing them, saying, 'Do not go in the way of the Gentiles, and do not enter any city of the Samaritans; but rather go to the lost sheep of the house of Israel'"** (Matthew 10:5-6). I couldn't imagine why God wouldn't allow the apostles to speak to the Gentiles and why He sent them only to preach to Israel.

Yet later in the same Gospel of Matthew, Jesus said, **"Go therefore and make disciples of all the nations (Gentiles), baptizing them in the Name of the Father and the Son and the Holy Spirit . . ."** (Matthew 28:19).

Obviously, these two examples point out a distinguishable change in God's plan. For some reason that was unfathomable to me as a baby Christian, God introduced some completely new revelation about how He and man are going to relate to each other. I could add many more examples like these if space permitted, but these should sufficiently illustrate the point.

What Is an Age?

Another indication that there have been distinguishable changes in God's plan for man is revealed in the term age or ages. The following New Testament usages of the word reveal this clearly.

Jesus spoke of **"this age and the age to come"** (Matthew 12:32). He also spoke of **"the end of the age"** (Matthew 13:39, 40-49; 24:3; Mark 10: 30). God revealed through the epistles many different ages in the history of His dealings with man. For instance, He speaks of **"ages past"** (note the plural) in Romans 16:25, Colossians 1:26, and Titus 1:2. He speaks of **"the present evil age"** in Galatians 1:3. Again, He speaks of **"the ends of the ages"** in Hebrews 9:26. In 1 Timothy 1:17, God is called the **"King of the ages."**

A very important element is added to the concept of successive ages in God's plan in Ephesians 3:9-11. It is a complex context, but the main point to the discussion is in verse 9, **"and to bring to light what is the administration of the mystery which for ages has been hidden in God, who created all things . . ."**

Several observations should be made of this statement.

First, the context in which the statement is presented. Second, Paul is now "bringing to light" the administration of this mystery in the present age. The word age as it is used here is defined as "a period of time in history or in the development of man." In the context this idea is connected with the term administration which is οἰκονομία (oikonomia).

As the word is used in this context where it is linked with the term age, it means that God has planned, ordered, arranged, and administered certain purposes within a sphere of definable periods of history. The two terms together (i.e., administration and ages) define the world as a household that is being administered by God in growing stages of Divine revelation.

It is important to add that the closest English equivalent to the Greek work oikonomia is *economy*. *Webster's Unabridged Dictionary* shows oikonomia as the root of economy and defines it as "an art of managing a household; the management of the affairs of a group, community or establishment with a view to insuring its maintenance of productiveness; God's plan or system for the governing of the world."[30] So, it is in the last sense that I am using the term economy and its synonyms, administration and dispensation.

Third, verses 10 and 11 reveal that **"God is teaching the angels His manifold wisdom through the mystery,**

---

30 Webster's *Third New International Dictionary of the English Language Unabridged* (Chicago: Encyclopedia Britannica, Inc., 1981)

the body of Christ, and that it is in accordance with the purpose of the ages (literal), which is made possible through Jesus our Lord." The main point here is that the ages are declared to have a definite Divine purpose which heretofore was hidden.

Taken literally, the Bible reveals that history from God's viewpoint has progressed through a number of ages in which there have been different revelations of God's will. For as we have seen, the Bible not only speaks of "this present age," but of "ages past and the ages future."

Inseparably linked with this is the revelation of God's arrangement, purpose and design with the ages via the term "administration" in the *New American Standard Bible.*

One of the most important verses of God's involvement with the ages is found in Hebrews 1:2, which literally says in the original, **". . . through Whom also He designed the ages."** This unique declaration reveals that Jesus actually planned and designed the various stages into which man's history would flow before time and space were created.

Explosive Emotion versus Reason

I realize that the subject of dispensationalism is an explosive one. A whole book could be written on this important matter which I am trying to summarize in one chapter. And on this point, I urge every serious Bible student to read Dr. Ryrie's excellent book, *Dispensationalism Today.*[31]

---

31 Charles C. Ryrie, *Dispensationalism Today* (Chicago: Moody Press, 1965)

Whatever your theological viewpoint, you have to come to grips with the two recurrent concepts: the economies and the ages. Apart from these concepts, the Bible cannot be understood as a consistent and cohesive whole. The only other alternative is to allegorize large portions of Scripture, which were clearly intended to be taken as normal statements of fact, in order to keep the Bible from contradicting itself.

The theological system that most adheres to a consistent, literal, grammatical and historical interpretation of the Bible is dispensationalism.

Dispensationalism Defined

No better definition of dispensationalism can be found that that of Dr. Ryrie: "A concise definition of dispensation is this: a dispensation is a distinguishable economy in the outworking of God's purpose. If one were describing a dispensation he would include other things, such as the idea of distinctive revelation, testing, failure, and judgment. But we are seeking a definition, not a description.

"In using the economy as the core of the definition, the emphasis is put on the Biblical meaning of the work itself (i.e., oikonomia). Economy also suggests the fact that certain features of different dispensations might be the same or similar. Differing political and economic economies are not completely different, yet they are distinguishably different. Communistic and capitalistic economies are basically different, and yet there are functions, features and items in these economies that are the same."[32]

Each one of the various dispensations or economies that are distinguishable in the Bible begins with a new revelation from God to man. The new revelation contains both responsibilities of how man is to relate to God and promises which enable man to perform them.

There is then a period of testing in the new revelations. Each economy reveals human failure to both appropriate the blessing and to obey the revealed responsibilities.

Each economy ends with a distinct Divine Judgment upon man for his failure, and then a new economy is introduced.

The German scholar, Eric Sauer, adds a very important observation about the succession of the various Biblical economies, "The Holy Scripture is plainly not a spiritual-divine-uniform 'block,' but a wonderful articulated historic-prophetic organism. It must be read organically, age-wise, according to the Divine ages.

"Thus a new period always begins only when from the side of God a change is introduced in the composition of the principle valid up to that time; that is when from the side of God three things occur:

"A continuance of certain ordinances valid until then;

"An annulment of other regulations until then valid;

---

32 *ibid.*

"A fresh introduction of new principles not before valid.

"Thus with the introduction of the present period of salvation there remains the general moral principles ruling the realm of the earlier period (Romans 8:4; 13:8-10), even though in a completely new spirit; for the Law is the unity (James 2:10), and as such is wholly abolished."[33]

The main points that should be emphasized from Sauer's statement are that the Bible is an organic, cohesive progress of living revelation that cannot be mechanically put into a philosophical straitjacket. But it falls into various Divinely initiated stages of history in which certain ordinances of past ages continue, certain regulations of the past are eradicated, and certain new principles are revealed and set up as the new governing force of living for God.

I wish to make it clear, however, that even though there are distinguishable economies, there has always been only one way of salvation presented by God for man. Man has always had to approach God and be forgiven and accepted by Him on the basis of faith alone. In other words, salvation always has been and always will be received by man on the basis of faith alone.

The way that a redeemed man is to live for God has changed in the various dispensations. But the way of salvation has not.

33 Erich Sauer, *The Dawn of World Redemption* (Grand Rapids, MI: Wm. B. Eerdmans Publishing Co., 1951), pp. 193-194

CHAPTER SEVEN

What Are the Dispensations or Economies?—God's Time Line

*O*ne of the best ways to explain further the principle of Biblical economies is to show what they are. Now it really isn't of utmost importance exactly how many there are. Nor is it fatal to the validity of the system that different people call the various economies different names.

The important thing is that they be distinguished and recognized. Even the avowed enemies of dispensational interpretation have to make distinctions between the way God deals with mankind in the dispensation of the law, the Church and the coming Messianic kingdom.

All dispensationalists generally agree upon the following list of Biblical economies. The chart at the end of this chapter will also aid greatly in seeing these things in perspective.

The Dispensation of Freedom or Innocence

God created Adam in a state of holiness which was compatible with His own character. But Adam had—as part of the image of God created in him—freedom of choice. It was through this attribute that the possibility of sin existed.

Some have said, "If God created man with the potential for sinning, then God is responsible for the failure." But what were the choices? God could have created man without freedom of choice and thus have had a robot. Man would not have been able to respond to God's love, nor could there have been fellowship. For one must be able to choose *not* to love in order to *be able* to love.

The only other possibility was for God to take a calculated risk and create a creature in His own image. That image gave man *intellect* by which he could understand God; *emotion* with which he could respond with feeling and passion; and *volition* or *freedom of choice* with which he could act upon his understanding and emotions. The other two facets of God's image in man are *moral reason or conscience* and *everlasting existence of his immaterial being*, called the "soul."

God took the calculated risk and created man in His own image, as defined above, in order that man could respond to Him in true love and fellowship.

The Angelic Factor

There is one other factor that is somewhat shrouded in the mist of eternity past which has to do with why man was created and why it is that history is organized that way. The Bible reveals that the angels are vitally concerned with how man responds to God. We know that the highest being God created was an archangel named Lucifer who through pride and a desire to be equal with God rebelled against God and led a revolt among the angelic creation (Ezekiel 28:11-17; Isaiah 14:12-15).

We know that Lucifer, who became known as Satan and the Devil, was instrumental in causing Adam and Eve to believe a lie about God's character, to reject the relationship they had with Him, to lose their unproven holiness, and to lose the most basic part of their being, called spiritual life. It was only through this spiritual nature that man could know God on a personal basis and understand Divine revelation (Genesis 3; John 3:1-18).

We know that all through the successive Biblical ages Satan and his angels (called demons) have relentlessly sought to prevent humans from understanding and accepting God's provision of forgiveness, and to neutralize and destroy those who do receive it (John 8:42-47; 2 Corinthians 4:3-4; Ephesians 6:10-18; 1 Peter 5:8).

We know that the angels who remained faithful to God rejoice over one fallen human being who comes to repentance and believes in God's salvation (Luke 15:7-10). We also know that the angels are learning about God's manifold wisdom by the way He is dealing with mankind through the Church (Ephesians 3:10-11). We also know that the angels stare intently at the way God's grace is being poured out upon the world through the Holy Spirit (1 Peter 1:12).

As I surmised in a much fuller way in my book, *Satan Is Alive and Well on Planet Earth,*[34] man was created in large measure for the purpose of resolving the angelic conflict. Apparently, God allowed Lucifer and his rebel angels time to repent. But after a period of grace, God brought judgment against Satan and his angels and sentenced them to eternal separation from God under a perpetual punishment. At that point Satan must have called God unjust and unloving.

---

34 Hal Lindsey, *Satan Is Alive and Well on Planet Earth* (New York: Bantam Books, 1972)

Although God was under no obligation to do so, He chose to demonstrate to His angels His perfect justice and unfathomable love by means of a vastly inferior creature called man. The crowning of grace is that God is going to elevate redeemed and glorified man not only to replace the angels who were banished with Satan, but He is going to make him ruler over the whole angelic realm (1 Corinthians 6:3).

God Had a Plan

When the first human parents fell, God instituted a plan of redemption that demonstrates to the whole universe the perfection of His character.

God demonstrates His justice in that even though He loved man, He did not compromise that justice by simply sweeping the rebellion of Adam and Eve under the rug. Instead, God demonstrated His wisdom by devising a way for a uniquely qualified Substitute (Jesus) to fully pay our debt to His violated law and thus provide a free pardon.

God demonstrated His perfect love by coming into the world, becoming a man, living a selfless and sinless life, so that He could qualify to take upon Himself the full measure of His own wrath against sin on behalf of every human being. All of this was done in order that rebellious man might receive a full pardon and eternal life by simply believing that the Lord Jesus died in his place. At the final judgment, this great act of salvation will silence all of God's accusers and cause all to bow and acknowledge that they deserve their punishment. So in the first dispensation man was free to do anything he chose, except that he was to tend the garden and not eat from one specific tree that God put off limits. When man failed, innocence and freedom from sin was lost. The immediate judgment was loss of the relationship with God and the loss of spiritual life. Nature was cursed so that it would be very difficult to provide a living. Man was cast from the paradise garden, woman was placed under man's authority, and child-bearing became much more difficult.

The Dispensation of Conscience or Self-determination

At the end of the previous economy, even in the midst of judgment upon man's failure, God introduced the way of forgiveness. Adam and Eve experienced a basic change in their being. They were still physically alive; but as God had warned, they had died spiritually the moment they decided to reject God's one commandment. There was an immediate experience of guilt that was evidenced by their becoming uncomfortable with being naked. They immediately tried to cover their sense of guilt with the work of their own hands. This was the first act of *religion*, for *religion is man's attempt to cover his sin by his own works.*

God graciously showed man the only acceptable way to cover his sin. God killed an animal and from its skin made coverings for their guilt. This, in very simple form, taught man that the consequence of his sin was the death of an innocent substitute of God's choosing. And from the substitutionary sacrifice God provided a covering for the effect of their sin. All they could do was receive it and throw away their own religious handiwork. This was the Gospel in childlike simplicity.

In this economy man was to recognize his need of forgiveness as well as understand how he was to live for God by the witness of his conscience. Man had conscience from the beginning, but now there was a great need for daily moral choices. Conscience now became the principal way God governed over mankind during this dispensation.

Man was responsible to respond to God through the inner promptings of his conscience. But man soon discovered the age-old art of rationalization. He soon made black white, white black and everything some shade of gray.

Finally, God evaluated the world of that day as follows: **"Then the Lord saw that the wickedness of man was great on the earth, and that every intent of the thoughts of his heart was only evil continually"** (Genesis 6:5).

God destroyed all mankind with the exception of eight persons who walked with Him and believed in His provision of forgiveness. The judgment that distinctly ended this period was a worldwide flood. Man had failed another period of testing.

The Dispensation of Civil Government

Noah was the patriarch of the world after the flood. The new revelation to govern this period included making the animals fearful of man. Man became an eater of meat as well as grains. A promise was given that there would be no more world floods. And man was given the ultimate authority for human government—-capital punishment.

This ultimate authority endowed human government with all lesser authority necessary for governing in the world. Human civil government became the Divine means of maintaining order. It also included the way to walk with God. Man's inability to govern properly became apparent early in this economy. Even Noah displayed moral weakness by getting stone drunk and improperly guiding his own family.

Instead of dispersing and subduing the earth as God had commanded, the people banded together in one place. Soon, the first world dictator arose (Nimrod, Genesis 10:8-12; 11:1-9) and then led all the inhabited earth into the first system of false religion. This new religion was based on astrology and worship of the stars.

The people built a tower at Babel (which later became the site of Babylon). This tower was an observatory for studying the stars and was a symbol of unity. It was totally devoted to astrology. More importantly, it was also the symbol of man's rejection of God and His truth.

Man used civil government as a unifying system to bring all people into a false religion and to stamp out the truth about God. Once again unregenerate man failed by taking the very vehicle that was to lead him to God and using it to blind himself to the truth.

God knew that any form of one-world government made it too easy for Satan to slip in a dictator who could then lead humanity away from the truth. The judgment that ended this economy was the sudden confusion of languages. This forced man to scatter and form nations. Soon afterward the nations began to deliberately erase the knowledge of God from their memory.

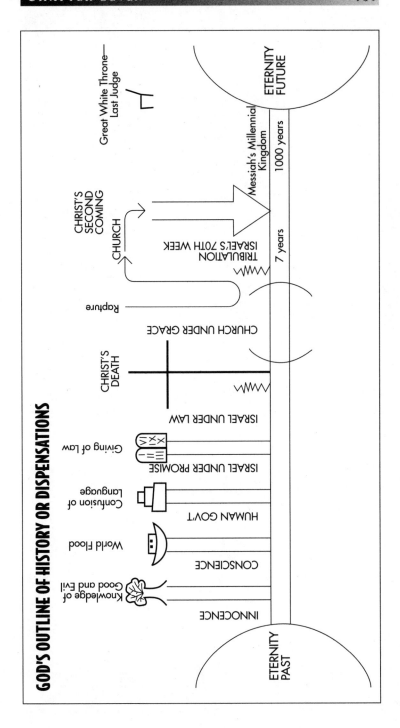

GOD'S OUTLINE OF HISTORY OR DISPENSATIONS

ETERNITY PAST

INNOCENCE

Knowledge of Good and Evil

CONSCIENCE

World Flood

HUMAN GOV'T

Confusion of Language

ISRAEL UNDER PROMISE

Giving of Law

ISRAEL UNDER LAW

CHRIST'S DEATH

CHURCH UNDER GRACE

Rapture

CHURCH

CHRIST'S SECOND COMING

Great White Throne—Last Judge

TRIBULATION ISRAEL'S 70TH WEEK

7 years

Messiah's Millennial Kingdom

1000 years

ETERNITY FUTURE

Precise As It Needs to Be

*O*n the history covered by the first three economies, issues are not as precisely distinguished in the Scripture as they are in the following dispensations. There just wasn't very much written about those early periods. Several thousand years of man's relationship with God is covered in the first 11 chapters of Genesis.

I want to carefully note that this is not the case with the following economies. The Scriptures from Genesis 12 to Acts 2 are specifically addressed to the special people created from one Divinely chosen man named Abraham. This portion of the Bible of course has application to all believers of all ages, but by strict interpretation, it was addressed specifically to the physical descendants of Abraham, Isaac and Jacob under two economies.

So the following dispensations that are noted are very clearly distinguishable. There is clear Scriptural differentiation of the principles that prevail in each one of the successive economies.

The Dispensation of Israel under Promise

A people and a promise characterize this economy. The term promise comes from the unconditional covenants that God made with an Assyrian man named Abram whom God renamed Abraham.

God's reason for introducing this new economy is clear. All nations were deliberately pushing the knowledge of God and the way of salvation out of their minds.

Romans 1:18-32 is certainly an applicable description of the course all nations took in that era.

So in order that the truth about God might be preserved upon earth, and that the way of salvation for all mankind might not only be kept but also developed, God elected to create a special nation through which all these things would be accomplished.

A Promise Is a Promise

God created this nation with a series of promises. God bound Himself with an oath to keep each promise. The following is a catalogue of the promises, which are also called covenants:

1 The Promise of a Nation: **"will make you a great nation . . ."** (Genesis 12:2a).

2 The Promise of Preservation of Abraham and His Descendants: **"I will bless those who bless you, and the one who curses you I will curse . . ."** (Genesis 12:3a).

3 The Promise of World Blessing Through Abraham's Seed: **"And in you all the families of the earth shall be blessed . . ."** (Genesis 12:3b).

4 The Promise of a **Specific Land** (Genesis 13:14-17; 15:18-21).

These promises were confirmed to both Isaac (Genesis 26:2-4) and to Jacob (Genesis 28:13-14). Ryrie gives an excellent analysis of the general character of this economy: "The responsibility of the patriarchs was simply

to believe and serve God, and God gave them every material and spiritual provision to encourage them to do this.
The promised land was theirs and blessing was theirs as
long as they remained in the land. But of course there was
failure soon and often."[35]

The Scripture that specifically deals with this economy
is Genesis 11:10 through Exodus 18:27. Some have ques-
tioned whether there truly are two dispensations distinguishable in God's dealings with Israel, since the promise
and the law were both given to the same people.

I believe the two dispensations are sharply distinguished in Galatians 3 in spite of the statement that the
Mosaic Law did not annul the promise that was previously
given. The distinction between the dispensation of
promise and the dispensation of law fits every principle of
definition given in the early part of this chapter.

Paul summarizes the failure of the people under the
promise, **"Why the law then? It was added because of
transgressions . . ."** (Galatians 3:19). The people failed to
live by faith in the promises that God had given them so
He placed them under specific laws. (For God's summary
of Israel's failure to believe His promises see Numbers
14:11, 22, 23.)

The Dispensation of Israel under Law

This economy began with dramatic and frightening
manifestations of God at Mount Sinai. God reviewed how

35 Ryrie, op. cit., pp. 60-61

He had graciously delivered them under the conditions of promise, **"You yourselves have seen what I did to the Egyptians, and how I bore you on eagles' wings, and brought you to Myself"** (Exodus 19:4).

Then God offered the Israelites the law, **"Now then if you will indeed obey My voice and keep My covenant, then you shall be My own possession among all the peoples, for all the earth is Mine . . ."** (Exodus 19:5). I believe, with many other theologians, that had the Israelites refused this offer of a law relationship and instead asked to remain under the gracious economy of promise which depended upon God answering faith, the Lord would not have forced the change.

But instead the people reacted with human pride and said, **"All that the Lord has spoken we will do!"** (Exodus 19:8). This confirmed the unbelieving heart which God saw and which caused the Lord to introduce the economy of law. The law was given to make man see how utterly incapable he is to live up to God's standards by human effort.

This is revealed in the following verses:

"And the law came in (for the purpose) that the transgression might increase . . ." (Romans 5:20).

"Therefore did that which is good become a cause of death for me? May it never be! Rather it was sin, in order that it might be shown to be sin by effecting my death through that which is

good, that through the commandment sin might become utterly sinful" (Romans 7:13).

The law was given to make sin *increase*, not decrease, because man is inherently blind to the sinful nature with which he is born. The law provokes this nature into life so that it becomes very exposed. The more we try to keep God's law, the more the sinful nature rebels. So man has to admit that he is inherently so sinful that he must look by faith to the Messiah Jesus to save him and to the Holy Spirit to enable him to live pleasingly for God.

God spoke to Moses about Israel's chances of living successfully under the law at the beginning, **"Oh that they (the Israelites) had such a heart in them, that they would fear Me, and keep all My commandments always, that it might be well with them and with their sons forever!"** (Deuteronomy 5:29).

It is obvious that the law was not God's preferred way to deal with man, but rather was a necessary historical lesson in the development of man's understanding of his total helplessness to establish a relationship with God by his own efforts.

God clearly anticipated Israel's failure under law when He predicted, through Jeremiah in the seventh century BC, **"'Behold, days are coming,' declares the Lord, 'when I will make a new covenant with the house of Israel and with the house of Judah, not like the covenant which I made with their fathers in the day I took them by the hand to bring them out of the land of**

Egypt, My covenant which they broke, although I was a husband to them' declares the Lord." In the rest of the statement, the Lord says that He will bring in three uniquely new factors: (1) "I will put My laws within them, and on their heart I will write it." (2) "All shall know Me, from the least of them to the greatest of them." (3) "I will forgive their iniquity, and their sin I will remember no more" (Jeremiah 31:31-34).

Israel's utter failure to live under the law is meant to be an historical lesson for all humanity. The law was never meant to be a way of salvation, but rather to show us how good we would have to be if we were going to help God save us. This is clearly stated in Romans 9:30—10:4. Once again, the only way of salvation in every dispensation has been by faith in God's provision.

The interruption of the dispensation was predicted by the Lord Jesus, "O Jerusalem, Jerusalem, who kills the prophets and stones those who are sent to her! How often I wanted to gather your children together, the way a hen gathers her chicks under her wings, and you were unwilling. Behold, your house is being left to you desolate! For I say to you, from now on you shall not see Me UNTIL you say, 'Blessed is He who comes in the name of the Lord'" (Matthew 23:39). This economy was in focus from Exodus 19 to Acts 1:26.

The rejection of the often promised and long awaited Messiah caused God to set Israel aside and to temporarily suspend this dispensation. I say *temporarily* suspend because according to the previously mentioned prophecy of Daniel 9:24-27, Israel still has allotted to her seven years to complete the six Divinely given responsibilities named in Daniel 9:24. These must be fulfilled under the same conditions that prevailed in the dispensation in which the first 483 years were acted out (or 69 weeks of years). This seven-year period, called the Tribulation by theologians, is actually the *completion* of the dispensation of Israel under Law.

The Dispensation of Grace

This dispensation was actually a mystery in the ages of the Old Testament. It had to be, or there simply could not have been a bona fide offer of the promised Messianic kingdom to the Israelites. One dispensational teacher calls this economy "the great parenthesis." Not because it is an afterthought of God, but because it was of necessity a Divinely kept secret (Ephesians 3:9). No Israelite would have taken Jesus' offer of an imminent kingdom seriously if an alternate plan had already been revealed and understood in the Old Testament. This would have already concluded their failure.

A Clear Distinction

Of all the various dispensations, the most clearly revealed differences are between the economy of law and of grace. One of the most important features of the new modus operandi for living under grace is the personal ministry of the Holy Spirit in and to every believer in Jesus Christ.

Since the fall of man, all the redeemed have experienced a spiritual birth when they believed. But the new ministries listed below are absolutely *unique* to the economy of grace. They all happen *once for all at the moment of salvation.*

There is the *baptism* of the Holy Spirit that joins each believer into a living union with Christ. This union is the most basic and essential meaning of the Church. The Church is the body of Christ composed of all believers. And we can only enter that body through the baptism of the Spirit (1 Corinthians 12:12-14). This first occurred in Acts 2 according to Peter in Acts 11:15-18.

- There is also the *indwelling* of the Holy Spirit. The Spirit takes up permanent residence in each believer at the moment of salvation (John 14:16, 17; 1 Corinthians 6:19-20; Romans 8:11).

- There is also the *sealing* of the Holy Spirit. The presence of the Spirit in the believer is God's seal or guarantee that we are His purchased possession and that He will certainly bring us into a glorified eternal state in His presence (Ephesians 1:13, 14; 4:30; 2 Corinthians 1:22).

- There are also *gifts* of the Holy Spirit. Each believer receives at least one or more spiritual abilities (gifts) with which to accomplish God's will for his life (1 Peter 4:10-11; 1 Corinthians 12:1-33). The gifts are permanent (Romans 11:29).

- Of these new ministries of the Spirit, only one is not received once and for all at the time of salvation. It is called *the filling of the Spirit.* It is a moment-by-moment ministry that must be continually appropriated by a submissive will and an aggressive faith. This is that ministry which enables the believer to effectively live for and serve God (Romans 8:1-4; Galatians 3:1; 5:16-18; Ephesians 5:18).

It is these new ministries of the Spirit that made it possible to remove the law principle and establish the grace principle. All of this was not possible until Jesus the Messiah completed His redemptive work at the Cross. Because He satisfied all of the demands of the law against us and then paid its ultimate penalty of death in our place, God can now remove us completely from under the law's demands. The Holy Spirit under grace now works the righteousness of the law through the trusting believer (Romans 8:4).

In the economy of grace God is no longer working in a special way only with Israel. Thanks to the Cross all nations, Jew and Gentile, are joined into a unique heavenly people called the Church. In the Church there is no national, racial or sexual distinction. All are one in Christ.

The Apostate Church

Even with such a heaven-high privilege the Bible predicts that the Church will fail, and all but a believing remnant will fall away from the faith (1 Timothy 4:1-4). Organized Christendom will have an outward façade of godliness, but will deny its power (2 Timothy 3:1-10).

Peter predicts that false teachers, masquerading as ministers of Christ, will infiltrate and take over the institutional
church and teach destructive heresies. They will malign
and nullify the truth, which is the Bible (2 Peter 2:1-2).
They will especially deny the prophetic Scripture and its
claim of the Lord's return (2 Peter 3:1-7). Not to digress
too much, I can testify that these prophecies have been
fulfilled before my eyes and in my hearing. The
Dominionists vigorously protest against this truth. I will
deal with their objections in chapter 22.

How the Church Ends

This dispensation began in unique way, and it will end
in a unique way. It began with the advent of the Holy Spirit
to take up personal residence on earth in each believer. It
will end with a complete reversal. The Lord Himself will
evacuate the Church so that the final seven years allotted to
Israel under the law in Daniel's prophecy can be fulfilled.

From the world's standpoint, the believers will just
VANISH without a trace. CNN will be trying to come up
with an explanation. World leaders will be grasping for
explanations. Satan will provide an explanation and **God
will cause a strong delusion to come upon the world so
that they will believe *the* lie** (2 Thessalonians 2:10-13).

More will be said about these very important aspects
of prophecy. But it is very important to stress again this
fact: since the Church in the economy of grace was necessarily a mystery hidden in God from all ages past, it

must be removed before God can finish His distinct program with Israel.

And since the focus of God will once again be upon the Jew, according to Daniel's final allotment of seven years, the Church must be removed. Otherwise the conditions that prevail during the age of the Church (i.e., where there is no difference between a believing Gentile and a Jew) would make such an arrangement impossible.

The Unparalleled Time of Global Catastrophe

The world conditions of the final seven years of Daniel's predicted time for Israel are often overlooked. Here are some Scriptures that show why the pre-Tribulation Rapture is called **the Blessed Hope.**

"This is what the LORD says: 'Cries of fear are heard—terror, not peace. Ask and see: Can a man bear children? Then why do I see every strong man with his hands on his stomach like a woman in labor, every face turned deathly pale? How awful that day will be! *None will be like it.* **It will be a time of trouble for Jacob, but he will be saved out of it"** (Jeremiah 30:5-7, NIV).

"Blow the trumpet in Zion; sound the alarm on my holy hill. Let all who live in the land tremble, for the day of the LORD is coming. *It is close at hand—a day of darkness and gloom, a day of clouds and blackness. Like dawn spreading across the mountains a large* *and mighty army comes, such as never was of old nor ever will be in ages to come"* (Joel 2:1, NIV).

"**At that time Michael, the great prince who protects your people, will arise.** *There will be a time of distress such as has not happened from the beginning of nations until then.* **But at that time your people—everyone whose name is found written in the book—will be delivered**" (Daniel 12:1, NIV).

"**For then there will be great distress, unequaled from the beginning of the world until now—and never to be equaled again. If those days had not been cut short, no one would survive, but for the sake of the elect those days will be shortened**" (Matthew 24:21-22, NIV).

There are three recurring themes in the context of all of these important prophecies: First, God's focus is centered on the nation of Israel. Second, it will be a time of unprecedented global catastrophe. Nothing in the past or the future will ever equal it again. Third, Israel will be delivered out of it and given her covenant promises. This has never happened before. This flies in the face of the arrogant Dominionists. If these prophecies are taken literally, they destroy their whole system.

The Dispensation of the Millennium

The Second Coming of Christ to the earth ends **"the time of Jacob's trouble"** and ushers in the Millennial

Kingdom promised to Abraham, Isaac and Jacob's descendants.

There will be an outpouring of the Holy Spirit upon all believers. Only believers will enter this kingdom. Satan will be bound for a thousand years. Jesus the Messiah will rule over the whole earth and set the atmosphere of the world system with righteousness. With all these blessings man will be expected to live out the standards of the King Messiah as described in the Sermon on the Mount of Matthew 5—7.

The curse of nature will be removed and man will have a perfect environment once more (Isaiah 11; 65:17-25; Amos 9:8-15; Micah 4:1-8; Zechariah 14:16-21).

But even with this kind of privilege some of the children of those who start the kingdom will not believe in the Lord Jesus and Savior. Evidence of unbelieving offspring shows up early in the Millennium (Zechariah 14:17-19 and so on). So, at the end, God will release Satan to bring out into the open the rebellion that He sees in their hearts. Satan will quickly raise up an army of unbelievers, but God will judge them quickly and directly (Revelation 20:7-10).

At this point, time ends. All mortal believers will be translated into immortality. All unbelievers from all economies will be raised to stand before the Great White throne for eternal condemnation.

A clear philosophy of history from God's viewpoint emerges out of these economies. Man is tested under all kinds of conditions throughout the dispensations. The first dispensation begins with a perfect environment and the last one ends with a perfect environment. Man fails in all environments, which demonstrates that environment is not the problem. (Thus God's viewpoint is totally the antithesis of communism, modern psychology and many other human philosophies.)

The dispensations show that the only answer is to be born again by faith so that man is changed from within. Then he masters the environment about him by God's enablement through faith.

Summing Up

Without an understanding and recognition of these various economies it is virtually impossible to interpret and harmonize the various stages of progressive revelation and the distinguishable responsibilities under which man has been tested before God. But more to the point of this book, I believe it's impossible to understand the time of the Rapture without this understanding.

God's Greatest Mystery

*O*ne of the central questions in settling just when the Rapture occurs is whether Israel and the Church are truly distinctive and separate works of God.

In fact, Walvoord points out this critical issue when he says, "It is not too much to say that the rapture question is determined more by Ecclesiology than Eschatology." To translate this, it means that the doctrines concerning the Church bear more on the Rapture question than the doctrines of prophecy.

Ryrie expresses a similar conviction, "Actually the question boils down to whether or not the Church is a distinct entity in the program of God. Those who emphasize the distinctiveness of the Church will be pre-Tribulationists, and those who de-emphasize it will usually be post-Tribulationists."[36] I have always admired Ryrie for his ability to state things in such stark simplicity. I must add that this also applies to the pre-Wrath and mid-Tribulation positions. They also have to minimize the distinctions between Israel and the Church.

I believe along with these men that the question of just when the Rapture occurs in relation to the Tribulation depends almost entirely on how unique and distinct God's program for the Church is from His program for the nation of Israel.

In fact, I believe that God's purpose for Israel and His

---

36 *Ibid*

purpose for the Church are so distinct and mutually exclusive that they cannot both be in force on earth at the same time, especially during the seven-year Tribulation.

Jew and Gentile Segregated Again

If this is so, then the Church must be removed before God can deal specifically again with Israel as defined in Daniel's prophecy (Daniel 9:24-27), because today there is no such thing as a Jew remaining a Jew in the Old Testament sense after believing in Jesus as Messiah.

The apostle Paul makes this very clear when he says of the believer today, **"For there is no distinction between Jew and Greek; for the same Lord is Lord of all, abounding in riches for all who call upon Him"** (Romans 10:12). And again Paul says, **"For all of you who were baptized into Christ have clothed yourselves with Christ. There is neither Jew nor Greek, there is neither slave nor free man, there is neither male nor female; for you are all one in Christ Jesus"** (Galatians 3:27-28).

From the call of Abraham until the birth of the Church, God divided the human race into two categories: Jews and Gentiles. From the birth of the Church until today, God has three categories: nonbelieving Jews, nonbelieving Gentiles, and the Church. This is clear throughout the New Testament Epistles, which were expressly written to the Church. But the following verse makes this concisely clear, **"Give no offense either to Jews or to Greeks or to the Church of God . . ."** (1 Corinthians 10:32).

In this present economy of God's dealing with man, there are unbelieving Jews, and there are unbelieving Gentiles. But the believer from either category becomes known as **the church of God** at the moment of salvation.

The Scriptures from both the Old and New Testament that apply to the Tribulation period deal with the believing Jew as Jew and the believing Gentile as Gentile. Even the great judgments the Messiah executes upon the survivors at the end of the Tribulation are segregated. The Gentile is judged in Matthew 25:31-46 and the Jew in Ezekiel 20:34-44. The conditions are the same as they were in the dispensation of Israel under law.

What Is the Church?

It is very difficult to discuss the Church today because the mere mention of the word conjures up all kinds of erroneous definitions as well as various emotions.

To most the Church is the building where the Christians meet. To others it is the organizations that make up the various denominations.

I'll never forget my first lesson on the Church that I heard as a young believer. An elderly lady sitting in a Bible class I was attending in Houston interrupted the teacher and said, "Pastor, there are young people in here desecrating the church sanctuary by chewing gum." The pastor, Robert Thieme—who has a knack for shocking statements—fired back, "Lady, the sanctuaries are chewing the gum."

That's probably the best lesson I've ever received on Ecclesiology, because I still remember it over 45 years later. The thrust of the statement, though humorous, is profound. For the Church is neither a building nor an organization. It is first and foremost a living organism called the body of Christ.

"And He put all things in subjection under His feet, and gave Him as head over all things to the church, which is His body, the fulness of Him who fills all in all" (Ephesians 1:22-23). And, **"Now I rejoice in my sufferings for your sake, and in my flesh I do my share on behalf of His body (which is the church) in filling up that which is lacking in Christ's afflictions"** (Colossians 1:24).

This body is made up of every true believer, Jew or Gentile, mystically joined in a living union with Jesus Christ Himself and with each other. God explains how we enter the Church, **"For by one Spirit we were all baptized into one body, whether Jews or Greeks, whether slaves or free, and we were all made to drink of one Spirit. For the body is not one member, but many"** (1 Corinthians 12:13-14). And, **"For all of you who were baptized into Christ have clothed your-selves with Christ. There is neither Jew nor Greek, there is neither slave nor free man, there is neither male nor female; for you are all one in Christ Jesus"** (Galatians 3:27-28).

The average professing Christian today has no under-standing of this truth, and yet it is the central teaching of the New Testament. I believe that ministers who act as if the goal of the ministry is to acquire real estate and build buildings that they erroneously call churches cause this confusion. Sometimes in the process they drive people away from the Gospel with high-pressure fundraising pro-grams to pay for these often unnecessarily large and pala-tial edifices.

Paul addressed churches that met in houses, but he never called the houses "churches." (See Romans 16:5 and Philemon 2 for example.)

This concept of the Church being the body of Christ is not just an illustration, but an actual organic reality. This is made wonderfully clear in an extreme case which Paul had to deal with in Corinth.

Some of the Corinthian believers had obviously gotten out of fellowship (not out of relationship) with God and slipped back into their old religious ways. I have stood among the ruins of ancient Corinth and looked up the mountain to the ancient temple of Aphrodite, the goddess of love, that dominates the skyline of the old city. Part of their worship at that temple involved having intercourse with the temple priestess-prostitutes.

It is extremely important to observe carefully how God deals with this problem among these true believers who were walking according to the flesh at this point. Listen to what God said,

"Do you not know that your bodies are members of Christ? Shall I then take away the members of Christ and make them members of a harlot? May it never be!

"Or do you not know that the one who joins himself to a harlot is one body with her? For He says, 'The two shall become one flesh.'

"But the one who joins himself to the Lord is one spirit with Him.

"Flee immorality. Every other sin that a man commits is outside the body, but the immoral man sins against his own body.

"Or do you not know that your body is a temple of the Holy Spirit who is in you, whom you have from God, and that you are not your own?

"For you have been bought with a price: therefore glorify God in your body" (1 Corinthians 6:15-20).

In the first place note that God doesn't question their salvation, but rather affirms that THEY ARE members of Christ's body.

Second, note that the whole basis of God's command for them to stop immediately their immoral behavior is: (1) **"Do you not know that your bodies are members of Christ?"** (2) **"Do you not know that your body is a temple of the Holy Spirit who is in you, whom you have from God, and that you are not your own?"**

Third, and most important, God says that when they have sexual relations with a prostitute, they are actually making the members of Christ to be members of a prostitute (1 Corinthians 6:15-16). There is only one possible way to understand the above statement. It is saying in the first place that the Christian is so joined in an organic union with Christ that Christ is actually involved in whatever our bodies do (see Ephesians 5:30, KJV).

In the second place, it is saying that whenever we have sexual relations with someone, we become one flesh with that person, thus we join Christ to them. Sobering thought, isn't it? By this definition, many people have been married in the eyes of God more than once.

A Very Special Word

God inspired the New Testament writers to take a common Greek word, ekklesia, (ἐκκλησία) and refine it into a highly technical and special meaning.

In its Greek usage outside of the Bible, ekklesia simply meant "a called-out assembly of people." It is used in this sense in the ancient Greek translation of the Hebrew Old Testament, called the Septuagint.

The Lord Jesus Christ was the first to use the term ekklesia in its new sense when He said, **"And I also say to you that you are Peter, and upon this rock I will build my church; and the gates of Hades shall not overpower it"** (Matthew 16:18).

Jesus chose a very special moment to unveil "His

Church." Up until this moment, the word ekklesia had never been used in this special sense. The occasion was Peter's public confession of Jesus as "the Messiah, the Son of the living God." Peter was the first of the disciples to publicly recognize this. (In the original Greek it is clear that the foundation of the Church is not Peter because the word "Peter" (Πέτρος) is masculine in gender. It does not agree with the word "rock" (πέτρα) which is neuter in gender, as it must if the term rock referred back to the term Peter. It is Peter's confession of faith in Jesus that is the rock on which the one true Church is built.

This was Jesus' private revelation to His disciples. It was also a prophecy because He said, **"I WILL build my church . . . "** The Church couldn't be built at this point because Israel had not made its final rejection of Jesus as Messiah, *and the means of forming the Church was not yet given.*

The One Who Builds the Church

Since the Church is the body of Christ, composed of a living union of all true Christians with Christ Himself, the Church could not begin to be built until the arrival of the One who had the power to effect this miraculous union. The Bible calls that person God, the Holy Spirit.

Jesus predicted the coming of the Holy Spirit to inaugurate His new ministries for this dispensation, **"I will ask the Father, and He will give you another Helper, that He may be with you forever; that is the Spirit of truth,**

whom the world cannot receive, because it does not behold Him or know Him, but you know Him because He abides with you, AND WILL BE IN YOU . . . In that day you shall know that I am in My Father, and YOU IN ME, AND I IN YOU" (John 14:16, 17, 20).

The final seven sublime words that I have emphasized describe the essence of what the true Church is in its universal sense. **"You in Me"** describes the union of each believer with Christ Himself. Paul later described it, **"For we are members of His body, of His flesh and of His bones . . . This is a great mystery, but I speak concerning Christ and the Church"** (Ephesians 5:30, 32, NKJV).

"And I in you" describes the permanent residence which Christ takes inside the believer at the moment of salvation. Paul later said, **". . . that is, the mystery which has been hidden from past ages and generations; but has now been manifested to His saints, to whom God willed to make known what is the riches of the glory of this mystery among the Gentiles, which is Christ in you, the hope of glory"** (Colossians 1:26-27).

The mystery of our union with Christ and His dwelling in us are the foundation of the true Church. For this reason, they could not have been revealed before it was obvious that Israel had rejected the Messianic claims of Jesus.

The Holy Spirit's ministry which miraculously forms the Church is defined as follows: **"For even as the body is one yet has many members, and all the members of the body, though they are many, are one body, so also is**

Christ." [This beautifully describes the Church universal.] **"For by one spirit we were all baptized into one body, whether Jews or Greeks, whether slaves or free, and we were all made to drink of one Spirit"** (1 Corinthians 12:12-13).

The Most Important Baptism

It is the baptizing work of the Holy Spirit that forms the Church. This is NOT water baptism. It is the Spirit of God taking each believer at the instant of salvation and immersing him into a living, inseparable union with Christ (Galatians 3:27-28; Colossians 2:12).

So the Church couldn't begin until the baptism of the Holy Spirit began. John the Baptist predicted that Jesus would instigate this baptism of the Spirit (Matthew 3:11). Jesus predicted that it would begin not many days from His ascension to the Father (Acts 1:5). The apostle Peter reveals that the baptism of the Spirit was first given to the Jewish believers on the day of Pentecost (Acts 11:15-16).

So the Church was born on the day of Pentecost when all of the new ministries of the Spirit that are unique to this dispensation were given.

The book of Acts reveals that God followed a specific order in initially giving the new Spirit ministries. They were first given to the Jewish believers since God previously had a covenant relationship with them (Acts 2).

Then the new ministries were initiated to the Samaritan believers who were part Jewish (Acts 8:14-17).

Next they were initially given to the non-Jews or Gentiles, who had no covenant claim to God at all (Acts 10:1-48 compared with 11:15-18).

After this transition period, the new ministries of the Spirit, for example, baptism, indwelling, sealing, gifting, and filling, were given to every believer when he believed. This is set forth in the epistles as the norm for every believer.

What we have been discussing is the Church universal. But there are a number of other shades of meaning given to the term "church" in the New Testament.

The Local Church

The Church is often simply designated by its location. In this sense it refers to the professing believers who meet together regularly in a certain village or city. For example "... the church in Jerusalem" (Acts 8:1); "... the church which is at Cenchrea" (Romans 16:1); "... the church of God which is at Corinth" (1 Corinthians 1:2).

A great many of these churches met in private homes. Twice the church that met in **Prisca and Aquila's home** is mentioned (Romans 16:5; 1 Corinthians 16:19). Others were mentioned as follows: **"greet ... Nympha and the church that is in her house"** (Colossians 4:15); **"to Philemon ... and to the church in your house"** (Philemon 2).

Local churches were also described in the plural in terms of geographical regions in which they were founded. Here are a few examples: **"And he [Paul] was traveling through Syria and Cilicia, strengthening the churches"** (Acts 15:41)**; ". . . as I directed the churches of Galatia"** (1 Corinthians 16:1)**; "the churches of Asia greet you"** (1 Corinthians 16:9); **". . . the churches of Judea which were in Christ"** (Galatians 1:22).

The previous references about the Church teach us the following truths:

First, though the Church assembled in various geographical locations, it is viewed as something distinct from both the building and the locale in which it met.

Second, these churches were simply designated by the name of the city, province or region in which they met.

Third, the local church was always considered to be part of the one true universal Church. For instance, it was **"the Church of God which is at Corinth,"** and **"the churches of Judea which are in Christ."** Though these churches were resident in a specific location, they were viewed as belonging to God and each one directly united with Christ.

Fourth, the New Testament reveals that not everyone in the local church is part of the true Church universal, the body of Christ. The apostle John writes to the local churches concerning former members who have abandoned the faith,

"They went out from us, but they were not really of us; for if they had been of us, they would have remained with us; but they went out, in order that it might be shown that they are not of us" (1 John 2:19).

These are dreadful words which John says, "... in order that it might be shown that they all are not of us."

The same apostle records the words of Jesus the Messiah to the seven churches of Revelation Chapters 2 and 3. In these letters, there are several exhortations to unbelieving individuals within those churches who are obviously not truly saved.

The clearest proof of this is the oft repeated promises to "the one who overcomes," Revelation 2 and 3. John defines this statement in his first epistle, "and who is the one who overcomes the world, but he who believes that Jesus is the Son of God . . . Whoever believes that Jesus is the Messiah is born of God . . ." (1 John 5:5 and 1a).

The Visible Church on Earth

The term "church" is also used in the New Testament to mean the totality of professing Christians without reference to locality. Used in this sense, the Church is practically equivalent to the term "Christendom." This usage embraces all the churches and individuals in them that profess to be Christian. It therefore includes true and false churches, believers, and unbelievers (Romans 16:16; 1 Corinthians 15:9; Galatians 1:13, and so forth).

CHAPTER TEN

The Mystery of Being "In Christ"

*T*he uniqueness of the Church mystery, **"which is Christ in you, the hope of glory,"** and **"now in Christ you who formerly were far off have been brought near by the blood of Christ,"** is central to proving the pre-Tribulation Rapture.

One of the exclusive new designations given only to the believer in the dispensation of grace is a simple prepositional phrase that is repeated some 165 times in the New Testament Epistles. This prepositional phrase is variously stated as **"in Christ," "in Christ Jesus," "in Him,"** or **"in God the Father"** and **"in the Lord Jesus Christ."**

These phrases describe the eternal, inseparable, personal union that each believer has with the Lord Jesus through the baptism of the Spirit. Virtually every benefit of salvation that the heavenly Father bestows upon the believer is transmitted through this organic union with Christ.

For example, we were given **"every spiritual blessing in the heavenly places in Christ"** (Ephesians 1:3).

We were given the very **"righteousness of God in Him"** (Corinthians 5:21). Since Jesus Christ is **"the righteousness of God,"** when we are made one with Him, His righteousness becomes ours.

"In Him we have redemption through His blood, the forgiveness of our trespasses, according to the riches of His grace" (Ephesians 1:7).

Christ's Death, Burial and Resurrection Become Ours

Because of being in Christ, His death and resurrection are as much an actual fact for the believer as they are to Jesus Christ Himself. Sin and the law have no more claim on Christ because He has already died under the full penalty of the law. Just so, the same thing is true of the believer because of his total union of life with Christ (Romans 6:3-14). Just as sin has no claim on Christ's new resurrection life, so sin has no claim on the one who is in union with Him. This is so difficult to believe that only the Holy Spirit can make us understand and receive it.

The Lord says, **"Even so consider yourselves to be dead to sin [the sin nature], but alive to God in Christ Jesus"** (Romans 6:11). If you want your life changed to a whole new sphere of victory, then begin to count as true what God says is true.

The Most True Thing

In the economy of grace, *the Christian way of life is a matter of becoming what God has already made you in Christ.* It simply depends upon learning what God says is true of us because of union with Christ, and then counting it true by faith. And remember, WHAT GOD SAYS IS TRUE ABOUT US IS THE MOST TRUE THING THERE IS ABOUT US.

Because of all that has been accomplished for us in Christ, God promises flatly, **"For sin [the sinful nature] shall not be master over you, for you are not under law,**

but grace" (Romans 6:14). In this new economy of grace, we are no longer under obligation to the law principle that could only demand but not enable. But we are under the principle of grace that doesn't demand, but gives new inner desires and enables (Philippians 2:13 and 4:13).

Now What?

You are probably saying, "What's all this got to do with the Rapture question?" Everything! All the unique and unparalleled ministries of the Holy Spirit to every believer make this economy absolutely distinct from all previous economies. These present ministries of the Holy Spirit also make this economy distinct from the conditions that are predicted for the believers in the seven-year Tribulation.

It is a shame that the post-Tribulationists, mid-Tribulationists and pre-Wrath teachers have to downplay this uniqueness in order to present their case.

Is the Church a Mystery?

In his effort to remove the distinction between the Church and Israel, Gundry first attacks the doctrine of the Church being a mystery, "Further, any argument for the exclusiveness (of the church) on such grounds runs up against the fact that the Church as such is never desig-nated a mystery."

Gundry's statement really begs the question. As dis-cussed earlier in this chapter, Paul in the Ephesian letter said that the mystery is **". . . that the Gentiles are fellow-heirs and fellow-members of the body, and fellow-partakers of**

the promise in Christ Jesus through the Gospel"
(Ephesians 3:6). All these mystery truths revolve around
and are only possible because of the removal of the Old
Covenant distinctions and the uniting of believing Jews
and Gentiles into the body of Christ. Since the body of
Christ is the Church and vice versa, anything that speaks
of the most basic features of the body of Christ is
speaking also of the Church. Therefore, the term **mystery**
rightly applies to the Church.

But the real point is that the Church is a new program
of God in which the Gentiles are made fellow heirs, united
in one body with the Jews who believe in Jesus as
Messiah. *If this new program had been revealed and
understood before the Messiah Jesus offered the Jews the
promised kingdom and Himself as King-Messiah, it would
not have been a bona fide offer.* How could they have
believed in an offer that assumed their unbelief and
already had a known program to replace them?

The Postmillennial Argument for the Church in Tribulation

Gundry levels three arguments against the pre-
Tribulationist view of dispensational distinction between
Israel and the Church. Gundry says, "A partial revelation of
the present age (that is, the dispensation of the Church under
grace) in the Old Testament, a connection (not necessarily
identification) between Israel and the Church, and a dispensational charge involving a transitional period open the door
to the presence of the church during the tribulation."

It is important to note at the outset that even if Gundry could prove these three allegations, it wouldn't necessarily put the Church in the Tribulation. But after carefully searching through each argument, I didn't find any evidence to prove that the Church in its unique sense as the body of Christ was anywhere revealed in the Old Testament. Only the Holy Spirit could interpret and apply the veiled Old Testament references to future salvation of Gentiles and make them understandable. The Israelite certainly didn't have any Old Testament revelation that would have made him comprehend this present economy of grace and the Church.

The fact remains that all Old Testament prophecies about Gentiles picture them in a subordinate role to the Jew in the Messianic kingdom. There is some justification for the old rabbinical teaching of Jewish supremacy in the Millennial Kingdom,

> **"And strangers will stand and pasture your flocks, and foreigners [Gentiles] will be your farmers and your vine dressers. But you will be called the priests of the Lord; you will be spoken of as ministers of our God. You will eat the wealth of nations, and in their riches you will boast"** (Isaiah 61:5-6).

The Old Testament prophecies quoted in the New Testament and applied to the Church do not prove that the body of Christ with all its unprecedented privileges was revealed even partially in the Old Testament. It was a "secret hidden in God" (Ephesians 3:9 and Romans 16:25-27).

Why Are Gentiles Mentioned in Old Testament Prophecy?

The New Testament writers used the prophetic references to Gentiles to prove that Gentiles were always included in God's plan of salvation. The false teaching of first century Judaism, which said that Gentiles couldn't even be saved, had to be refuted by the Old Testament Scriptures that they claimed to accept. This false teaching was so tenacious that it even carried over to the early Jewish believers and the apostles (see Acts 10:34-35; 11:1-18).

This error persisted in the first Church Council of Acts 15:1-29. Some of the converts from Judaism insisted that Gentiles had to become Jewish proselytes to be saved. The apostle James quotes Amos 9:11-12 only to show that Gentiles were always included in God's purposes.

In summary, the Old Testament references to Gentiles only have meaning when parts of these prophecies were selected by the omniscient Holy Spirit and applied to certain aspects of this economy's doctrine. But none of these Old Testament prophecies revealed anything about the body of Christ, the Church, before the Holy Spirit interpreted and applied them.

But there is no getting around the following clear declaration of Paul, **"Now to Him who is able to establish you according to my gospel and the preaching of Jesus Christ, ACCORDING TO THE REVELATION OF**

THE MYSTERY WHICH HAS BEEN KEPT SECRET
FOR LONG AGES PAST, BUT NOW IS MANI-
FESTED, and by the scriptures of the prophets,
according to the commandment of the eternal God,
has been made known to all the nations, leading to
obedience of faith . . ." (Romans 16:26-27).

What About Dispensational Transitions?

Gundry also contends that since there have been transitional periods in changing from one dispensation to
another, there will necessarily be a transition period
between the dispensation of grace and the Tribulation
which, according to him, will put the Church into the
Tribulation.

Even if this premise could be proven, it wouldn't
follow that the Church would go all the way through the
Tribulation to the very end as he claims.

There was a transitional period during the change
from law to grace. It was necessary because the economy
of grace introduced such radically new conditions. The
change from law to grace as a principle of living; the
change from God dealing almost exclusively with the
Israelites to dealing with Gentiles on an equal basis; the
change from a selective, conditional and limited ministry
of the Holy Spirit to an unconditional permanent ministry
to every believer—all required some time to inaugurate.

God graciously gave time for the Jews not only to
understand the above changes, but also to overcome the

false doctrines with which they had been indoctrinated. The epistle to the Hebrews, written sometime between AD 66 and 69, was God's final warning to them. In AD 70 Judaism was no longer an option, because the temple was destroyed by the Romans. With this destruction, animal sacrifice according to Mosaic Law was rendered impossible. God left those who rejected His Messiah with no pretext to continue in a system of worship that had been made null and void by His once for all atonement.

But the change from the economy of grace back to Daniel's final predicted seven years of Tribulation does not need such a transition. The reason is that it is not the introduction of new conditions, but rather a return to old conditions previously known *and still followed to some degree by Orthodox Judaism today.* The only hint of transition is the prophetic signs that telegraph the approach of the era that precedes Christ's Second Advent.

The Close of the Great Parenthesis

Since this economy was not understood in the Old Testament times, and since there was only an expectation of a time of Tribulation ending with the coming of the Messiah to set up the promised Messianic kingdom, the interim economy of grace with its main feature of the Church has to be removed even more suddenly and miraculously than it began. The Word of God certainly promises just that. The instantaneous translation of living saints through the Rapture will close the dispensation of grace.

God's great parenthesis of history that was hidden in God will be closed in "the twinkling of an eye." The whole body of Christ on earth, composed of every living believer in Christ, will suddenly "be snatched out" of the earth to meet the Lord in the air. Without experiencing physical death, we will be instantly translated into immortality.

There, we will join the rest of the body of Christ composed of all believers who have died from the day of Pentecost until that moment. There has never been such a family reunion as this one for which we are bound!

The Restrainer Must Go

More will be said about this later, but the removal of the Church is synonymous with the removal of **"the Restrainer"** of 2 Thessalonians 2:4-12.

As I will demonstrate later, **the Restrainer of lawlessness** who prevents the Roman Dictator called the Antichrist from being unveiled, can only be the Holy Spirit. Since the day of Pentecost, the Spirit of God has been personally resident in the world through the indwelling of the body of Christ that is composed of every believer.

Because of this special, unique residence in the world the Holy Spirit has been restraining **"the mystery of lawlessness"** as well as the Antichrist, **"the man of lawlessness."** But when the body of Christ is removed, the Spirit of God in His present ministry is **"taken out of the way"** (2 Thessalonians 2:7).

Here is the first evidence of this. The Tribulation is characterized by the most rampant human lawlessness of all time. The present restraint of the Holy Spirit is obviously removed.

There is ample evidence that the Holy Spirit does minister according to the conditions of the previous economy of law during the Tribulation.

It is important to note that in the Old Testament the Holy Spirit did convince people of their need for salvation, give the new birth and work through certain chosen vessels such as the prophets. The Scripture predicts that He will work in the same way during the Tribulation.

Second, one of the clear examples of the limited ministry of the Spirit during the Tribulation is the severe lack of spiritual perception on the part of the believers at the judgment that occurs just after the Second Advent of Christ (Matthew 25:31-40). Certainly a believer who is indwelt by and filled with the Holy Spirit would understand what Jesus meant when He says, **"I was hungry, and you gave Me something to eat; I was thirsty, and you gave Me drink; I was a stranger, and you invited Me in; naked, and you clothed Me; I was in prison, and you came to visit Me."**

A believer today in the dispensation of grace understands through the Spirit's teaching the verse that says, **". . . he who receives whomsoever I send receives Me"** (John 13:20a). The Tribulation believer however doesn't manifest this rather simple spiritual insight.

I praise God for a man like John Darby who in the early 19th century through diligently studying the Scripture found that the Church of his day had completely overlooked the large body of revelation about the uniqueness of the Church as the body of Christ. Darby's greatest contribution was his teaching on the uniqueness of the Church, the Body of Christ.

The coming chapters will help define how the Church and the Tribulation relate to each other. It will also help establish God's chronology of the Tribulation—Daniel's Seventieth Week.

CHAPTER ELEVEN

History of the Future

*F*ew people today doubt that history is moving toward some sort of climactic catastrophe. As I have discussed in previous books, current events are moving toward a showdown between the major world powers. Many secular scientists, statesmen, and military experts believe that the world is heading for a global holocaust, involving an all-out nuclear war. The only variable with most of these experts is when.

Of far greater significance is the fact that all the predicted signs that set up the final fateful period immediately preceding the Second Coming of Christ are now before us. We are on the verge of this period, which will last seven years. Students of prophecy have commonly called this time "the Tribulation" because of its awful worldwide judgments. Though the term "Tribulation" may not be the best, I'll use it for the sake of easy identification.

There is more prophecy pertaining to these seven years than any other comparable time period with which the Bible deals. Moses, Isaiah, Jeremiah, Ezekiel, Daniel, Zechariah, most of the so-called Minor Prophets, as well as almost the entire book of Revelation, prophesy about this period. The Tribulation is also the topic of Jesus' most extensive prophetic discourse (see Matthew 24 and 25; Mark 13; Luke 21:15-36).

The sheer volume of prophecy devoted to the Tribulation shows how important it is to God. Since we live in the general time of its occurrence, it is of immense importance to know what the Bible says will happen.

In this chapter I'm going to seek to arrange the events of the Tribulation in chronological order. I approach this task with a true sense of humility and reliance upon God's Spirit, for it is the most demanding of all Biblical interpretation. What is summarized here represents hundreds of hours of my own study over a period more than 40 years, as well as the work of a number of other Biblical scholars.

The Duration of the Tribulation

The prophet Daniel gave the framework of the Tribulation era in Daniel 9:24-27. He was given a revelation concerning the main course of Israel's future. God decreed that 70 weeks of years were allotted to the people of Israel. The prophecy is specifically concerned with the future of (1) the **people of Israel** and (2) the **city of Jerusalem** (Daniel 9:24).

God's Prophetic Stopwatch

Around 530 BC Daniel prophesied that Israel's special allotted time would begin with a decree to restore and rebuild the city of Jerusalem. This decree was actually given by Artaxerxes Longimanus of Persia in 445 BC. Imagine that God had a great stopwatch with 490 years on it. He started the watch counting down the allotted time on the very day Artaxerxes issued the decree to restore and rebuild Jerusalem and its Temple.

Daniel predicted that from the giving of this decree until Messiah the Prince appeared would be 69 sabbatical years (seven years each), or 483 Biblical years. The Bible uses the lunar year of 360 days. Scholars have carefully worked out the chronology from ancient records and found that exactly 173,880 days (that is 483 x 360 days) later, Jesus of Nazareth allowed Himself for the first time to be publicly proclaimed Messiah and heir to the throne of David (recorded in Luke 19:29-44).

The context of this prophecy is that Israel had been put in exile for failure to keep 70 Sabbatical years (2 Chronicles 36:15-23). So just as God tested Israel for 490 years prior to their exile, so He allotted 490 more years for them to finish the purposes for which He had created them.

Two Critical Historical Events

The prophecy then forecast that two historical events would take place after the 483 years, but before the final seven allotted years. First, the Messiah would be "cut off" or killed, and have nothing that was due Him as heir to David's throne. Second, the city of Jerusalem and the temple, which was rebuilt by the Jews who had returned from Babylonian exile, would both be destroyed.

Jesus was crucified five days after being publicly presented as Messiah, and Jerusalem and the temple were destroyed some 37 years later by Titus of Rome in AD 70.

God obviously stopped "the prophetic stop watch" after it had ticked off 483 years. The predicted destruction of Jerusalem happened far outside the predicted bounds of the last remaining week of years, so the clock could not have just continued ticking consecutively.

Because Israel failed to accept her Messiah and instead **"cut Him off"** by crucifying Him, God stopped the countdown seven years short of completion. During the ensuing parenthesis in time, God turned His focus to the Gentiles and created the Church.

The Last Week

It is the remaining seven years of the prophecy that shed so much light upon the Tribulation period. The following are events that must occur to implement the covenant or treaty predicted in Daniel 9:27:

- The Antichrist is unveiled immediately after the Restrainer is taken out of the way.
- In order for the Antichrist to sign the Security Treaty with Israel, he must first take over ten of the strongest nations in the EU so that his political power base will support such a treaty. This will necessitate a short interim period between the removal of the Restrainer/Rapture and the signing of the treaty.
- The final seven year countdown, also called the Seventieth Week of Daniel, begins with the signing of a protective treaty between Israel and the Antichrist, who will come from the revived Roman Empire (9:27). Daniel 9:26 predicted that

the Coming Prince would be **of the people** who destroyed Jerusalem in AD 70, i.e., Roman.

- Israel must rebuild the temple at the beginning of this time, because sacrifice and offerings will be resumed. This type of observance of Mosaic law and worship can only be done in a temple rebuilt on its ancient site in old Jerusalem.

- After three and one-half years the Roman Dictator will betray Israel and set up "**the Abomination of Desolation**." This refers to the desecration of the temple. The Antichrist will enter the Holy of Holies and will erect there a statue of himself, and proclaim himself to be God (Matthew 24:15; 2 Thessalonians 2:3-4; Revelation 13:14-15).

Jesus, speaking of this event, warned that it signals a great intensification of tribulation upon the earth. This will continue to escalate for the remaining three and one-half years (Matthew 24:15-22).

I have gone into some detail on Daniel 9:24-27 because it clearly illustrates that the final seven years, or the Seventieth Week, specifically pertains to God's unfinished business with the Israelite people and Jerusalem. It is a time when God's special focus is back on the Israelites as a people distinct from the Gentiles and the Church. It is an allotment of time in which Old Testament covenants to Israel are to be fulfilled and completed.

It therefore does not seem to be a time when the Church, with its distinct calling and purpose, could be present. For if the Church were present, there could be no distinction between Jew and Gentile as I have already proved in chapters nine and ten.

A Distinct and Special People

Yet in Daniel's prophecy about the Tribulation period, as well as the Revelation Chapters 6-18, the Israelites are again dealt with as a distinct, separate, and special people. Remember this very important point, for much will be said about it later.

Events Just before the Tribulation

It is apparent that sometime before the seven-year Tribulation begins, the Antichrist will receive a mortal wound, be miraculously healed, be indwelt by Satan, and take over the ten nations out of what we now know as the European Union (Revelation 13:3). These things must first occur in order to give him the political position and power base from which to sign the protection treaty with Israel, which officially begins the Tribulation.

A False Prophet, or pseudo-Messiah to Israel (Revelation 13:11-17), will be manifested before the Tribulation begins, for he is the leader of Israel who will make the covenant with the Roman Dictator (the Antichrist).

The great falling away or apostasy of the professing false Christian Church also takes place before the beginning of the Tribulation which is sometimes called "the Day of the Lord" (2 Thessalonians 2:3).

CHAPTER TWELVE

VANISHED

Into Thin Air

*A*s I've discussed, there are many complex issues that are related to establishing the chronology of the book of Revelation. In this chapter, several other specific passages in the book which contribute to answering the Rapture question will be analyzed.

The Promise to the True Church

Philadelphia. As in the case with all seven of the letters to the churches in Revelation Chapters 2 and 3, this letter obviously has an application which goes far beyond the time of the original addressees.

The context indicates in Revelation 3:10 there is an extraordinary promise given to the church of that day that also applies to the end times of the Church. This is true first because the next verse says, **"I am coming quickly; hold fast what you have, in order that no one take your crown"** (Revelation 3:11). This verse has to refer to the coming of Christ for the Church because it uses a warning that is consistently associated with it in this book (see 22:7, 12, 20).

Second, verse 11 also mentions rewards and the receiving of a crown. This is definitely to be given at the "Bema" or judgment seat of Christ. Paul speaks of receiving a crown on "that day" (2 Timothy 4:8). Peter speaks of the "unfading crown of glory" that will be given to faithful elders "when the Lord comes" (1 Peter 5:4). This definitely ties the context to the time of Christ's coming for the Church.

The third reason why this promise must apply to the end times of the Church is given in verse 10 itself. The promise is said to apply to **"that hour which is about to come upon the whole world, to test those who dwell upon the earth."** So the time period concerns a test which God will send upon the whole world. It is obvious that such a global "test" has not yet occurred.

The What, Who, and Why of the Test

It is important to understand just what the original Greek word translated "test" means. The original word is πειράζω. Dr. Gingrich says that the word is used here in the sense of *"to try, to make trial of, to put to the test, in order to discover or reveal what kind of person someone is."* Often the purpose of the trial is to bring out the evil that is in someone. For this reason it is sometimes translated "temptation."

In this context it is best understood as putting the world under severe trial to reveal its evil heart. The trials are launched against **"the whole inhabited earth,"** which is further defined as **"those who dwell upon the earth."** The apostle John makes this a technical descriptive clause to mark out a certain class of people.

Listen to what John says about **"those who dwell upon the earth"**:

- They are the ones who murder the Tribulation believers (6:10).
- The wrath of God contained in the judgments called the "three woes" will specifically fall upon them (8:13).

- They will murder the two special prophets of God (who I believe will be Moses and Elijah) and rejoice over their deaths (11:10).
- The message given by these two prophets will torment them (11:10).
- They will worship the Roman Antichrist, and their names are not in the Lamb's book of life (13:8, 12).
- They will be deceived by the miracles of the False Prophet from Israel (13:14).
- They will be intoxicated and blinded by the false one-world religious system (17:2).

From this survey we can easily see why God is going to have an hour of testing for this group. It is to so demonstrate the hard, evil hearts of **"those who dwell upon the earth"** that God's judgment of them will be shown as totally just.

There is also a very important contrast in Revelation between **"those who dwell upon the earth"** and another special group called **"those who dwell in heaven."**

Let us first consider who **"those who dwell in heaven"** are. First, they cannot be angels because of a statement made in Revelation 12:12 about this same group of "heaven dwellers." It says, **"For this reason, rejoice, O heavens and you who dwell in them, woe to the earth and the sea, because the devil has come down to you, having great wrath, knowing that his time is short."** God's angels would not be exhorted to rejoice because they are not dwelling on earth during the devil's unrestrained wrath. Satan couldn't hurt them.

Second, this is not a reference to the departed souls of those massacred during the Tribulation. Though a non-resurrected believer's soul does go to be consciously with the Lord after he dies, he is never said "to dwell in heaven" until after he receives a resurrection body. Furthermore, it would make no sense for the devil to blaspheme the souls of those whose bodies he has just murdered.

Third, there is a direct contrast made between **"those who dwell on earth,"** who are unbelievers, and **"those who dwell in heaven."** The implication is that the "heaven dwellers" are believers.

So the question is: If they are not angels, and they are not the souls of departed believers, *who are they?*

I believe the answer is that they are the translated (Raptured) saints of the Church who are now dwelling in heaven in glorified bodies. This explanation gives an intelligent reason for why the devil would take the time to blaspheme them. After all, he couldn't very well hide or sweep into a corner the news of millions of Christians vanishing. So Satan must give an explanation to his followers lest they slip into the other camp.

I believe the Holy Spirit has given us here a clear clue as to the whereabouts of the missing Church.

The Church of Philadelphia

The prophetic application of the letter to the Church in Philadelphia is to the true Church in the last stage of church history. It is contrasted with the Laodicean church that depicts the predominant apostate church of the last stage of church history.

It is to the true Church that God says, "Because you have kept the work of My perseverance, I also will keep you from the hour of testing, that hour which is about to come upon the whole inhabited earth [literal], to test those who dwell upon the earth" (Revelation 3:10).

Gingrich, quoting the great Greek scholar Walter Bauer, brings much light to the meaning of "the word of My perseverance." He says that it literally means **"because you have kept the word concerning patient expectation of Me."** This would mean that the promise is to those who patiently expect the Lord's coming. This certainly fits the context.

However, I believe that it also means that they have persevered in clinging to the truth of God's Word under much opposition.

Now because of this perseverance, God promises**, "I will keep you from the hour of testing that is coming upon the whole inhabited earth."** The post-Tribulationist vigorously disputes the meaning of this promise. Some even try to make it have no clear meaning at all.

There are three important aspects to analyze in this promise. First, what does the word keep mean? Second, what does it mean to be kept from the hour of testing? Third, what length of time is meant by the term "hour?"

The verb "to keep" "tereo" (τηρέω) means **"to protect,"** in this instance according to Bauer. God makes a solemn promise to those who are faithful to His Word. He says, **"I will protect you. . . ."**

This protection is not just from the testing, but from the time of the testing. This is often overlooked by those who dispute the application of this verse. The major area of dispute is over the exact meaning of the preposition translated "from" which is the word ek in the original.

The Greek preposition ἐκ in most circumstances means a separation from within something. There are only two instances in the New Testament where ἐκ is used with the verb τηρέω. Both of them are in the writings of the apostle John.

The first instance is in John 17:15 where Jesus prayed for His disciples, **"I do not ask Thee to take them out of the world, but to keep (τηρέω) them from (ἐκ) the evil one."** The idea is that Jesus wants the believer to be protected from falling under the authority of the evil one (Satan). It is clear that the disciples were not in Satan's clutches at the time Jesus prayed the prayer. So in this case ἐκ used with τηρέω means to be protected from coming under Satan's power.

The only other instance these words are used together is here in Revelation 3:10. The same author, John, is expressing the same idea. He is saying that God will protect the believer *from the time* of the testing, not just from the testing.

The meaning of **"the hour of worldwide testing"** must be understood in the light of the main focus of the book of Revelation. Revelation specifically details the judgments, events and personalities of the seven years of Daniel's Seventieth Week. It begins with the worldwide deception and takeover by the Antichrist of Rome. It ends with the worst holocaust of all time. Its purpose is to bring the sons of Abraham, Isaac and Jacob to faith in the true Messiah and to judge the unbelievers from all nations called "those who dwell upon the earth." So **"the hour"** must apply to the whole seven-year Tribulation where all these things fall upon the world.

Search for the Missing Church

I mentioned earlier a very important piece of evidence in Revelation which supports that the Church is translated before the beginning of the Tribulation period.

The Book of Revelation, which, as I've said, is the only book in the Bible specifically written to detail the events and phenomena of the Tribulation, nowhere mentions the Church as present on earth during the Tribulation. This point gains even more significance in the light of the fact that the Church is mentioned 19 times in Chapters 1 through 3.

The voice from heaven says to the apostle John, **"come up here, and I will show you what must take place"** after these earthly scenes.

Revelation makes continual reference to the believers who are on earth during this time, so there is every reason to expect that the term Church would be mentioned if these believers were the Church. There is one striking case where the Church certainly should have been mentioned if it were on earth.

There is a formula that is addressed to the Church seven times in Chapters 2 and 3. It says, **"He who has an ear, let him hear what the Spirit says to the Churches"** (Revelation 2:7, 11, 17, 29; 3:6, 12, 22). This exact formula is repeated again during the Tribulation in Revelation 13:9 and 10, **"If anyone has an ear, let him hear. If anyone is destined for captivity, to captivity he goes; if anyone kills with the sword, with the sword he must be killed. Here is the perseverance and the faith of the saints."**

This is an extremely strong evidence for the Church's absence. In Chapter 13:9 the formula is given to alert Tribulational believers to hear and take heed to the life and death instructions to them of 13:10. In verse 10, believers of that period are instructed not to resist being taken captive for their faith by the Antichrist, nor are they to resist with weapons. If they use weapons, God says that they will be killed by them.

Instead the believers are instructed to persevere in their faith in Jesus Christ whether they die as martyrs or survive until the Second Advent up to the Lord.

Now this is a very clear situation where the term "church" should have been used. Because it is speaking to all the believers of that time about vital survival instructions. But even though the formula is exactly the same as the one given in Chapters 2 and 3, the word "church" is left out of verse 9.

Who Moved the Lamp?

When the apostle John is caught up to heaven in Revelation Chapter 4, he sees seven lamps of fire burning before the throne of God (verse 5). Those seven lamps first appeared on earth in Chapter 1, verses 12 through 20. In verse 20 they are identified as the seven symbolic churches. I believe that these seven lamps are the Church, which has just been raptured into heaven. Here they are called the seven spirits of God because John is emphasizing that the Spirit indwells the churches.

The Bride in Heaven

The Church doesn't specifically reappear until just before the Second Coming of Christ to the earth in Revelation 19:7-16. As previously mentioned, the bride is in heaven already rewarded and prepared for the great wedding feast. The Lord Jesus Christ begins His Second Coming to earth.

The bride of Christ then accompanies Him to the earth on white horses wearing the white robes of her righteous deeds.

The post-Tribulationists have to go all out to try and explain away the sequence of events in this passage. Concerning this passage Ladd says, "So the vision of the bride prepared for the wedding feast is prophetic. In vision, John sees the bride ready for marriage; but this is not a vision of what shall be after Christ returns. Then will occur the resurrection of the dead in Christ—both saints and martyrs (20:4). The final proof that this is a prophetic vision is the fact that the dead in Christ are not yet raised; their resurrection occurs after the return of Christ (20:4)."[37]

Ladd not only has to do violence to the immediate context of Revelation 19:7-16 to come up with such a far-fetched interpretation, but he also has to do damage to the whole structure of the book of Revelation.

First of all, there is a chronological sequence of events in Revelation Chapter 19. The bride of Christ not only is seen in heaven already prepared for her wedding feast, but afterward the same bride returns with Christ in His second advent to earth (19:4).

Second, the Book of Revelation moves through the Tribulation in a definite chronological order except for the interludes where the cameo sections explain the history and future of the personalities, organizations and events that culminate in the book. When Ladd says that John sees "the bride of Christ [the Church] in vision," he seems to think that this eliminates any necessity for following the normal, logical, chronological, and temporal sequences that are established throughout the book. What Ladd doesn't recognize here is that the whole Book of Revelation is a vision. But that doesn't remove the fact that the visions have a definite chronological sequence. If this

---

37 George E. Ladd, *The Blessed Hope* (Grand Rapids: Wm. B. Eerdmans Pub. Co., 1956), p. 102

logic were followed, the book is nothing more than an incoherent collection of visions that cannot possibly be understood.

Third, Ladd's own quote brings out the error of his interpretation. In fact, it is an extremely strong evidence for the Church's Rapture long before the second advent of Christ.

An Embarrassing Resurrection

As previously quoted, Ladd says, "The final proof that this is a prophetic vision is the fact the dead in Christ are not yet raised; their resurrection occurs after the return of Christ" (20:4).

Ladd seems to be so determined to prove his view that he must not have carefully evaluated the implications of the above statement.

First, if God intended for this book to be intelligible at all, Chapters 19 and 20 have a very definite chronological sequence:

The armies of the Antichrist, the False Prophet and all the kings of the earth unite to fight Christ's return (19:19).

The Antichrist and the False Prophet are both taken and cast alive into the lake of fire. Christ returns with His bride, the Church (19:7-16, 20).

All the rest of the armies with their kings are slain by Christ and given to the scavenger birds (19:21).

Satan is bound for a thousand years (20:1-3).

The martyred Tribulation believers are resur-rected.

There is absolutely nothing in this context to indicate to an unbiased reader that this passage is anything other than a consecutive narrative of future history.

Now here is the point. Ladd agrees that this resurrection of Tribulation saints takes place *after* the return of Christ. If the Church is on earth during the Tribulation, and if the Church is raptured immediately before the Second Coming of Christ, then how is it that these Tribulation believers (who are the Church according to his view) are resurrected after the Second Coming? The Scripture says that **"the dead in Christ shall rise first, then we who are alive and remain until the coming of the Lord shall be caught up together with them in the clouds to meet the Lord in the air"** (1 Thessalonians 4:16-17).

If the Church were on earth and raptured just before the Second Coming (as post-Tribulationists must say), then all martyred Tribulation saints would be part of the Church and, therefore, have to be raised before the living believers could be translated into immortality. And all this, according to post-Tribulationists, occurs just before the Second Advent.

This is a major evidence that the Church must be snatched up to meet the Lord long before the end of the Tribulation and the Second Advent.

Is God a Bigamist?

Gundry argues, "Israel is sometimes likened to a bride (Isaiah 49:18; 16:10; 62:5; Jeremiah 2:32; Hosea 2:19-20) and the Church is likened to a wife (Ephesians 5:22-23). We should not expect to find rigid consistency in the Biblical use of metaphors. To press woodenly the marital relationship of both Israel and the Church to the Lord would be to say that God is a bigamist."

Gundry's whole argument is misleading because Israel is never once said to be the bride of the Lord Jesus Messiah. God's attitude toward Israel is illustrated by various aspects of a bride's jewelry, by a bridegroom's excitement over his bride, and so forth.

But the Church is actually said to be the bride of Jesus Christ. In Ephesians 5:22-32, God says that though it is a great mystery, marriage is intended to be an earthly illustration of the believer's heavenly union with Christ. God says, "**. . . because we are members of His body, of His flesh, and of His bone. For this cause a man shall leave his father and his mother, and shall cleave to his wife; and the two shall become one flesh. This mystery is great; but I am speaking with reference to Christ and the Church**" (Ephesians 5:30-32, NKJV).

The Hebrew marriage custom underlies the New Testament declaration of the Church as the bride of Christ. Ryrie traces the steps of the Hebrew marriage custom of that era.

First, betrothal (which involved the prospective groom's traveling from his father's house to the home of the prospective bride, paying the purchase price, and thus establishing the marriage covenant); second, the groom's returning to his father's house and remaining separate from his bride for 12 months during which time he prepares the living accommodations for his wife in his father's house; third, the groom's coming for his bride at a time not known exactly to her; fourth, his return with her to the groom's father's house to consummate the marriage and to celebrate the wedding feast for the next seven days (during which the bride remained closeted in her bridal chamber).

"In Revelation 19:7-9 the wedding feast is announced, which, if the analogy of the Hebrew marriage means anything, assumes that the wedding previously took place in the father's house. Today, the church is described as a virgin waiting for her bridegroom's coming (2 Corinthians 11:2); in Revelation 21 she is designated as the wife of the Lamb, indicating that previously she has been taken to the groom's father's house. Pre-Tribulationists say that this requires an interval of time between the Rapture and the Second Coming."

All of the symbols and imagery used in the New Testament were based upon the common Hebrew culture of the day. Otherwise there would be no hope of understanding the rich use of parable, allegory and illustrations. Therefore, the standard Hebrew marriage tradition of that time gives insight into the Church as the bride of Christ, particularly in Revelation Chapters 19 and 21.

Summary

I believe that these passages we have examined contribute significantly toward the case for a pre-Tribulation Rapture. The promise of being kept form the hour; the identity of those who dwell in heaven; the Church's absence from earth in Chapters 4 through 19; the bride's presence in heaven before the Second Coming, all fit into the pattern of a pre-Tribulation Rapture scenario.

Now let us look at the evidence in 1 and 2 Thessalonians.

CHAPTER THIRTEEN

THE THESSALONIANS AND THE RAPTURE

The Thessalonian Legacy

*T*he two New Testament letters that mention the Rapture most were both written to the same people. These letters are 1 and 2 Thessalonians.

These were the apostle Paul's earliest epistles. Both letters were written from Corinth in about the year AD 50, shortly after Paul's departure from Thessalonica (Acts 17:1-15 and 18:1-11).

Many important insights come from these early letters. First, it is nothing short of amazing how many Christian doctrines Paul taught these people who formed the church located in Thessalonica. He brought them from being idol-worshiping pagans to understanding the following major theological subjects in about four weeks: election (1 Thessalonians 1:4); the Person of the Holy Spirit (1:5, 6; 4:8; 5:19); assurance of salvation (1:5); the Trinity (1:5, 6); conversion (1:9); the Christian walk (2:12; 4:1); sanctification (4:3; 5:23); the day of the Lord (5:1-3); the three dimensions of man's nature (5:23); resurrection (4:14-18); Rapture of the Church (1:10; 2:19; 3:13 4:14-17; 5:9, 23); the coming apostasy (2 Thessalonians 2:3); the advent of the Antichrist (2 Thessalonians 2:3-12); the second advent of Christ and world judgment (2 Thessalonians 1:7-10).

These are only part of what Paul must have taught them. Can you imagine today someone going to a city dominated by false religion, winning many to faith in Christ, founding a church, and then communicating all the above truths in four weeks? No wonder Paul said concerning his ministry there, **"For our Gospel did not come to you in word only, but also in power and the Holy Spirit and with full conviction . . ."** (1 Thessalonians 1:5).

The All-Time Greatest Bible Conference

A second insight is that even though Paul had such a short time with them, he fully taught the whole scope of prophecy as it relates to the Rapture, the Second Coming of Christ and the world events that precede and follow. This fact alone should silence the many critical theologians and ministers who say that this subject is irrelevant to Christian living and shouldn't be taught. Paul has so thoroughly taught eschatology (prophecy) that he could refer to some advanced concepts and say, **"Do you not remember that while I was still with you, I was telling you these things"** (2 Thessalonians 2:5).

The whole underlying occasion for writing these two letters sprang from the area of prophetic subjects. In 1 Thessalonians, Paul primarily answers the questions of whether believers who have died will be reunited with those who are still living at the time of the Rapture and are translated (1 Thessalonians 4:13-18).

In 2 Thessalonians, Paul primarily writes to reassure the Thessalonian believers that they are not already in "**the day of the Lord**" and/or the Tribulation or the Seventieth Week of Daniel. (*The first seven years of "the day of the Lord" coincide with the Tribulation period.*)

The Problem of Lazy Brethren

A second occasion for writing both letters was the problem of those who misapplied the practical meaning of Paul's teaching concerning the "any moment" possibility of Christ's return which is commonly called the doctrine of imminence.

Two things should be observed about the way Paul dealt with this error. First, Paul doesn't deny or tone down his teaching that Christ's coming for the Church could be near. Some people think that no one should teach that Christ's coming could be very near because it could cause some to drop out of jobs, school, get married prematurely, and so forth, becoming generally irresponsible. However, the possible misapplication of truth is never a justification for not teaching it. Some people misapply the truth of salvation, but shouldn't we continue to teach it?

Second, Paul shows that even if Christ were to come today, we should live responsibly and maintain a good testimony to the end. It has been my experience that most believers are motivated to greater dedication, faith and spiritual production by the hope that the Lord Jesus could come at any moment during their lifetime.

In 1 Thessalonians Paul reminds these idle believers of his example before them (2:9-10). He exhorts them to work, supply their own needs and maintain a testimony to the nonbelievers (4:11-12). Paul's first priority was to win people to Christ and to build them up in the faith. This, he tells us, is the proper response to the expectation of the Lord's imminent return.

The Rapture is mentioned in every chapter of 1 Thessalonians. Such an amazing emphasis of this doctrine in the earliest Epistles underscores its importance.

The Rapture Delivers from Wrath

Paul says in Chapter 1, **"And to wait for His son from heaven, whom He raised from the dead, that is Jesus, who delivers from the wrath to come"** (1 Thessalonians 1:10).

Dr. Morris comments on the term, **wait:** "The word for **'to wait'** is found only here in the New Testament. The Grimm-Thayer Greek dictionary suggests that in addition to the thought of waiting for someone expected, it includes 'the added notion of patience and trust.' Findlay thinks it implies 'sustained expectation.'"[38]

I agree with Dr. Morris. The root meaning of the Greek verb, ἀναμένειν, is that of a persistent, sustained and expectant waiting. And since it is also an infinitive in the present tense, the linear action of the present verb tense added to the root meaning of the word adds tremendous emphasis on the continuing action and tenacity of waiting.

So the emphasis is that the believer should *constantly expect and await Christ's return*. It is to be our primary motivating hope that inspires and sustains us to live for

---

38 Leon Morris, *The First and Second Epistles to Thessalonians* (Grand Rapids: Eerdmans Pub. Co., 1959)

God, especially in adversity. The Thessalonians were undergoing extreme persecution. Paul reminds them that even though the present conditions are severe, the Lord will deliver us from the coming wrath of God upon the unbelieving world, which will be much more severe.

"The Wrath to Come"

The purpose of this coming of "**the Lord from heaven**" is to deliver the true Church from "**the wrath to come.**" *Not from just any wrath, but from the predicted wrath of the Tribulation.* The verb "**to deliver**" is ῥυόμαι in the Greek. It means "to rescue or save someone from a terrible situation in which he is helpless." This same term is used, for example, in 6:13 ("**deliver us from the evil one**"), and also in Colossians 1:13 ("**He [Christ] delivered us from the domain of darkness**"). This is a perfect term to describe the Rapture because it truly is a deliverance from human history's worst period of suffering and spiritual darkness under which mankind is totally helpless.

Rapture, Reunion, and Crown (2:19-20)

In Chapter 2, Paul says concerning the Rapture, "**For who is our hope or crown of exultation? Is it not even you, in the presence of our Lord Jesus at His coming? For you are glory and joy**" (2:19, 20).

The apostle speaks of those whom he has introduced to Christ as his crown of exultation when the Lord Jesus comes in the Rapture. I believe that when the Rapture occurs we will be reunited with all those we helped come to faith in Christ. They will be part of our reward and crown at the Rapture. What a joyous thing to contemplate!

Rapture and an Unblamable Heart (3:12-13)

Paul says of the Rapture at the end of Chapter 3, **". . . May the Lord cause you to increase and abound in love for one another, and for all men, just as we also do for you; so that He may establish your hearts unblamable in holiness before our God and Father at the coming of our Lord Jesus with all His saints"** (3:12-13).

If we allow the Holy Spirit to produce God's kind of love in us now, then we will have an unblamable heart of holiness when the Lord Jesus comes for the Church.

Paul also adds that all of the believers of the Church who have died will be with the Lord when He returns. This is explained in more detail in Chapter 4.

The Great Body Snatch (4:13-18)

Paul gives his main reason for writing 1 Thessalonians at the end of Chapter 4. Since I have previously commented on these verses, it is sufficient to simply list the main points here.

First, believing loved ones who have died will not only join us in the Rapture, they will receive their resurrection bodies a split second before our translation. The Thessalonians were confused about whether they would see their dead loved ones again (4:13-15).

Second, the living believers will be snatched up bodily to meet the Lord and departed saints in the air and instantly transformed from mortal to immortal (4:16-17).

The Day of the Lord (5:1-11)

Paul answers another prophetic question that bothered the Thessalonians. He introduces the important section with the Greek phrase περὶ δὲ ("**now as to**" in NASB) which literally means "**but concerning**" or "**now concerning.**" This was Paul's standard form for answering the questions of the ones to whom he was writing (see 1 Corinthians 1:11; 7:1; 7:25; 8:1; 12:1; 16:1). It was his custom to introduce a new subject and a new answer in this manner.

Let us carefully read the entire passage:

"**Now as to the times and epochs, brethren, you have no need of anything to be written to you. For you yourselves know full well that the day of the Lord will come just like a thief in the night. While they are saying, 'Peace and safety!' then destruction will come upon them suddenly like birth pangs upon a woman with child; and they shall not escape. But you, brethren, are not in darkness, that the day should overtake you like a thief; for you are all sons of light and sons of day. We are not of night nor of darkness; so then let us not sleep as others do, but let us be alert and sober. For those who sleep do their sleeping at night, and those who get drunk get** drunk at night. But since we are of the day, let us be sober, having put on the breastplate of faith and love, and as a helmet, the hope of salvation. For God has not destined us for wrath, but for obtaining salvation through our Lord Jesus Christ, who died for us, that whether we are awake or asleep, we may live together with Him. Therefore encourage one another, and build up one another, just as you also are doing" (1 Thessalonians 5:1-11).

The question concerned the "times" (χρόνοι) and "seasons" (καιροῖ) of prophetic events that precede and lead up to the Second Coming of the Lord (5:1). Chronoi refers to the specific times of prophetic events in chronological order. Καιροῖ, on the other hand, views the characteristics of the events themselves.

Paul's Answer

First, Paul reminds them that they already **"know perfectly"** about the subject (5:2). This stands in contrast to their ignorance about the subjects of the previous section (4:13-18). It also continues to amaze me as to how much they were taught in such a short time.

Second, Paul groups their entire question about specific prophetic events and their characteristics under one all-inclusive prophetic period—**"the day of the Lord."** He had obviously taught them that the day of the Lord began with and included all of the specific events that count down to the Lord's return to earth. So Paul focuses his answer on how and under what world conditions **"that day"** will begin. The following is a brief survey of what the Bible teaches about the day of the Lord.

The Day of the Lord in the Old Testament

This phrase is used about 20 times in the Old Testament. The parallel terms, **"the last days"** and **"in that day"** occur 14 times and more than 100 times, respectively. Walvoord writes, "A study of numerous Old Testament references to the Day of the Lord and 'the Day,' as it is sometimes called, should make it clear to anyone who respects the details of prophecy that the designation denotes an extensive time of Divine judgment on the world. Among the texts are Isaiah 2:12-21; 13:9-16; 34:1-8; Joel 1:15—2:11, 28-32; 3:9-12; Amos 5:18-20; Obadiah 15-17; Zephaniah 1:7-18." After a thorough study, Walvoord concludes, "Based on the Old Testament revelation, the Day of the Lord is a time of judgment, culminating in the Second Coming of Christ, and followed by a time of special Divine blessing to be fulfilled in the millennial kingdom."[39]

Day of the Lord in the New Testament

Almost all the teaching concerning the Day of the Lord in the New Testament is in this passage and in 2 Thessalonians 2:1-12. The following is a summary of what these two passages teach about "the Day of the Lord."

---

39 John F. Walvoord, *The Blessed Hope and the Tribulation*, pp. 111, 113

First, it will come **"like a thief in the night"** upon the unbelieving world. This metaphor means that it will come with surprise and speed.

Second, it will come when the world is saying **"peace and safety."** When the Antichrist is revealed by being miraculously raised from a mortal wound (Revelation 13:3), he will give superhuman answers to the world that will be in a state of fear and insecurity. They will almost instantly receive him as world leader and rest in the pseudo-peace and security he initiates.

Third, sudden destruction is associated with it. The judgments of the Day of the Lord will be like birth pangs seizing a pregnant woman (5:3). Once they begin, there is no escape. But they increase in frequency and severity until the birth is over. So it will be with these judgments. The most extensive and chronological development of the judgments is in the Book of Revelation.

Antichrist's Unveiling Closely Connected to Beginning of the Day of the Lord

Fourth, it begins shortly after the Antichrist is revealed, which is immediately after the removal of the Holy Spirit's restraining ministry (2 Thessalonians 2:1-12). *This passage connects the beginning of the Day of the Lord closely to the Antichrist's revelation.* (Since the Holy Spirit has been personally resident on earth in every believer since the day of Pentecost, this is tantamount to saying the Church is raptured. You can't remove the Holy Spirit without removing the vessels in whom He dwells.) *Remember this in connection with the pre-Wrath Rapture theory.*

Fifth, the Day of the Lord will not take the believers by total surprise for two reasons:

The believer is a child of light and of the day. This means that he has the illumination of the Holy Spirit and the prophetic Scripture (Daniel 12:8-10). Peter spoke of this very illumination, **"For we did not follow cleverly devised tales when we made known to you the power and the coming of our Lord Jesus Christ, but we were eyewitnesses of His majesty . . . and so we have the prophetic word made more sure, to which you do well to pay attention as to a lamp shining in a dark place, until the Day dawns and the morning star arises in your hearts"** (2 Peter 1:16, 19). So the believer will not be taken by total surprise. As I have taught many times, the believer *cannot* know the day or the hour, but in these last days it has been revealed that he will know the general time (Matthew 23:32-36). However, if the believer of this economy were left in **the Day of the Lord** with all of its specific signs, he could calculate the day of the Lord's return.

The Day will not overtake the believer like a thief because **"he is not destined for wrath, but for the obtaining of salvation through our Lord Jesus Christ"** (5:9). We will be delivered from the wrath that begins with the Day of the Lord by the Rapture.

The post-Tribulationists and pre-Wrath teachers have more problems than a one-armed paperhanger trying to fit the beginning of the Day of the Lord in at the very end of the Tribulation.

First, they have the problem of holding off all the Divine judgments until after the Rapture (which they say is simultaneous with the Second Advent), and then having them all fall before the Second Coming. This means that at least most of the seal and trumpet judgments, plus all of the bowl judgments, would have to occur in less than five minutes. This view would also have to compress the invasion of the king of the North (Daniel 11:40-45; Ezekiel 38-39) and the kings of the East (Revelation 16:12) into that short period.

Second, they have to explain why the unbelievers of that time will proclaim **"peace and safety"** (5:3) in the midst of the concentrated wrath of God. **"Peace and safety"** is contrasted with the sudden destruction that follows. So Gundry's interpretation that they are only wishing for peace and safety doesn't make sense.

Third, the fear and concern the Thessalonians have about being already in the Day of the Lord (2 Thessalonians 2:1-5) cannot be reconciled with the post-Tribulation view. Unless **"the Day"** started near the time of the Antichrist's unveiling, the passage wouldn't make sense. It would have been obvious to the Thessalonians that they could not be in the Day of the Lord if it were only at the very end.

All of us must admit that there are some things that are difficult to reconcile on this issue. But the pre-Tribulation view harmonizes all of the scriptural evidence best, and answers the most questions satisfactorily.

Sanctified and Completed at the Rapture

Paul mentions the Rapture again in his closing prayer for the Thessalonians. Paul prays, **"May God Himself, the God of peace, sanctify you through and through. May your whole spirit, soul and body be kept blameless at the coming of our Lord Jesus the Messiah. The one who calls you is faithful and he will do it"** (5:23, 24, NIV).

Paul reveals a beautiful truth in this prayer. It is God who sanctifies us. The verb **"to sanctify"** (ἁγιάζω in the Greek) has a common root with the term **"holy."** It literally means *to set something apart for God's possession and use.* The word was used in ancient Greece even to describe inanimate objects that were offered to the ancient temple gods.

Paul's prayer is that God will progressively set apart our whole being to Himself. Paul then gives a promise of assurance that God will see that this is accomplished in our lives because He is faithful. The end result is that we will be blameless when we are caught up to stand before our Lord Messiah in the Rapture.

Summary of 1 Thessalonians

Here is a summary of the main principles taught in 1 Thessalonians concerning the Rapture:

1. The doctrine of the Rapture was taught even to young believers.

2. The Rapture will deliver believers in the Lord Jesus from the predicted time of wrath which is part of the beginning of the "**Day of the Lord**" (1:10; 5:9).

3. All living believers will suddenly be caught up to meet the Lord in the air, and will be reunited with their loved ones who have died.

4. The believer will not know the specific time of the Rapture (5:4-5).

5. The Day of the Lord will come with sudden destruction upon the unsuspecting, nonbelieving world while it is proclaiming peace and safety (5:2-3). The Rapture delivers believers from this period of destruction, as we noted in (2).

6. The hope of the Rapture and its deliverance from wrath is given as a source of comfort and encouragement to the believer (1:10; 4:18 and 5:11).

As the world spins virtually out of control from crisis to crisis, this hope burns ever brighter. May the impact of the incredible promises of deliverance from wrath we have just studied not be lost in the technical details, but cause hope to spring alive in you.

CHAPTER FOURTEEN

LIGHT FROM A FORGED LETTER

*S*econd Thessalonians contains a very important passage with regard to the chronology of events related to the Rapture. Whether you are a pre-, mid-, or post-Tribulationist, the Rapture interpretation of this letter is crucial.

The apostle Paul clearly states his main reason for writing the letter in Chapter 2, verses 1 and 2:

"Now we request you, brethren, with regard to the coming of our Lord Jesus Christ, and our gathering together to Him, that you may not be quickly shaken from your composure or be disturbed either by a spirit or a message or a letter as if from us, to the effect that the day of the Lord has come."

The phrase **"as if from us"** brings out the real problem that this letter seeks to correct. Someone had brought a message to them, representing it as from Paul, which said that the Day of the Lord had already begun.

Paul begins to correct the grave error by appealing to **"the coming of the Lord Jesus Christ."** He specifies carefully which aspect of His coming by the qualifying phrase **"and our gathering together to Him. . . ."** This could only refer to the Rapture when Christians will be caught up to be with Christ.

Because Paul begins this important section of the letter by holding up the promise of the Rapture first, it is obvious that it has an important bearing on whether the Day of the Lord has indeed already come.

The fact that Paul holds up the Rapture as yet to occur seems to remind the Thessalonians of its chronological relationship to the Day of the Lord. Since the Rapture hasn't occurred, the Day of the Lord could not already be present.

The Terrifying Forgery

Two words describe the Thessalonians' reaction to the forged message. The first is the verb saleuo, [σαλεύω] which is translated "**shaken**." It means to shake or agitate something. It is a violent term that is used sometimes to describe an earthquake. We have a slang expression today that captures this idea. We say, *"He's all shook up,"* meaning that someone is thoroughly shaken from his emotional moorings. The people had been shaken from what they had been taught and had become thoroughly confused.

The second term describing the impact of the forgery is translated "**disturbed**." The original Greek word (θροεῖσθαι) means "**to be frightened**." It is in the present tense and the passive voice, which means they were gripped by a continuing state of fear.

Gundry disagrees with this premise. He says that the Thessalonians were only a little agitated, not fearful. He also says that their agitation was due to some believers who had erroneously understood that the Lord's coming was near and had quit their jobs. This misses the point of the context altogether. The Thessalonians were in a state of fear, not just agitated. They were confused and fearful because they thought they were already in the Tribulation, not because a few quit their jobs.

A Crucial Question

The following question helps reveal what Paul must have taught them. If Paul had told them that the Rapture followed the Day of the Lord, these people would not have been troubled but rather rejoicing because the Lord's coming for them would have been very near. They would have faced the Tribulation with hope and steadfastness, knowing that the Rapture was less than three and one-half years away, if Paul had taught a mid-Tribulation Rapture or less than seven years away if he had taught a post-Tribulation Rapture.

But, if Paul had instructed them that the Rapture preceded the Day of the Lord, and afterward a forged message was received that said they were already in that Day, then their panic becomes completely understandable.

I believe this scenario best explains the conditions that underlie the epistle. This whole context reflects that Paul had taught them a pre-Tribulation scenario for the Rapture.

Paul sets up a threefold denial of any message coming from him that said the Day of the Lord had begun. He lists the three different ways that a false message could have been communicated and denies them all. He sent neither a spirit, nor a verbal message, nor a written letter with such a teaching. Paul's usual way of communication was a written letter. For this reason he urges them to check out any letter presented as being from him by verifying his handwritten greeting and signature (3:17-18). He also wanted them to know that this letter correcting the forgery was not itself a forgery.

Two Imperative Historical Signs

Paul reminds them of two world-shaking events of prophecy which must happen just before the Day of the Lord can begin. He obviously selects these two events because they are of such magnitude that they could not occur unnoticed.

About this Paul says,

"Let no one in any way deceive you, for it [the Day of the Lord] will not come unless the apostasy comes first, and the man of lawlessness is revealed, the son of destruction, who opposes and exalts himself above every so-called god or object of worship, so that he takes his seat in the temple of God, displaying himself as being God. Do you not remember that while I was still with you, I was telling you these things?" (2 Thessalonians 2:3-5).

The Great Apostasy

The first event which precedes the Day of the Lord is "the apostasy." In this context, the word (ἀποστασία in Greek) means to deliberately forsake and rebel against known truth from and about God.

The definite article before the term "apostasy" clearly indicates that it is a definite event, not just a progressive rebellion. The article also points out that this fact has been taught to them before.

There are many New Testament warnings about a progressive apostasy in the last days which would grow in intensity within professing Christendom. Apostasy was perceptible even in the early Church as shown in verse 7, where it is called "**the mystery of lawlessness**." But "**the apostasy**" is a reference to a climactic event when the professing church will completely revolt against the Bible and all of its historical truths.

The ultimate act of apostasy on the part of professing Christendom sets the stage for the second great sign, which apparently happens almost simultaneously.

The Unveiling of the Antichrist

With all restraint of lawlessness removed (that is, the rejection of God and His truth), the door is opened for Satan to reveal his masterpiece, the Antichrist. This unveiling is portrayed by the opening of the First Seal in Revelation Chapter 6. This event constitutes one of the greatest judgments of all time against man. He is called here **"the man of lawlessness"** and **"the son of destruction."** The exact meaning of these titles **is "the man who brings lawlessness"** and **"the son who brings destruction."**

What accurate insight these two descriptive titles give us. The Antichrist, who will spring forth from the modern remains of the ancient Roman culture and people, will cause the worst period of lawlessness and destruction the world has ever seen.

Daniel's prophecies about this world dictator give more insight into this aspect of his awesome career:

"And he will speak out against the Most High and wear down the saints of the Highest One, and he will intend to make alterations in times and in law; and they will be given into his hand for a time, [and two] times, and half a time [three and one-half years]" (Daniel 7:25).

"And in the latter period of their rule [Gentile world power], when the transgressors have run their course, a king will arise insolent and skilled in intrigue. And his power will be mighty, but not by his own power [he will have Satan's powers], and he will destroy to an extraordinary degree and prosper and perform his will; he will destroy mighty men and the holy people. And through his shrewdness he will cause deceit to succeed by his influence; and he will magnify himself in his heart, and he will destroy many by means of peace . . ." (Daniel 8:23-25a).

These Scriptures teach us that the Antichrist will alter times and laws to his own purpose. He will also be a master of deceit, and will deceive the whole world into following him. While capitalizing on the world's desire for peace and security (1 Thessalonians 5:3), he will bring them under his control and ultimate destruction.

Paul gives a threefold summary of this Messianic counterfeit.

First, he opposes and exalts himself above every so-called god or object of worship. The Antichrist will seek to destroy all truth about God and even the gods of other religions.

Second, he will take his throne into the holy of holies of the third Jewish temple which must be rebuilt upon its ancient site.[40] This act will fulfill Daniel's and Jesus' prophecy concerning the **"abomination of desolation"** which officially begins the last three and one-half years of the Tribulation period (Daniel 9:27 compared with Matthew 24:15).

Third, he will proclaim and display himself as being God. This is the ultimate blasphemy. He will take secular humanism into the religious sphere by deifying man. He will not only deceive the world into accepting him as the supreme political dictator, but will also demand worship (Revelation 13:4 and 15).

A Necessary Prelude

Another line of prophetic chronology makes it absolutely necessary for these two events to precede the Day of the Lord. This was previously mentioned briefly, but bears repeating here.

The Roman Dictator must be unveiled a short while

---

40 It has recently been discovered that the Holy of Holies lies approximately 100 meters north of the Dome of the Rock. This means that the third temple could now be built without disturbing the third holiest Muslim shrine

before the actual beginning of Daniel's Seventieth Week, which also begins the Day of the Lord. This is necessary because, as stated before, it begins with the signing of a guarantee of protection for Israel between the Roman Dictator of the revived Roman Empire and the leader of Israel called the False Prophet.[41] The Roman Antichrist must have time to be revealed, take over the ten-nation European confederacy and establish himself as the world leader before he can have a power base from which to make the covenant with the Israeli leader.

Such momentous events necessitate an interlude between the revelation of the Antichrist and the official beginning of the Day of the Lord.

The Restrainer

After reminding the Thessalonians of the two signs just mentioned, Paul takes up another prophetic personality of whom he assumes their previous knowledge.

The apostasy and the Antichrist refer to future events. The conditions described by "the Restrainer" relate to the present time and to what is holding back these two fateful events.

Paul admonishes them by saying,

"And you know what restrains him [Antichrist] now, so that in his time he may be revealed. For the mystery of lawlessness [apostasy] is already at work; only He who now

41 See Revelation 13:11-18, 19-20

restrains will keep on doing so until He is taken out of the way. And then that lawless one will be revealed . . ." (2 Thessalonians 2:6-8a).

The apostle had taught this subject so well that he could say, **"you know."** Then he refers to the most critical subject of the who context, **"the Restrainer."**

The root verb for **"restrainer"** (κατέχω) literally means "to hold down or suppress something." It is translated in the sense of Romans 1:18 where it speaks of the unbeliever suppressing the truth.

In verse 6, the Restrainer is called an influence by the use of the neuter gender (τὸ κατέχον) in the present tense participle form of the verb to restrain. But in verse 7 a singular masculine gender (ὁ Κατέχων) is used to describe the Restrainer, thus showing that he is also a person.

The Duration of the Restrainer's Mission

The apostle Paul said that the Restrainer would keep on restraining both the mystery of lawlessness and the advent of the man of lawlessness continuously until He literally **"takes Himself out of the midst."** This translation is demanded by the middle voice of the Greek verb. Immediately after the Restrainer removes Himself from His mission, the Antichrist will be revealed. The masculine participle is also in the present tense. So a literal translation would be, **"Only He who is now restraining will keep doing so until He takes Himself out of the way, then that Lawless One will be revealed."**

Now let us list the characteristics of the Restrainer.

First, the Restrainer must be both a worldwide influence and a Person. This suggests omnipresence.

Second, the Restrainer must be a supernatural Person to be able to restrain from Paul's time to the present hour.

Third, the Restrainer must be a powerful Person to hold back two such mighty forces as worldwide apostasy and the Antichrist's advent.

Fourth, the Restrainer must have some logical reason for terminating the restraint of lawlessness and the Antichrist's advent, which agrees with the Biblical record.

Fifth, the Restrainer must have a logical reason to restrain lawlessness and the man of lawlessness.

Who Is the Restrainer?

There have basically been three different major views as to who or what "the Restrainer" is.

Is the Restrainer Human Government? (Mid-Tribulation Position)

Some have said that the Restrainer is human government. Those who held this view in past history were not generally noted for their adequate view of the prophetic Scripture.

Mary Stewart Relfe was one of the Bible teachers who held this view. She wrote, "The Church was already in severe persecution at the hands of Rome, so Paul chose not to invite more suffering by naming the Roman power. He had previously in person identified it. Rome was so powerful that Paul knew another Super World Dictator professing to be above all could not rise to power until Rome was removed. Likewise, we know this power which has prevented the revealing of the Wicked One has been subsequent government structures. When the government of the world becomes unable to enforce law and order (or **'is taken out of the way'**), this condition will give rise to the revelation of this Wicked One World Leader, who will himself bring about some semblance of law and order. He will be revealed to the Christians in 2 Thessalonians 2:3 at the outset of the last seven years, but his wickedness will not be revealed to the world until midweek."[42]

There are a number of problems with this view. In fact Relfe's statement quoted above has some inner contradictions. This view must be rejected for the following reasons:

It doesn't adequately explain the use of the masculine gender for the Restrainer in verse 7 (ὁ κατέχων). If the Restrainer were an impersonal force, the neuter gender would have continued to be used in verse 7. The deliberate switch to the masculine singular in verse 7 indicates that the Restrainer is definitely a person.

Human government doesn't have enough power to restrain Satan, who is second in power and intelligence only to God. Nor does it have the power or a logical reason for restraining **"the mystery of lawlessness"** which we have previously seen is that progressive development of the rejection of God and His truth. To say that the wicked

---

42 Mary Stewart Relfe, *When Your Money Fails*, p. 216

Roman Empire, or any other form of human government, has restrained Satan's relentless attack against God's truth borders on the preposterous.

The most powerful argument against this view is this. The Scriptures teach exactly the opposite. Satan and his demons are not ruled by human government, but rather totally control it. According to the following passages, Satan and his demons rule over this present world system. **"We know that we are of God, and the whole world lies in the power of the evil one"** (1 John 5:19). Apart from God's Restrainer, they manipulate and guide unbelieving government leaders (see Ephesians 2:1-3; cp. Daniel 10:12, 13).

The thing that truly baffles me is how Relfe can say, "Rome was so powerful that Paul knew another Super World Dictator professing to be above all could not rise to power until Rome was removed."[43] This doesn't make sense. First of all, Satan could have simply taken possession of the Caesar of that day and made him the Antichrist. How in the world could the Roman government, a human power, have prevented Satan, a superhuman person with awesome powers, from doing this? Secondly, the government that the coming Dictator will take over is a revived form of the old Roman Empire.

This view doesn't explain adequately the reason for "the restrainer getting Himself out of the midst." Human government will reach its zenith under the Antichrist. Human government doesn't end until the Second Coming

---

43 *ibid.*

of Jesus the Messiah to set up God's kingdom on earth. And, human government can't get itself out of the way as the translation of the verb's middle voices requires.

This view just doesn't harmonize with the Bible as a whole, nor answer the demands of the context.[44]

Is the Restrainer Satan?

Another view is that the Restrainer is Satan. This would fit the need of the Restrainer to be both an influence and a person. It could also explain the purpose clause of verse 6 that says, "**so that in his** [the Antichrist's] **time he may be revealed**." The idea (in this view) is that Satan would restrain the Antichrist's revelation until the most opportune time in order to ensure his successful reception.

Hogg and Vine, who hold this view, interpret verse 7 as follows,

"Until he be taken; as shown in the notes, there is nothing in the text to justify taken. Γινομαι means to become, to come to be. Naturally then, the meaning of the phrase is to come into being, or to appear, rather than to be removed, or to disappear."[45]

Hogg and Vine go on to make the following amplified translation of verses 7 and 8 to support their view, "For the secret of (the spirit of) lawlessness is already working; only (there is) the Controller at present (who will hold it in check) until he (the man of lawlessness) may become

---

44 *ibid.*
45 C. F. Hogg and W. E. Vine, *The Epistles to the Thessalonians,* p. 242

(successfully manifested) out of the very midst (of the situation that will develop, so not risking defeat by a premature attempt to capture the key position). And then (but not until then) the Lawless One shall be revealed whom the Lord Jesus shall slay, etc."[46]

There are serious flaws in this view. First, the normal meaning of the Greek verb, κατέχω, is to restrain or suppress something that is in active opposition to the restraint.

Second, the clear meaning of verse 7 is that the Restrainer is an obstacle to **"the mystery of lawlessness,"** not at all holding it in tactical check.

Third, the antecedent of **"He is taken out of the way"** is clearly the Restrainer. To make the "he" refer to the Antichrist rather than the natural antecedent is grammatically extremely improbable.

This view doesn't agree with the simple meaning of the context. The most serious flaw of this view in the light of the context is that it makes Satan be in opposition to himself. About that situation Jesus said on another occasion, **"Every kingdom divided against itself will be ruined, and every city or household divided against itself will not stand. If Satan drives out Satan, he is divided against himself. How then can his kingdom stand?"** (Matthew 12:26-27, NIV).

---

46 This view best explains the purpose clause, "so that in this time he [Antichrist] may be revealed" (verse 6). The verb "to be revealed or unveiled" (αποκαλυπτω) is used three times in this context, each time in the passive voice. This indicates that the Antichrist is revealed by God's permission into his fateful historic role.

Is the Restrainer the Holy Spirit?

The third major view is that the Restrainer is the Holy Spirit. Relfe takes a strong exception to this, "The recent pre-Tribulation doctrine teaches that this 'he' is the Holy Spirit. There are many blatant inconsistencies which render this untrue."[47]

With due respect, this not a recent view. Some noted early Church leaders believed that the Holy Spirit is the Restrainer. Alford, in Volume III of his scholarly commentaries, mentions the following men on pages 57 and 58 (I am indebted to Gundry for this insight). The first was John of Constantinople who was also known as Chrysostrom (AD 347-407). He was called Chrysostrom (golden mouth) because of the eloquence of his preaching. He is known to history as the greatest Greek-speaking Christian preacher of all time.[48] A second early Church leader who believed this view was Theodore of Mopsuestia (AD 350-428). And another was Theodoret, Bishop of Cyprus (AD 390-457).[49]

Gundry says in favor of the Spirit restraining role, "Far from being novel, the view just might reflect apostolic teaching . . . the charge of novelty against this view, as we have seen, does not survive investigation. We may ask why Paul should not have openly mentioned the Holy Spirit. But what reason would have prompted him to do so? For

---

47 Relfe, op. cit. p. 216
48 Earle E. Cairns, *Christianity Through the Centuries,* pp. 151-153
49 *Ibid.,* p. 153

they knew what he was writing about in (verses 5 and 6a). No other passage of Scripture teaches that the Spirit holds back the appearance of the Antichrist. But neither does any other Scripture teach that Satan, the Roman Empire, or human government holds back the Antichrist."[50]

Interpreting God the Holy Spirit as the Restrainer best answers the grammatical, contextual and theological questions involved in 2 Thessalonians for the following reasons:

It best answers the usage of both the neuter and masculine singular gender to describe the Restrainer. The Spirit is a worldwide restraining power, which explains the use of the neuter gender. Furthermore, since the Greek word for spirit (πνεῦμα) is neuter, the neuter pronoun is regularly used to refer to Him. However, the distinct personality of God the Spirit is also frequently emphasized in the same context with the neuter by referring to Him.

The Holy Spirit is almost always referred to by a title that describes His particular function or ministry. For instance, He is called **"the Spirit of Truth"** (John 14:17); **"the Helper"** (John 16:17); **"the Spirit of life in Christ Jesus"** (Romans 8:2). These titles mean the Spirit who teaches truth gives us help and empowers us with the life of Jesus. So it is very normal for Paul to simply refer to Him as the Restrainer to people he had thoroughly taught on the matter.

This view is also the most consistent with the Holy Spirit's historic role revealed in the Bible. Theologically,

---

50 Henry Bettenson, *The Early Christian Fathers*

the third person of the Trinity, the Spirit of God, is the active agent in implementing the common plan of the Triune God. For instance, He is the active agent in God's program of creation and salvation.

It takes a person of superior power to restrain a supernatural person and his superhuman program. Jesus called Satan "**the ruler of this world** [system]" (John 14:30). And in another place it says that the unbeliever is under Satan's authority and control: "**In which you formerly walked according to the spirit of this age, according to the prince of the power of the atmosphere** [of thoughts and customs]**, of the spirit that is now energizing the sons of disobedience**" (Ephesians 2:2, literally translated).

Satan has a highly organized army of fallen angels that are called demons. It is through this means that he exercises worldwide power in programs such as "**the mystery of lawlessness.**" God reveals about this world-governing system, "**For our struggle is not against flesh and blood, but against the rulers, against the powers, against the world forces of [behind] this darkness, against the spiritual forces of wickedness in the heavenly places**" (Ephesians 6:12).

Satan even has his own corps of dedicated ministers within the Church who are spreading the mystery of lawlessness, "**For such men are false apostles, deceitful workers, disguising themselves as apostles of Christ. And no wonder, for even Satan disguises himself as an angel of light. Therefore it is not surprising if his**

servants also disguise themselves as servants of righteousness . . ." (2 Corinthians 11:13-15).

To say that human government could restrain these
things is ludicrous. Satan has no logical reason to do so.
The person of the Spirit of God is the only one with the
motive and power to confront such a person and his system.

Is the Restrainer the Archangel Michael?

Since this idea is only developed by Marv Rosenthal
in his pre-Wrath Rapture view, I'll comment on the identification of Michael as the Restrainer in that chapter. At
this point, suffice it to say the angel Michael has none of
the supernatural attributes nor power to do the things
attributed to the Restrainer in this chapter.

CHAPTER FIFTEEN

Revelation's Chronology and the Rapture

*D*own through history, the Book of Revelation has inspired more wonder, curiosity, bewilderment and sometimes even fear, than any other book of the Bible. It is unquestionably the most difficult to analyze and interpret.

But no other book gives us more clues as to how to find the meaning. There are certain keys given in the book itself that are of enormous help to us in interpreting it.

However difficult it may be, the Book of Revelation is the most important factor in understanding the events of the seven cataclysmic years immediately preceding and leading to the Second Coming of the Lord Messiah Jesus. It is the only extended portion of Scripture that systematically deals with this topic. Revelation Chapters 4 through 19 deal exclusively with the Tribulation period. Revelation is the " Grand Central Station" of all the prophecies that deal with the Tribulation. It puts them all together into perspective.

Why Revelation Is Relevant to Rapture

No other single book is more important to the issue of when the Rapture occurs. Revelation's chronological sequence establishes just when and upon whom "the wrath of God" falls. The mid-Tribulationist, post-Tribulationist and the pre-Wrath proponents must establish that "God's wrath" only falls at or near the very end of the Tribulation. They all admit that the Scripture does say that God's wrath will not be poured out upon the Church.

The following are some of the important keys to interpreting Revelation:

The *first key* is the use of Old Testament symbols. Most of the symbols used in Revelation are either explained somewhere else in the Bible, or, as we will see in the second key, they are explained in the context itself.

For example, the symbols used in Revelation 12:1 and 2 are explained in Joseph's dream of Genesis 37:9 and 10. Jacob, Joseph's father, interprets the dream as follows: the sun is Jacob; the moon is Rachel; the eleven stars are the sons of Jacob who fathered the tribes of Israel; the twelfth star is Joseph. So the symbols show that the "woman" of Revelation Chapter 12 is Israel, composed of the 12 tribes descended from Jacob's 12 sons.

The *second key* is that symbols are often explained by the immediate context. The great dragon and the serpent of Revelation 12 is identified in Revelation 12:9 as the Devil and/or Satan. Another example is the great harlot, called Babylon the Great, of Revelation 17:3-7, which is identified in 17:18. **"She is the great city that is reigning over the kings of the earth."** When the apostle John wrote this, the great city reigning over the kings of the earth was Rome. So Rome is clearly labeled *"mystery Babylon"* by the prophetic symbol of Revelation.

Risking Treason

Parenthetically, the above use of symbols illustrates one of the reasons for the symbols in the time of Revelation's writing. Had the apostle openly labeled Rome as the center of all heresy and corruption, the Roman Emperor would have had him and all the Christians executed for treason.

The *third key* is John's testimony of how he actually saw and heard the things about which he writes in his prophecies.

At the beginning of the book, John records the vision given him by the Lord Jesus Christ.

"I was in the Spirit on the Lord's day, and I heard behind me a loud voice like the sound of a trumpet, saying, 'Write in a book what you see, and send it to the seven churches . . .'" (Revelation 1:10-11a).

All the way through the rest of the book the apostle continually testifies that he saw and heard the things about which he wrote. And then at the end of the book John bears his final solemn testimony about how he received the content about which he wrote, **"And he said to me, 'These words are faithful and true'; and the Lord, the God of the spirits of the prophets, sent His angel to show to His bond-servants the things which must shortly take place . . . and I, John, am the one who heard and saw these things . . ."** (Revelation 22:6, 8).

In a real sense, John was a time traveler who was whisked to the 21st century, and then returned to the first century to describe what he saw.

Describing the Indescribable

The *fourth key* is this: John actually saw and heard the

things that are future to us. Time and space are God's creation. It was nothing for God to time travel John up to the beginning of the 21st century and cause him to witness the horrible marvels of the scientific age we live in. But just think of the problem presented to John when he has returned to the first century and commanded to write as an eyewitness about all he had seen, heard and felt.

How in the world would a first century man describe the highly advanced scientific marvels of warfare at the end of the 20th century? John had to use phenomena with which he was familiar to give visual and audible illustrations of what he was witnessing. Picture John viewing Intercontinental Ballistic Missiles with multiple independently targeted thermonuclear warheads streaking through the atmosphere. How could he explain the awesome destruction of many thermonuclear warheads exploding in close proximity of time and location? How would he describe a main battle tank, an attack helicopter spraying chemical weaponry or a nuclear naval battle?

How do you describe such weapons when, in your world, men, horses or jackasses pulled along the most advanced mobile weapons of war? The most advanced artillery of his day was a crude catapult that threw huge rocks. The only missiles he had ever seen were flaming arrows shot from a bow.

I believe John does a tremendous job under the inspiration of the Holy Spirit. He used composites of things with which he was familiar to portray all these things. If you are interested in seeing these descriptions decoded, get a copy of my book, *The Apocalypse Code.*

The Divine Outline

The *fifth key* to interpreting Revelation is the outline that Jesus gave John at the time He commissioned him to write it. Actually, the Lord Jesus instructed the apostle exactly how he was to structure the book,

"Write therefore the things you have seen, and the things which are, and the things which shall take place after these things" (Revelation 1:19).

In checking commentaries on the Book of Revelation written from some two centuries ago until the present, I found that the vast majority of writers recognized that Revelation 1:19 is intended to be the outline of the book. It is obvious to any interpreter who takes the book normally and believes it at face value. This is of considerable importance because most post-Tribulationists try to explain this outline away so that they can strengthen their case for the Church being in the Tribulation.

The Things Which You Have Seen . . .

This covers Chapter 1 where John describes the risen Lord Jesus' appearance to him and the phenomena that occurred during that visitation. It is described in the past tense.

The Things Which Are . . .

This describes Chapters 2 and 3. These chapters are described by a present tense of the verb for being (εἰμί in the Greek) which stresses the present state of things in history. I believe, along with many scholars, that these seven letters were not only written to seven literal churches with real problems, but also that they have a prophetic application to Church history.

Many factors convinced me of this interpretation.

- First, why were these seven churches selected? There were hundreds of other churches in Asia at this time. There were thousand of churches worldwide. So why just these particular seven?

- Second, why were these seven churches arranged in this order?

- Third, why were the conditions in the churches arranged in such a way that they described discernable, successive epochs of Church history accurately?

- Fourth, why place seven practical letters of instruction to churches in this book and in this position if they have no prophetic application?

I believe that these seven churches were selected and arranged by our omniscient Lord because they had problems and characteristics that would prophesy seven stages of history through which the Church universal would pass.

The Things Which Shall Take Place after These Things . . .

This third division of the book's Divinely given outline is clearly intended to convey things that will happen after the events covered by the first and second divisions.

The future tense of the verb γίνομαι contrasts sharply with the present tense of the verb εἰμί used for the previous section. The idea is "**what shall come to be after these things**." This statement obviously describes things that will occur after the first two sections.

"**After these things**" is the translation of the Greek words μετὰ ταῦτα. The phrase is first used in Revelation 1:19 and not used again until 4:1. It clearly indicates that there is a shift into future things under different conditions from those described in the first three chapters and that this is the place where the outline begins its futuristic phase.

That this is a shift to things future to the Church age described in Chapters 2 and 3 is apparent because of these factors:

- First, as I just mentioned, Revelation 4:1 is the first place that μετὰ ταῦτα is used after it is given the special meaning in 1:19. Therefore, as the antecedent of that special meaning given in 1:19 it must be understood as the place where the outline shifts to things that are future to the first two parts of the outline. Writers call this a plot point.

- Second, in Revelation 4:1, μετὰ ταῦτα is used twice. A voice from heaven leaves no doubt as to its meaning in the latter part of verse 1, "**Come up here, and I will show you what must take place after these things.**"

- Third, John is caught up to heaven to see things that are definitely future to our present experience.

John is actually representative of the whole Church in heaven. It is a preview of the Rapture and what we will see in heaven when we get there.

- Fourth, not one reference is made again concerning the Church on earth until after the Second Coming of the Lord Jesus Christ. Since the Church is mentioned 19 times in the first three chapters under the Divine outline of "**the things which are**," and since the Church is not mentioned or implied as being on earth even once after the statement **"Come up here, and I will show you what must take place after these things,"** I conclude that it is the end of the Church age that is meant here, and the Church is in heaven until it returns as the bride of Christ in Revelation 19:7-14.

An Amazing Similarity

The similarity of the terminology used in both 1 Thessalonians 4:16-17 and Revelation 4:1-2 supports the contention that the Church is taken to heaven here. Both passages speak of a trumpet sounding, of a shout of command, of being caught up to heaven, and of an instantaneous translation of the believer. I believe, along with many scholars, that the apostle John's experience here is meant to be a prophetic preview of what the living Church will experience in the Rapture. I believe one day very soon, we will experience and see what John did some 1,900 years ago.

CHAPTER SIXTEEN

GOD'S WRATH UPON EARTH BEGINS

The Consecutive Order of the Judgments

*O*ne of the most critical elements in understanding the Book of the Revelation is recognizing the order in which the book unfolds. For example, it is important to understand whether the seal judgments and the trumpet judgments are in consecutive order or whether or not they unfold concurrently.

I believe the seal, trumpet and golden bowl judgments unfold in consecutive order. The fact that the seventh seal and seventh trumpet actually open up the next series of judgments unmistakably indicates that they are in consecutive order. There is even a lull of grace between each new series to give opportunity for repentance. There is no question that each series is more severe than the previous one. For instance:

- The fourth seal judgment kills a fourth of the world's population (6:7-8).
- The sixth trumpet judgment kills a third of the earth's population (9:18).
- The second trumpet judgment kills a third of all the life in the planet's oceans (8:8-9).
- The second bowl judgment kills all life in the planet's oceans (16:3).

The consecutive order of these judgments makes the scenarios necessary for the mid-Tribulation and pre-Wrath views impossible.

Who Is Worthy to Open the Seal Judgments?

Also critical to when the Rapture occurs is just who

opens the seals and thus unleashes these judgments upon the world. It is also imperative to understand exactly when the Second Seal is opened in the Tribulation. I will seek to answer these questions over the next few chapters.

The Tribulation Begins

When the Antichrist and the Israeli pseudo-Messiah sign the treaty of protection for Israel, the last seven years of Daniel's prophecy begins (Daniel 9:27 and 11:36-39). From that point the final countdown resumes on God's prophetic stopwatch.

Remember, the Bible uses lunar years of 360 days in length. There will be exactly 7 x 360, or 2,520 days, until the Second Coming of Jesus the Messiah.

At the very beginning of this time frame, there will also occur the most important and incredible manifestation of God's grace for this period. One hundred and forty-four thousand Jews around the world will miraculously be brought to faith in their true Messiah, the Lord Jesus. According to Revelation 7:1-4, this will occur before any harm comes upon the earth, the sea, or any vegetation. This means that the conversion must be right at the beginning of the Tribulation.

The context indicates that the evangelistic successes of these elect and chosen people from the 12 tribes of Israel (excepting the tribe of Dan) will be awesome (Revelation 7:9-17). Believing martyrs from the Tribulation that are too great in number to be counted will be standing before

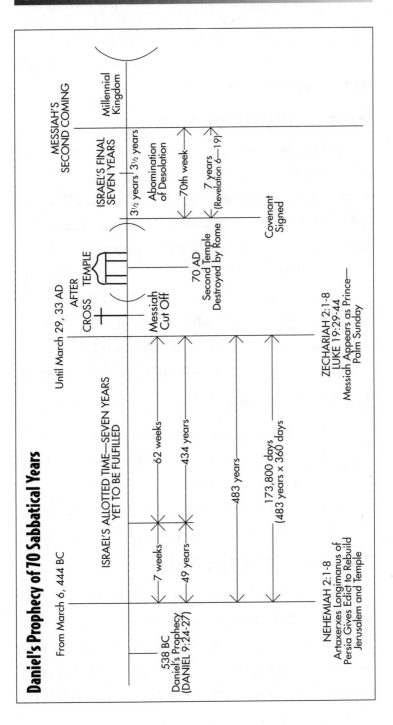

Daniel's Prophecy of 70 Sabbatical Years

From March 6, 444 BC

Until March 29, 33 AD

MESSIAH'S SECOND COMING

Millennial Kingdom

ISRAEL'S FINAL SEVEN YEARS

3½ years | 3½ years

Abomination of Desolation

70th week

7 years (Revelation 6—19)

Covenant Signed

AFTER CROSS TEMPLE

Messiah Cut Off

70 AD Second Temple Destroyed by Rome

ISRAEL'S ALLOTTED TIME—SEVEN YEARS YET TO BE FULFILLED

7 weeks
49 years

62 weeks
434 years

483 years

173,800 days
(483 years x 360 days)

538 BC
Daniel's Prophecy
(DANIEL 9:24-27)

NEHEMIAH 2:1-8
Artaxerxes Longimanus of Persia Gives Edict to Rebuild Jerusalem and Temple

ZECHARIAH 2:1-8
LUKE 19:29-44
Messiah Appears as Prince—Palm Sunday

God's throne. The fact that the great throng of martyrs are placed in close juxtaposition to the 144,000 Jews indicates that they are converts of their witness.

Two Prophets Shake the World

Revelation 11:3-13 traces the most unusual mission of two prophets. God sets them uniquely apart by calling them **"His two witnesses"** and by granting them **"His own authority."** I believe that these two will be none other than Moses and Elijah, who will be sent to prepare Israel for the true Messiah and to expose the pseudo-Messiah. They will shake up not only Israel but also the world for 1,260 days, or the first three and one-half years of the Tribulation.

Apparently the world at large will hate their message of warning and exposé, because all rejoice at their death.

An Important Observation

It should be noted that all the witnesses introduced in the Book of Revelation to minister during the Tribulation are Jews. This is in keeping with the fact that the Church is gone and the Israelites are once again God's representatives on earth. It is their responsibility to evangelize the world.

The First Series of Judgments Begins

The first series of judgments to be unleashed on the world are called "the seven seals," and are recorded in the Book of Revelation. These "seals" are fixed on a great scroll that contains God's decreed judgments. The scroll is progressively unrolled with the breaking of each seal.

Are the Seal Judgments Part of God's Wrath?

The whole point of Revelation Chapter 5 is to show that no one in the universe is worthy to unleash God's judgment on the unbelieving world except the Lord Jesus Christ. He is worthy to judge because He died for those who reject the pardon He purchased for them with His own blood. Jesus Himself claimed this right, **"Moreover, the Father judges no one, but has entrusted all judgment to the Son, that all may honor the Son just as they honor the Father. He who does not honor the Son does not honor the Father, who sent him . . . And he has given him authority to judge because he is the Son of Man"** (John 5:22, 23, 27).

So from the very first judgment, God the Son is pouring out the wrath of God. If you are going the pre-Wrath route, then you have to go back to the beginning of the Tribulation.

How Marvin Rosenthal and the pre-Wrath teachers can say that God's wrath doesn't begin until near the end of the Tribulation is a mystery. When Jesus unleashes the Antichrist on the world, is He only partially ticked off? Or when He unleashes the fourth seal that kills more than 1,500,000,000 people is He just getting His anger warmed up?

The First Seal: Antichrist Revealed

The first seal is broken at the beginning of the Tribulation. It releases the Antichrist of Rome to begin his mission of world conquest. He will bring all nations under his authority, using the revived Roman Empire (Greater EU) as his economic and political power base (Revelation 6:1-2; Daniel 8:23-25).

General Conditions of the First Half of the Tribulation

The fear of war will apparently be stopped by the negotiating genius of the Roman Dictator. He will find solutions to such problems as Russia's desire for world conquest, the Sino-Russian split, the enmity between the Arab and the Jew, the poverty-spawned revolutions of the Third World, and the forthcoming international economic collapse.

Listen to what the Holy Spirit foretells the people of the world will say: **"Who is like the beast (Antichrist), and who is able to wage war with him?"** (Revelation 13:4). **"While they are saying, 'Peace and Safety!'"** (1 Thessalonians 5:3). In fact, Daniel shows that the Antichrist will use people's desire for peace to gain control of the world.

> **"And through his (Antichrist) policy also he shall cause craft (deceit) to prosper in his hand; and he shall magnify himself in his heart, and by means of peace shall destroy many...."**

This man will know how to use the world's desire for peace to his own diabolical ends. The Messiah-rejecting world will be given over to his deceptions as a Divine judgment (2 Thessalonians 2:9-12).

Persecution will begin to spread worldwide upon those who believe in the Messiah during this first half of

Daniel's Seventieth Week. Many false teachers and prophets will arise, and millions of true believers will be massacred. The Antichrist's apostate world religion will apparently spearhead the persecution (see Matthew 24:9-14 and Revelation 17:14).

The Midpoint of the Tribulation

Many things begin to happen quickly as the midpoint of Tribulation is reached. This very important time is signaled by a very specific event. In the middle of Daniel's Seventieth Week the Roman Dictator will break his covenant with the Israelis and stop the offering of sacrifices and temple worship. He will then desecrate the temple by entering the holy of holies and proclaiming himself to be God (2 Thessalonians 2:4).

This act is technically known in the Scripture as the **"abomination of desolation."** Jesus said that this would be the sign for believers living in Israel to flee to the mountains (Matthew 24:15-20) because this would be the beginning of unprecedented catastrophes. Listen to His warning: **"For then there will be a great tribulation, such as has not occurred since the beginning of the world until now, nor ever shall. And unless those days had been cut short, no life would have been saved; but for the sake of the elect, those days shall be cut short"** (Matthew 24; 21-22).

Jesus' warning for the believing Israelites to flee for protection coincides with the prophetic promise of protection in Revelation 12:6, 13-17.

"And the woman [Israel] fled into the wilderness where she had a place prepared by God, so that there she might be nourished for one thousand two hundred and sixty days" [three and one-half years] (12:6).

"And when the dragon [Satan] saw that he was thrown down to the earth, he persecuted the woman who gave birth to the male child [Jesus]. And the two wings of the great eagle were given to the woman, in order that she might fly into the wilderness to her place, where she was nourished for a time [one year] and times [two years] and half a time [one-half year], from the presence of the serpent [Satan].

"And the serpent poured water like a river out of his mouth [symbolic of invading armies of Ezekiel 38—39] after the woman, so that he might cause her to be swept away with the flood. And the earth helped the woman, and the earth opened its mouth [great earthquake] and drank up the river which the dragon poured out of his mouth" (12:13-17).

Many believe that this place of protection for believing Israel will be the ancient fortress city of Petra, which is carved out of the rock of a protected canyon in southern Jordan. Since the signing of the peace treaty between Israel and Jordan, many Israelis are already making preparations in this area. Until the peace treaty, Petra was on the wrong side of the Jordan and completely inaccessible to *any* Jew. But God's time clock is no respecter of politics. When the time is right, so is the political situation!

CHAPTER SEVENTEEN

The Second Seal Opened—War Begins

*S*hortly after the **"abomination that causes desolation,"** the second seal is opened, **"and another, a red horse went out; and to him who sat on it, it was granted to take peace from earth, and that men should slay one another; and a great sword was given to him"** (Revelation 6:4).

Up until this point, the Antichrist has kept a pseudo-peace going on earth. But now war begins, and his careful alliances are shattered. The second seal unleashes the following:

First, the Muslim armies led by Russia launch an all-out attack against Israel (Daniel 11:40). The present Oslo Peace Accords will never bring a lasting peace. Anyone who takes the time to study the history of Islam and its teachings about "the divine imperative from Allah to take back holy places that have been captured" will see this.

Jerusalem, My Glory

This war will start over a dispute concerning Jerusalem (Zechariah 12:2-3). Since the signing of the 1993 Oslo Accords, the Palestinian Authority has made no secret of its ultimate intention of declaring a Palestinian state with Jerusalem as its capital. The Israeli government is adamant in its intention not to relinquish a single square inch of Jerusalem. Israel's official position over Jerusalem was articulated by then-Prime Minister Benjamin Netanyahu when he said, "Jerusalem—an undivided Jerusalem—will remain the eternal capital of Israel—forever."

Second, Russia and its Muslim allies seize upon this excuse and launch an all-out invasion of the Middle East by land, sea and air (Ezekiel 38:8-17; Daniel 11:40-41).

The Russians then continue through Israel into Egypt and take it over in a classic double cross. The Russian commander will apparently plan to take over Africa as well (Daniel 11:42-43).

At this point the Russian invasion is stopped. News from the north troubles the commander. As he looks northward from Egypt, he faces Europe and sees the mobilizing of the Western armies led by leader of the revived Roman Empire.

The Russian leader will also be troubled by news from the east. An Asian confederacy led by the People's Republic of China declares war on Russia and starts their thrust toward the Middle East (Daniel 11:44; Revelation 16:12). It appears that the Asian confederacy also uses this as an excuse to attack the Antichrist-led West.

The Russian/Muslim confederacy returns to Israel to make a stand against the combined Western and Asian forces. It is here that the Russians and their satellite countries will be annihilated (Daniel 11:45; Ezekiel 38 and 39; Joel 2:20).

All of this will take considerable time, at least many months. In the same time frame the remaining seals of Revelation are opened.

The Third Seal—Global Economic Catastrophe

The opening of the third seal brings worldwide economic collapse. After war breaks out in the Middle East, oil from the Persian Gulf will be halted and worldwide economic chaos will set in. Food will become scarce and very expensive (Revelation 6:5-6).

The Fourth Seal—One Fourth of Mankind Perishes

The opening of the fourth seal brings death to one fourth of the world's population. The enormity of this tragedy can hardly be imagined. In the space of a few months over one and a-half billion people will perish through war, famine, epidemics and breakdown of society (Revelation 6:7-8). All of these things will be the natural repercussions of the war in the Middle East.

The Fifth Seal—Massacre of Saints

The opening of the fifth seal unleashes a horrible persecution of believers. The Roman Antichrist and the Israeli False Prophet launch a wholesale slaughter of believers (Revelation 13:5-7). They have an ingenious method of exposing believers. The Antichrist and False Prophet use economics to achieve absolute control of the people. They will institute a monetary program by which every person in the world receives a number whose prefix is 666. This begins during the first half of the Tribulation. Without this number, no one is able to buy, sell or hold a job. But to get this number, a person has to swear allegiance to the Roman Antichrist. A true believer in the Messiah cannot do this, so he is exposed and has no means of survival (Revelation 13:13-18). The persecution which begins during the first half of the Tribulation (Matthew 24:9-13) now achieves full force.

Computers have made it possible for the first time in history to do exactly what is predicted here. Plans are already being made for a cashless society in which all people will have credit electronically transferred by computer instead of currency. Today it is already possible, through the use of ATM's, Value Added Cards, credit cards and Electronic Funds Transfers for an individual to live his entire life conducting normal business without ever handling hard currency of any type.

The Sixth Seal—First Nuclear Exchange

The opening of the sixth seal begins what all nations fear—nuclear war. Apparently warfare has been fought conventionally up until this point. But the Russian leaders, in this desperate situation, decide to launch a first strike. Ezekiel 39:6 says that fire is unleashed upon Magog (the cryptic name for Russia) and the "coastlands," which in ancient times referred to the great, faraway Gentile civilizations. Today the term would mean "continents." I believe that this is forecasting a nuclear exchange between Russia, Europe, and the United States.

The world is horrified, but the worst is yet to come.

CHAPTER EIGHTEEN

The Seventh Seal—Another Series of Judgments

*T*he seventh seal is opened and there is a lull in judgment as God gives mankind a chance to repent. The seventh seal actually releases the seven trumpet judgments, which are much more severe than the first six seals (Revelation 8:1-2).

It is important to note that God gives a gracious interlude between each series of judgments, which shows His reluctance to pour out more of His wrath. But as I've noted, each series of judgments is more severe and timed closer together.

With the sounding of the seven trumpets judgment greatly increases in speed, scope and severity.

The Trumpets—A Judgment of Thirds

The *first trumpet* bring a burning of one third of the earth's surface, one third of the trees, and all the grains and grasses on earth (Revelation 8:7). This could be caused by firestorms started by the numerous nuclear explosions of the sixth seal.

The *second trumpet* gives a foreview of a great nuclear naval battle. Convoys of merchant ships and warships are all destroyed. It appeared to the apostle John to be caused by a great burning mountain cast into the sea. I believe this is an excellent first-century description of the hydrogen bomb. A third of all ships and life in the sea is destroyed by the nuclear battle (8:8-9).

"Wormwood"

The *third trumpet* brings a poisoning of one third of all the world's fresh water. This could be caused by another nuclear exchange resulting in fallout, which would poison the fresh water with radiation.

"And the third angel sounded, and a great star fell from heaven, burning like a torch, and it fell on a third of the rivers and on the springs of waters; and the name of the star is called Wormwood; and a third of the waters became wormwood; and many men died from the waters, because they were made bitter."

In this light, it is interesting to note the Chernobyl disaster in the Ukraine. The name "Wormwood" has a Ukrainian equivalent. "Wormwood" in the Ukrainian language Bible is rendered *"Chernobyl."*

The *fourth trumpet* is a judgment against light reaching the earth. Light from the sun, moon and stars is diminished by one third. I believe this is a result of the debris spread into the upper atmosphere by the blast of hundreds of nuclear warheads. This would block out light from space. Just imagine how this will add to the panic and terror already gripping the earth (8:12).

The *fifth trumpet* is very difficult to discern. Whatever it is, some very vicious demons who have been bound until that time will be closely involved. Unbelievers will be so tormented by this judgment that they will seek death but be unable to find it. This will last for five months (9:1-12). This could be the result of some form of biological warfare. Russia already has a formidable arsenal of chemical weapons that could easily produce the symptoms given here.

The *sixth trumpet* coincides with the prophecy of Daniel 11:44 where news from the east troubles the Russian commander. The vast Chinese army and its Asian allies mobilize to contest the Russian/Muslim invasion of the Middle East and Africa. The activity at the Euphrates River, which was the ancient boundary between east and west, indicates that the Asian power is incited to war by some especially powerful and vicious demons who were bound there (9:13-14).

John Knew Beijing's Troop Strength

This army numbers 200 million. Only China could raise such an army and has already claimed that number of men under arms. As they move toward the Middle East, they wipe out one third of earth's population. They do this with fire and brimstone, which again seems to indicate a massive use of nuclear weapons (9:15-18). Considering the fact that Beijing had already stolen virtually all of America's nuclear secrets before the 20th century drew to a close makes this scenario all the more likely, even when viewed from a secular perspective.

Can you imagine the horror of these times: With one fourth of mankind killed by the fourth seal of judgment, and one third killed by this one, it brings the total of the earth's population destroyed to one half. And all of this occurs in a period of less than three years. No wonder Isaiah said of this time, **"The inhabitants of the earth are burned, and few men are left"** (Isaiah 24:6). And again, **"I will make mortal man scarcer than the gold of Ophir. Therefore I shall make the heavens tremble, and the earth will be shaken from its place at the fury of the Lord of Hosts"** (Isaiah 13:12-13).

A Shocking Survey of World Opinion

As terrible as all this is, the *real* holocaust is yet to come. It staggers the imagination to consider the hardness of the human heart reflected in the Divine survey of mankind's attitude after all these judgments take place. But listen to the Holy Spirit's preview of the world's attitude.

"And the rest of the men which were not killed by these plagues yet repented not of the works of their hands, that they should not worship devils, and idols of gold, and silver, and brass, and stone, and of wood: which neither can see, nor hear, nor walk: Neither repented they of their murders, nor of their *sorceries, nor of their fornication, nor of their thefts.*"

Another interesting play on words was interjected by the Holy Spirit at this point. Throughout the Bible, except in the Book of the Revelation, the word "sorceries" is translated from the Greek word "μαγεία," *magea,* meaning "magic arts." But in the Book of the Revelation, *the book specifically written to the last generation*, the word translated into the King James Version as "sorceries" comes from the Greek word φαρμακεία, "pharmakea," which means the "use or administration of drugs." And one thing social studies tells us that *drug abusers often turn to prostitution or theft to support their expensive habits.*

CHAPTER NINETEEN

VIGNETTES
AND BOWLS
OF TOTAL
DESTRUCTION

Vignettes of the Main Characters and Movements

*I*nterspersed between the three series of judgments, in typical ancient Hebrew style, are many historical sketches of the main subjects who are the prime movers during the seven years of Tribulation. These masterfully written vignettes display the wisdom and genius of the Holy Spirit who inspired them. They sometimes reach far back into history to trace why certain things occur, or they will reach into future history to show their final outcome and influence on the other events of the Tribulation.

The Seventh Trumpet–Bowl Judgments Unleashed

When the seventh trumpet sounds, it is very near the end of Daniel's Seventieth Week (Revelation 11:15). There is another gracious delay of events on earth before the judgments of the seventh trumpet strike. Meanwhile, in heaven the Lord Jesus, the Messiah, proclaims His right to the title deed of the earth and inaugurates His kingdom.

Mankind is given one last chance to repent before the most horrible and extensive judgments of all time hit the earth. During this time Babylon, the great worldwide religious system ruled from Rome, is destroyed by the Antichrist and his ten-nation confederacy (see Revelation 17:16-18 and 18:1-24).

A Reaping unto Life and a Reaping unto Death

There are also two "reapings" of the earth at this time. The first is a final great evangelistic movement whose purpose is to bring the last group of souls to salvation. The second will bring the rest of the unbelieving world into a final great war whose vortex is centered near Jerusalem and throughout the Jordan Valley (Revelation 14:12-20).

Apparently all those who are going to believe in the Messiah have done so by this time. The choice of whether to receive or reject the 666 mark of allegiance to the Antichrist will have been made. Only someone who believes and understands the truth about Jesus and the Bible will have the reason and courage to stand up to the consequences of rejecting this mark. Those who do receive it cannot be saved (see Revelation 14:9-12). The die is cast. At this point, the eternal destiny of every living human being will already be determined by their own choice.

The Seven Golden Bowls of God's Wrath

About these final judgments John the apostle wrote, **"And I saw another sign in heaven, great and marvelous, seven angels who had seven plagues, which are the last, because in them the wrath of God is finished . . . and one of the four living creatures gave to the seven angels seven golden bowls full of the wrath of God, who lives forever and ever"** (Revelation 15:1-7).

These seven horrifying judgments are all predicted in Revelation Chapter 16. Whereas the previous judgments had some restraint, these are worldwide and unrestrained.

- The *first bowl* brings cancer upon all those who have received the 666 mark on them. This could be a natural aftermath from the radiation of so many nuclear explosions. It appears that God will supernaturally protect the believers from this plague.
- The *second bowl* turns the sea to blood and every living thing in the ocean dies.
- The *third bowl* turns all fresh water on earth to blood.
- The *fourth bowl* judgment intensifies the sun's rays, causing horrible heat waves. Global weather patterns are already changing. Just imagine what the numerous nuclear explosions will do to the ecology.
- The *fifth bowl* brings a special judgment of thick darkness upon the throne of the Roman Dictator.

Terror Times 200 Million

The *sixth bowl* is terrifying indeed. The mighty 200-million-man Oriental army has now reached the Euphrates River, which has dried up so that their advance can be quickened. It seems that this army will also take advantage of the confusion caused by the darkness in the Antichrist's capital. Satan, the Antichrist, and the False Prophet use demonic power to deceive all the nations on earth to gather for a suicidal war. Since by this time the Russians will have destroyed the Arab armies, and Russia in turn will have been destroyed (Ezekiel 39:1-6; Daniel 11:45), the last battle will be fought between the Western armies and the Chinese-led Eastern army.

The vortex of this enormous battle will be fought at the place called in Hebrew Har-Mageddon and in English, Armageddon. This is the area around the ancient city of Meggido, which overlooks a great valley in northern Israel.

The Death of All Cities

The *seventh bowl* judgment seems to be primarily against cities. The greatest earthquake in the history of mankind occurs. Then all the cities of the Gentile nations are destroyed (Revelation 16:19). Apparently the earthquake will affect the whole world. Just think of it. Cities like New York, London, Paris, Tokyo, and Mexico City, all destroyed!

And remember these are not cleverly devised myths we are talking about. Four fifths of all Bible prophecy has been fulfilled in history. The last one fifth relates to the end times and is beginning to fit into place. Even as I write these words I am overwhelmed by the horrors that will befall this unbelieving generation.

The Second Advent of the Messiah

Shortly after the final bowl judgment, the personal, awesome return of Messiah Jesus, the Lord of Lords and King of Kings, begins. These are some of the characteristics of His return:

- *First*, it will be sudden and instantaneous. **"For just as lightning comes from the east, and flashes even to the west, so shall the coming of the Son of Man be"** (Matthew 24:27).

- *Second*, Jesus will personally return in bodily form and will be visible to all the world,

  "Then the sign of the Son of Man will appear in the sky, and then all the tribes of the earth will mourn, and they will see the Son of Man coming on the clouds of the sky with power and great glory" (Matthew 24:30).

  "Behold, he is coming with clouds, and every eye will see Him, even those who pierced Him; and all the tribes of the earth will morn over Him" (Revelation 1:7).
- *Third*, His return will be with power and great glory.
- *Fourth*, all people will mourn over Him, though for most of the survivors it is not in repentance. Hearts are so hardened by this point that the armies fighting each other join forces and try to prevent the Lord Jesus' return: **"and I saw the beast** [the Roman Antichrist] **and the kings of the earth and their armies, assembled to make war against Him who sat upon the horse, and against His army"** (Revelation 19:19). This reveals the incredible truth that these men hate the Lord even more than they hate each other. So, demonstrating hardened hearts beyond comprehension, they join forces and attack the Lord Himself.
- *Fifth*, His return will be with catastrophic judgment and devastating, unprecedented destruction upon those who resist Him:

"For the Lord's indignation is against all the nations, and His wrath against all their armies; He has utterly destroyed them, He has given them over to slaughter" (Isaiah 34:2).

"For I will gather all the nations against Jerusalem to battle. . . . Then the Lord will go forth and fight against those nations, as when He fights on a day of battle" (Zechariah 14:2-3).

"And those slain by the Lord on that day shall be from one end of the earth to the other. They shall not be lamented, gathered, or buried; they shall be like dung on the face of the ground" (Jeremiah 25:33; see also Revelation 19:11-16).

- *Sixth,* He will return with His bride, who is already prepared and adorned with her rewards.

"'Let us rejoice and be glad and give glory to Him, for the marriage of the Lamb has come and His bride has made herself ready.' And it was given to her to clothe herself in fine linen, bright and clean; for the fine linen is the righteous acts of the saints.

"And he said to me, 'Write, "Blessed are those who are invited to the marriage supper of the Lamb." And he said to me, 'These are true words of God.' . . . And I saw heaven opened; and behold, a white horse, and He who sat upon it is called Faithful and True; and in righteousness He judges and wages war. . . . And the armies which are in heaven, clothed in fine linen, white and clean, were following Him on white horses" (Revelation 19:7-9, 11, 14).

This Bride's Not Blushing Anymore

These verses clearly show that the bride of Christ, who is already judged and rewarded before the Second Advent, is also the army that comes with Him when He returns to judge the earth. Remember this, for much more will be said about who this bride of Christ is and why she is already in heaven and rewarded before the Second Advent of Jesus.

- *Seventh*, He will return to set up the kingdom of God on earth. This kingdom was offered and rejected in His first coming, postponed during the present age, and to be set up at His Second Coming (see Matthew 4:17; 23:37-39; Acts 1:6; Zechariah 14:9-21; Daniel 7:26-27; Revelation 19:11-20).

The Enormity of the Tragedy

At this point, it's important to take stock of the enormous loss of life during the seven years of Daniel's Seventieth Week.

First, there will be many who will die during the persecution of believers in the first half of the Tribulation (Matthew 24:9-14).

Second, there will be a minimum of over one and a-half billion people killed under the judgment of the fourth seal (Revelation 6:7-8).

Third, there will be **"a multitude of believers too great to be numbered"** massacred during "**the great Tribulation**" of the last half of Daniel's Seventieth Week (Revelation 6:9-11 compared with 7: 9-17). Since there are numbers like 200 million used in Revelation, this must be an enormous group, too large to be numbered.

Fourth, one third of the remaining population will die under the sixth trumpet judgment (Revelation 9:15). Assuming that the population of the earth at the beginning of the Tribulation will be over six billion, three billion people will die in the fourth seal and sixth trumpet judgments alone. Think of it! The death toll works out to over three billion!

Fifth, in the great worldwide destruction of cities that occurs during the seventh bowl judgment, many millions more will surely be killed.

Sixth, vast numbers around the whole world will die during the actual coming of the Messiah according to Jeremiah 25:33 and other passages.

In summary, it would appear that those who survive *could be as few as 50 million*. No wonder God warned through the prophets about the end, **"I will make mortal man scarcer than pure gold"** (Isaiah 13:12); **"the inhabitants of the earth are burned, and few men are left"** (Isaiah 24:6); and Jesus Himself said, **"unless those days had been cut short, no one would be left alive"** (Matthew 24:22).

Why have I gone into all this horror? I believe it is of

utmost importance to squarely face exactly what the Scriptures predict about this period. Those who say that the believers in the Church are going to go through all these catastrophes never really bring out what that means.

It's No Wonder

It's easy to see why they minimize the unprecedented terrors of the Tribulation. Against the backdrop of such terrifying events, it's rather difficult to get people excited about the nearness of Christ's return.

In the light of these prophecies, very few who begin the Tribulation will live to see His coming anyway. So how could anyone inspire the hope and comfort that is promised in Paul's teaching of Jesus' imminent return (1 Thessalonians 4:15-18)? Ladd, Gundry, and other post-Tribulationists talk about that hope being the prospect of seeing and being with the Lord in eternity. That is the hope normally promised to those who will die and be resurrected. But the Rapture is a hope presented to the living, not the dead. There is an enormous difference in the hope (if you can call it that) of the post-Tribulationists and the pre-Tribulationist hope presented around the mystery of the translation (Rapture) of living saints.

CHAPTER TWENTY

REVELATION'S ORDER OF JUDGMENTS

*B*y far the most important aspect of interpreting Revelation is just how the seven seal judgments, trumpet judgments, and bowl judgments relate to each other.

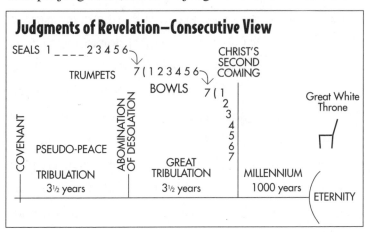

If the judgments occur in consecutive order, then it tends to support the pre-Tribulation Rapture. This chart illustrates the way I believe they occur.

If the judgments are concurrent, then it tends to support the mid- and post-Tribulation views. The chart below illustrates Gundry's view of the order of judgments.

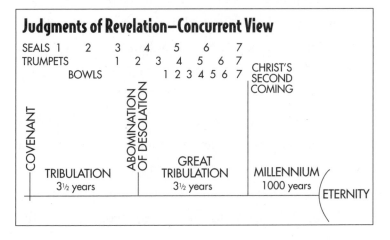

Since the post-Tribulationists agree that the Church cannot suffer Divine wrath, they have to jam as many of the severe judgments as possible into the short time-frame of the actual Second Coming. If it can be demonstrated that Divine wrath falls on the earth prior to the Second Coming, then their theory contradicts itself.

Gundry states, "Thus, God's wrath will not stretch throughout the whole Tribulation. Those passages in Revelation which speak of Divine wrath deal, rather, with the close of the Tribulation. Not until the final crisis at Armageddon, when Jesus descends (and the Church is caught up if post-Tribulationism is correct), will God pour out His wrath upon the unregenerate."

Whatever the order of judgments is, it has to fit into the whole pattern of Tribulation events predicted in the other prophetic passages of the Bible. I do not believe that the post-Tribulationists' scheme of Revelation's chronology can be harmonized with either the rest of the Biblical Tribulation prophecies or those of Revelation.

Let us first observe that all the judgments in the Book of Revelation are presented as judgments of God on a Christ-rejecting world no matter who or what the agency of judgment may be.

The scroll of seven seals, which contains the judgment of the seals, is presented as so dreadful in Chapter 5 that no one in heaven or on earth is worthy to open them except the Lord Jesus, the Messiah Himself. So the authority and source for the unleashing of the seal judgments is the

Lord. So how can anyone say that they are not God's wrath upon man?

The first seal unleashes the Antichrist to go forth and establish his control upon the earth. He will begin the seven years of Tribulation by signing a covenant guaranteeing Israel's security and the Middle East's peace (Daniel 9:27).

During this seal the Antichrist will apparently conquer through ingenious plans for world economic recovery and prosperity and world peace. In Daniel's prophetic description of the Roman Dictator, he says, **"and by means of peace [he] shall destroy many . . ."** (Daniel 9:25b, KJV).

No one can read 2 Thessalonians 2:9-12 and fail to see the clear connection between the Divinely permitted unveiling of the Antichrist, attended by Satanic miracles and a deluding influence from God, and the resulting condemnation of all on earth who reject God's truth. This passage clearly shows the Antichrist to be the chief vehicle of God's judgment on the world. The Antichrist himself is one of the greatest expressions of God's wrath, for he is the one who will slaughter believers and lead the whole world to destruction.

World Peace for Three and One-Half Years

There are several indications that the first half of the Tribulation will be a time of world pseudo-peace established by the Antichrist of Rome. In addition to the verse just quoted, Revelation records the progress of the Antichrist, **". . . and they worshiped the beast [Roman**

Antichrist], saying, 'Who is like the beast, and who is able to wage war with him?'" (Revelation 13:4). This verse reveals at least two profound insights into world conditions during the first half of the Tribulation.

First, the people will give absolute authority to the Antichrist because of fear of war and anarchy caused by economic catastrophe.

Second, the Antichrist will stop war so that the world will extol him because they believe that no one can make war against him.

Another very important clue is Ezekiel's prophecy of Israel's condition just before the great northern power [Russia and her allies] invades, **"Thus says the Lord God, 'On that day when My people Israel are living [in false] security, will you not know it? And you [Russia] will come from your place out of the remote parts of the north [extreme north], you and many peoples with you, all of them riding on horses, a great assembly and a mighty army'"** (Ezekiel 38:14-15, NASB).

God's Blazing Wrath in the Second Seal

For those who say God doesn't pour out His wrath (even on the unregenerate, as Gundry says) on the world till the very end, listen to God's response to this invasion:

"'It will come about on that day, when Gog [Russia] comes against the land of Israel,' declares the Lord God, 'that My fury will mount in My anger. And in My zeal and in My BLAZING WRATH I declare

that on that day there will surely be a great earthquake in the land of Israel. . . . And with pestilence and with blood I shall enter into judgment with him; and I shall rain on him, and on his troops, and on the many peoples who are with him a torrential rain, with hailstones, fire, and brimstone. And I shall magnify Myself, sanctify Myself, and make Myself known in the sight of many nations; and they will know that I am the Lord"' (Ezekiel 38:18, 19, 21-23, NASB).

Now when does all this happen? We know the following factors:

1. Israel will be at peace under the Antichrist's protection (Daniel 9:27; Ezekiel 38:11, 14).

2. Israel has reinstituted the sacrifices of the Mosaic law and rebuilt her temple. (Daniel 9:27; cp. Matthew 24:15-20).

3. The world is at peace (Revelation 13:4).

4. War begins when the Pan Muslim army attacks Israel because of a dispute over Jerusalem (Zechariah 12:2-3), and then Russia (King of the North) joins them and immediately launches an overwhelming attack into the Middle East (Daniel 11:40-45).

5. This war has to begin when **"the abomination of desolation"** predicted by Daniel in 9:27 is set up in the holy of holies of the Jerusalem temple (Matthew 24:15). Jesus Christ is the one who says to the believing Jew of the day to flee the city to a

prepared place of safety (Revelation 12:6, 13-17) because **"there will be a great tribulation, such as has not occurred since the beginning of the world until now, nor ever shall. And unless those days had been cut short, no life would be saved"** (Matthew 24:21-22).

We know absolutely that "the abomination of desolation" is set up in the middle of the seven-year Tribulation (Daniel 9:27). Therefore, the Great War of Ezekiel 38 and 39 must begin in the middle of the Tribulation.

The second seal must, therefore, occur at the middle of the Tribulation, because the second seal specifically **"takes peace from the earth, and men begin to slay each other with a great sword"** (Revelation 6:3, 4).

Therefore, the opening of the second seal must be the same as the Great Russian/Muslim invasion of Israel predicted in Ezekiel 38:8-16, Daniel 11:40-45, and Joel 2:20.

Parenthetically, the second seal also proves that the earth was in a period of pseudo-peace prior to its opening, because it **"takes peace from the earth."** You can't take away something that wasn't there. Also, the symbol of the **"great sword"** means weapons of mass destruction today. The expression **"slay one another"** is σφάξουσιν. It doesn't mean just to kill, but **"to savagely slaughter one another."**

Armageddon Isn't One Battle, but a War

The battle plan given in Daniel 11:40-45 definitely reveals that the war that begins in the middle of the

Tribulation escalates into a global conflict. Ezekiel 38 and 39 indicate the same thing.

Dr. Pentecost accurately states the issue, "It has been held commonly that the battle of Armageddon is an isolated event transpiring just prior to the second advent of Christ to the earth. The extent of this great movement in which God deals with 'the kings of the earth and of the whole world' (Revelation 16:4) will not be seen unless it is realized that the 'battle of that great day of God Almighty' (Revelation 16:14) is not an isolated battle, but rather a campaign that extends over the last half of the Tribulation period. The Greek word polemos (πόλεμος), translated 'battle' in Revelation 16:14, signifies a war or campaign, while mache (μάχη) signifies a battle, and sometimes even single combat. This distinction is observed by Trench *(New Testament Synonyms),* and is followed by Thayer *(Greek-English Lexicon of the New Testament)* and Vincent *(Word Studies in the New Testament).* The use of the word polemos (campaign) in Revelation 16:14 would signify that the events that culminate in the gathering at Armageddon at the Second Advent are viewed by God as one connected campaign."[51]

Looking at war in terms of today's unbelievably destructive weapons, it is easy to understand the horrible carnage and devastation that is predicted in the prophecies about this period. These prophecies indicate something that is very important from a military perspective. The war that begins

---

51 J. Dwight Pentecost, *Things to Come* (Findlay, OH: Dunham Publishing Co., 1958)

with the Pan Arab and Russian invasion of the Middle East is portrayed as beginning with conventional weapons. It is only after the Russian army is beginning to lose that the prophecies begin to intimate the use of nuclear weapons. And most important of all, the nuclear war escalates in stages until it becomes an all-out worldwide nuclear holocaust. This is the exact sort of military strategy that is being planned by the major powers today, that of a case-by-case escalation.

The seal, trumpet and bowl series of judgments in Revelation harmonize perfectly with this scenario if they are interpreted as unfolding successively. The judgments increase in frequency and severity with each new series. This is consistent with God's revealed character, for He is slow to anger, not willing that any should perish. Therefore, the progressive increase in severity is consistent with the successive scenario of judgments in the Old Testament prophecy.

The Seventh Seal and Trumpet

The seventh seal and seventh trumpet give very important insight as to whether the seal and trumpet judgments occur successively or concurrently.

A close examination of the opening of the seventh seal reveals that it isn't the same kind of judgment as the previous six seals. There is an interlude of silence mingled with the prayers of the saints in heaven and temporary restraint of judgment on earth. God gives the earth a chance to repent before the next series of judgments.

But the crucial thing to observe is that the seventh seal actually unleashes the next series of judgments which are the seven trumpets. Any normal reading of the following verses clearly reveals the idea of succession.

"And when He broke the seventh seal, there was silence in heaven for about half an hour. And I saw the seven angels who stand before God; and seven trumpets were given to them" (Revelation 8 1-2).

Likewise, the sounding of the seventh trumpet does not send forth a single specific judgment as the first six trumpets did. Instead there is another interlude in heaven and a lull in judgments upon earth. In heaven, God announces His claim of ownership over the earth and that His Messiah is about to begin His reign over it. Then there are more of the combined historical-prophetical cameos in Chapters 12 through 14.

We find that the next chronological movement of Tribulation events takes place in Chapter 15. Here we are introduced to the seven angels who have the seven last plagues which *finish* God's wrath (15:1).

From this, observe first that these seven bowl judgments are the direct result of the sounding of the seventh trumpet. This is true because these are the next and only judgments which occur after that trumpet is sounded.

Second, observe that it says the seven bowl judgments are the last ones. This indicates that they are the last in a series of previous judgments.

Third, observe that it says in these seven bowl judgments **"the wrath of God is finished"** (15:1). This indicates clearly that the wrath of God doesn't begin with these judgments, as Gundry and the post-Tribulationist crowd contend, but rather that they finish it. From this, it is evident that all the judgments of the Book of the Revelation are considered God's wrath against man.

The bowl judgments occur in very rapid succession. In terms of magnitude and scope, they are unprecedented. Whereas the trumpet judgments, for instance, destroyed a third of life in the sea, the bowl judgment destroys all life in the sea (16:4).

I believe that a normal analysis of the structure of Revelation leads to the conclusion that the three series of judgments are consecutive to each other and that the seventh judgment of the first two series simply introduces the next series.

There is a strong Semitic style of writing in the book of Revelation. This is evidenced by the many historical-prophetic cameos that explain why certain things happened in history and culminate in the Tribulation.

These cameos are interspersed in the chronological unfolding of the seven years in the form of the three series of judgments. In true Semitic style, history is moved forward a bit, then explanatory sections that flash both backward and forward in time are added. Then history is moved forward again, etc.

CHAPTER TWENTY-ONE

INVENTING
HISTORY

"The Book of Revelation is not about the Second Coming of Christ. It is about the destruction of Israel and Christ's victory over His enemies [Israel] in the establishment of the New Covenant Temple. In fact, as we shall see, the word coming as used in the Book of Revelation NEVER REFERS TO THE SECOND COMING. Revelation prophesies the judgment of God on apostate Israel."

—David Chilton, *Days of Vengeance*

Chilton's words betray the single biggest problem with Christian Reconstructionist or Dominionist theology. (Within the Charismatic movement, they are sometimes called the "Kingdom Now" Movement. For the purposes of this chapter, since they are virtually indistinguishable doctrinally, we'll use the *Dominionist*.) In order to make their scheme work, the Book of Revelation had to have been written prior to AD 70. Consequently, the Dominionist movement has to put John in exile on the Isle of Patmos no later than sometime in the 60s.

They run into some problems on this point. The majority of authorities in both the early and contemporary church put John's vision as recorded in Revelation in the middle of the last decade of the first century, with the majority dating it at about AD 95. This should truly put the Dominionists on the horns of a dilemma, because they proudly portray themselves as the authorities on early church history and use it liberally as their authority for many of their novel interpretations.

The unanimous witness of early church fathers like Ireneaeus, Clement of Alexandria, Origen, Victorinus, Jerome and Eusebius all fix the date as the mid-90s during the reign of the Roman Emperor Domitian. Beyond that, the very contents of the Book itself confirm the dating.

Paul wrote to the churches of Asia (Colossians, Ephesians, 1 Timothy and 2 Timothy) during the AD 60s. By the time John records Jesus' letters to the seven churches, the apostasy and spiritual deterioration were much more pronounced.

The apostle John himself did not even arrive in Asia until the mid-60s. That makes his writing to the seven churches of Asia somewhat problematic. For the Dominionists' dating scheme to work, John would have had to replace Paul as leader of the churches in Asia, settle, be exiled to Patmos and write the entire Book of the Revelation before Nero's death in AD 68. AD 68 is the latest date the Christian Reconstruction Movement can accept and still remain contestants in the Dating Game.

Also, in AD 60 or 61, the city of Laodicea was demolished in an earthquake. It had a long-term effect on the city and kept Nero busy with the rebuilding project until the day of his death. Jesus' letter to the church at Laodicea is unique in that He specifically mentions their material prosperity. That is totally inconsistent with a Laodicea struggling for its very existence as it digs out from a catastrophic earthquake.

But, by AD 95, Laodicea had been rebuilt and was one of the most prosperous cities in the known world. Emperor Domitian was in power, and the persecution of Christians had spread all the way to Asia. John's letter was constructed to encourage the suffering Christians of the post-Temple era. Its form and tone are totally inconsistent with any period earlier than the decade of the AD 90s.

I dealt with this subject, together with the other problems surrounding Christian Reconstructionism and Dominion theology, in greater detail in my book *The Road to Holocaust*.[52] Another excellent source of information on this subject can be found in *The Dictionary of Premillennial Theology* edited by Mal Couch of Dallas Theological Seminary. Thomas Ice, Director of the Pre-Tribulation Research Center has also written extensively on this subject and published his work on the Internet.[53]

The Earliest Roots of Dominion Theology

The early American settlers known as the Puritans were the earliest known Dominionists. They fled England and settled in America, hoping to establish a theocratic government that would rigidly adhere to Old Testament laws. Reconstructionists believe that it is up to man to establish the kingdom of God on earth. That effort brought America the Salem witch trials, public floggings, the stock and pillory and other pleasantries. It was the

---

52 Lindsey, Hal. *The Road to Holocaust* (New York, NY: Bantam Books, 1989)
53 http://www.novia.net/~todd/tt10.html

Puritan reconstruction efforts in early American history that gave the enemies of Christianity so much ammunition with which to attack the Church. The ACLU is fond of pointing to this oppressive period to justify their case for the separation of church and state.

Road To Holocaust

I have seen how good, born-again Christians become increasingly more anti-Semitic in their thinking after having been infected with replacement theology. By the time he reached old age, even the great reformer, Martin Luther, went on record making some stunningly anti-Semitic statements, many of which were quoted by the Nazis to legitimize the Holocaust. Simply stated, replacement theology is the view that the Israelite has been permanently replaced as the instrument through which God works and that national Israel does not have a future in the plan of God.

I will demonstrate in this chapter the fact that God's covenant with Abraham was and is eternal. Replacement theology takes the self-serving view that the Church inherits the promises and blessings originally given to Israel. The movement does allow Israel continued ownership of the curses that went along with those promises and blessings, but otherwise cuts it out of God's future outline of history. The father of the modern Reconstruction Movement, R. J. Rushdoony, explains the replacement this way:

"The fall of Jerusalem, and the public rejection of physical Israel as the chosen people of God, meant also the deliverance of the true people of God, the Church of Christ, the elect, out of the bondage to Israel and Jerusalem."[54]

It then follows that Israel is a pariah, even in the eyes of God, so it therefore becomes a religious duty to hate them. After all, if you can't hate the guys that God hates, what kind of Christian are you, anyway? Or so the thinking goes. It's a time-honored tradition, hating Jews for no apparent cause.

David Chilton elaborates further, saying "ethnic Israel was excommunicated for its apostasy and will never again be God's Kingdom[55] [and] the Bible does not tell of any future plan for Israel as a special nation."[56]

For the Jews, the situation created by the adoption of replacement theology by Christians can be summed up with a quote by Raul Hilberg I used in my book *The Road to Holocaust*. Describing the plight of the Jew throughout the Diaspora, one Jew made this comment, "First, we were told, **'You're not good enough to live among us as Jews.'** Then we were told, **'You're not good enough to live among us.'** Finally, we were told, **'You're not good enough to live.'"**

---

54 Rousas John Rushdoony, *Thy Kingdom Come: Studies in Daniel and Revelation* (Fairfax, VA: Thoburn Press, 1970) p. 82
55 Chilton, David, *Paradise Restored* (Tyler, TX: Reconstruction Press, 1985) p. 224
56 *ibid.*

Is God a Liar?

The same people who would willingly deny Israel's place in the plan of God eagerly claim the Old Testament as part of the Holy Scriptures. To them, as to all Christians, the Bible is made up of two sets of Books, divided into the Old and New Testaments. The word "testament" is the same as the word "covenant." That's why we call someone's last written wishes his "last will and testament." The execution of a will is a solemn, legal responsibility that has high penalties attached for those who fail to execute it faithfully and to the letter. The "will" part is the wishes of the deceased, but it is the "testament" part—the *covenant* relationship between the testator and executor— that is a legally enforceable and binding agreement.

Genesis Chapter 15 records the covenant between God and Abram. (God had not changed his name to Abraham at this point.) God had originally promised Abram in Genesis 12 that, if he would leave Ur in the land of the Chaldees [modern Iraq] and go to a land that God would show him, it would be given unto him and his seed forever. Abram did as God commanded. Abram grew impatient with God's promise. An old man of nearly 90, he still had no seed to inherit the Promised Land. The Bible records it this way:

"And Abram said, Behold, to me thou hast given no seed: and, lo, one born in my house is mine heir. And, behold, the word of the LORD came unto him, saying, This shall not be thine

heir; but he that shall come forth out of thine own bowels shall be thine heir. And he brought him forth abroad, and said, Look now toward heaven, and tell the stars, if thou be able to number them: and he said unto him, So shall thy seed be."[57]

The next verse is key, so look closely: **"And he believed in the LORD; and he counted it to him for righteousness."**[58]

When God imparts righteousness to men, He can then enter into covenant relationships that would otherwise be impossible to reconcile with perfect justice. But God imparted righteousness to Abram by his faith. We, the Church, are also justified by faith in Christ, making it possible for us to partake of the new covenant with Christ. Abram believed God, and God counted it for righteousness.

Signed, Sealed and Delivered

Abram asked the Lord for a legal deed to his new land, (verse 8) and God instructed him to prepare a blood covenant. A blood covenant, by the custom and practice of Abram's day, seems bizarre, but it was the equivalent of a signed contract. Today, if someone breaks a contract with someone else, they can be sued in court. But God and Abram entered into a *blood* covenant, the most solemn and binding covenant possible.

---

57 Genesis 15:3-5
58 Genesis 15:6

"And he said unto him, Take me an heifer of three years old, and a she goat of three years old, and a ram of three years old, and a turtle-dove, and a young pigeon. And he took unto him all these, and divided them in the midst, and laid each piece one against another: but the birds divided he not."[59]

Abram took these animals, killed and quartered them, and arranged them as God instructed. You can imagine his excitement! Abram knew the blood covenant custom. The two parties to the contract were required to walk together between the aisles formed by the dismembered animal carcasses. Hands joined, the parties' would recite the terms of the contract together. Once concluded, if either party failed to live up to his part of the bargain, he would end up like one of those animals lining the path. So Abram waited patiently for God to show up. But as he waited, the Bible says a deep sleep fell upon him, and he saw the contract consummated in a vision.

"And it came to pass, that, when the sun went down, and it was dark, behold a smoking furnace, and a burning lamp that passed between those pieces."[60]

There, did you see it? When the time came for God to execute His covenant with Abraham's seed (Israel) *He walked the path alone!* Since God signed, in effect, *both*

59 Genesis 15:9-10
60 Genesis 15:16

sides of the deal, Abram (and his seed) were released from any obligation to do anything in order to fulfill their part of the deal. Under ordinary circumstances, if Abram and his seed failed to live up to God's standards, the contract would be void. Voiding the contract meant somebody had to die to fulfill the terms of the blood oath. Of course, Abram (and his seed, every last one of them) fell short of God's standard. (As has every human being who ever lived, with the exception of Jesus, I hasten to add.) But the terms were clear. Somebody had to die. Since the only One who was party to both sides was God, He was the guilty party under the law. God paid the penalty for Abram's failure, and that of his descendants, at the Cross.

"Think not that I am come to destroy the law, or the prophets: I am not come to destroy, but to fulfil" (Matthew 5:17).

"And for this cause he is the mediator of the New Testament, that by means of death, for the redemption of the transgressions that were under the first testament, they which are called might receive the promise of eternal inheritance."[61]

"For this is the covenant that I will make with the house of Israel after those days, saith the Lord; I will put my laws into their mind, and write them in their hearts: and I will be to them a God, and they shall be to me a people. . . . For I will be merciful to their unrighteousness, and

---

61 Hebrews 9:15

**their sins and their iniquities will I remember no
more."**[62]

Clearly, the Cross marked the birth of the new
covenant, but it also validated the old covenant with Israel
forever. But God also makes it clear, using the New
Testament so there could be no doubt. In the Book of
Acts, the term Israel is used 20 times, and the word church
(ekklesia) is used 19 times, yet the two groups are always
distinct and separate. After Pentecost, the world was
divided into *three* groups, where previously there had only
been Jew and Gentile. But Paul writes in 1 Corinthians
10:32, **"Give none offence, neither to the Jews, nor to
the Gentiles, nor to the church of God."** Note that there
are now *three* groups, the Jews, the Gentiles, and the
Church.

Gary North made an unconscious admission when he
wrote in the publisher's preface to David Chilton's *Days
of Vengeance,* "For over two decades, critics chided the
Christian Reconstructionists with this refrain: 'You
people just haven't produced any Biblical exegesis to
prove your case for eschatological optimism.'"

Don't Bother Us with Facts

The fact is that for over two decades the Reconstructionists did have a huge superstructure of philosophically
based eschatology with no exegetical foundation. Chilton
was given the assignment of finding some Biblical passages

---

62 Hebrews 8:10, 12

on which the system might be based. Speaking from any point of view, that was not the best atmosphere for objectivity.

Chilton's books, far from establishing Dominion theology on a Biblical foundation, rather illustrate that they have no objective literal base of interpretation to justify their system. I found several attacks against Premillennialists, but unfortunately no definitive responses to the exegetical base of our doctrine. As I will demonstrate later, Chilton used the same technique as his colleagues before him. He built his system more upon attacking the Premillennialists than positively establishing his own system.

North revealed a further weakness in the Dominionist system when he admitted that "the final major work lacking for Reconstructionism is a book on hermeneutics." Hermeneutics, which means the science of interpretation, should be a foundational study, not the final capstone effort.

Summary

The arrogance of the Dominionists, particularly considering the weakness of their position, is staggering. But note this point. The pre-Tribulation position remains valid, even when applying the Dominionist's dating game. On the other hand, any dating of the Book of Revelation that dates it past AD 70 utterly demolishes the entire Dominionist argument. Take care that you are not led astray by a teaching that says we are going to conquer the world and that Christ's return is somehow connected to our good behavior. No matter how good and positive that might sound, it isn't true.

Over and over, we are commanded to be **"looking for the blessed hope and the appearing of the glory of our great God and Savior, Jesus Christ"** (Titus 2:13). There is a promise of a special crown for those who love and long for Christ's appearing (2 Timothy 4:8).

Don't let anyone steal your blessing. Instead, listen to the words of the apostle Paul, who wrote, "**Prove all things, and hold fast to that which is good**" (2 Thessalonians 5:21, KJV). Or the apostle John, who warned, **"Beloved, do not believe every spirit, but test the spirits to see whether they are from God; because many false prophets have gone out into the world"** (1 John 4:1).

I put it to you to decide for yourself. What spirit would motivate anyone to teach something that makes God a liar?

CHAPTER TWENTY-TWO

Optimism Versus the Truth

> "The traditional pessimillennialists [North's term for Premillennialists] have issued a clarion call: 'Come join us; we're historical losers.' They have built their institutions by attracting people who are content to remain historical (pre-Second Coming) losers."[64]
>
> —Gary North, Preface to *Days of Vengeance*

*O*ne of the most deceptive teachings against the pre-Tribulation Rapture has been a recent movement that believes there will be no Rapture or Tribulation at all. I have already mentioned the Reconstructionists or Dominionists several times. But because they have created so much confusion, especially among Charismatics, I will devote more space to them.

The Charismatic churches that have previously embraced the doctrines of *positive thinking, positive confession,* and *motivational science* have been the most susceptible to the Reconstructionists' doctrine. The reason is obvious. Those who preach Dominion doctrine continually talk about it being "the only optimistic and positive view of future history." This "new Gospel of optimism" has redefined what victory for the Church must be in terms of human standards and earthly goals.

---

64 Gary North, "Publisher's Preface" in David Chilton, *Days of Vengeance: An Exposition of the Book of Revelation* (Fort Worth, TX: Dominion Press, 1987) p. xxix

But is this "new doctrine of optimism," which teaches that the Church is going to perfect itself and conquer the world before Christ returns, really based on God's Word? To me, this is the only question that counts. If "optimism" is not based on God's truth, it is a cruel hoax. I believe that whatever God truly predicts will always be a ground of hope and optimism that never disappoints. God's plan and purpose can never be understood in mere terms of the human reason.

What Is Ultimate Success for the Church?

One of the main errors of the Dominion movement is their definition of what is success for the Church, and just what is its goal and destiny. From their point of view, success is gradually taking dominion over the entire world-system, and substantially establishing the Kingdom of God before Christ personally returns to the earth.

David Chilton states the Dominion view clearly: "The Bible give us an eschatology of dominion, an eschatology of victory. This is not some blind 'everything-will-work-out-somehow' kind of optimism. It is a solid, confident, Bible-based assurance that, before the Second Coming of Christ, the gospel will be victorious throughout the entire world."[65]

Gary North, with his customary "humility," clarifies the Dominionists' view concerning those who look for a tribulation and the return of Christ to establish God's Kingdom:

---

65 David Chilton, *Paradise Restored: An Eschatology of Dominion* (Tyler, TX: Reconstruction Press, 1988), p. 5

"They [Premillennialists] begin with the presupposition that God has not given His church the vision, program and first principles to defeat God's enemies, even with Christ's victory over Satan at Calvary as the foundation of the Church's ministry."[66]

But what the Dominionists fail to consider is that Satan's defeat at the cross did not eliminate man's freedom of choice. Nor has Satan been bound from operating on earth during this age. The apostle John makes it clear that the world-system is still under Satan's control: "... **the WHOLE WORLD [system] is under the control of the evil one**" (1 John 5:19b). The Scriptures do not say that Satan will be bound until the personal, cataclysmic intervention of the Lord Jesus at His Second Advent (Revelation 19:11—20:11).

North continues his attack against the Premillennialists: "If their followers ever sit down and read *Days of Vengeance*, Christian Reconstructionism will pick off the best and the brightest of them. Why? BECAUSE EARTHLY HOPE IS EASIER TO SELL THAN EARTHLY DEFEAT, at least to people who are not happy to accept their conditions as historical losers"[67] (emphasis mine).

There is one thing that is very true about North's statement: earthly hope is indeed easier to sell to the fleshly minded than earthly defeat. Those who are looking

---

66 Gary North, Publisher's Preface to *Days of Vengeance*
67 *ibid.*

at life from the human viewpoint and don't understand what the Bible teaches about our true hope will readily swallow their false hope of optimism.

But the Bible says that our hope is not in this world: **"If only for this life we have hope in Christ, we are to be pitied more than all men"** (1 Corinthians 15:19). And again, **"For our citizenship is in heaven, from which also we EAGERLY WAIT for a Savior, the Lord Jesus Christ"** (Philippians 3:20, NASB).

These Scriptures, and many more like them, do not reflect an earthly focused hope, but a heavenly one. This does not mean that we sit around doing nothing, but it does mean that our ultimate hope is not in an earthly theocracy under the Law of Moses established by men.

Snatching Defeat from the Jaws of Victory

A big factor the Dominionists forget is that Satan's judgment at the cross has not yet been executed to the point of him being bound. Satan is clearly portrayed in the Bible as being active right up to the Second Coming of Christ.

God does not view the snatching of Christ's bride out of the world as defeat. This is one of the most pernicious deceptions of Dominion teaching. They define from the human viewpoint what they think is victory, and then make that the criterion by which the Bible must be interpreted. What an editor for the *London Economist* once wrote about a different subject aptly applies to them,

"They proceed from an unwarranted assumption to a foregone conclusion."

What Is Victory for the Gospel?

The Bible simply does not teach the basic premises upon which much of Dominion theology is built. Jesus commanded us to preach the Gospel to the entire world. But victory in evangelism was never promised to result in the conversion of all or even a majority who heard. The LORD warned, **"Enter through the narrow gate. For wide is the gate and broad is the road that leads to destruction, and MANY enter through it. But small is the gate and narrow the road that leads to life, and only a FEW find it"** (Matthew 6:13-14). And in another place He said, **"For many are called, but few are chosen"** (Matthew 24:14, NASB).

Humorously, the Reconstructionists become more dispensational in their approach to interpreting these verses than C. I. Scofield himself. They contend that the above verses only applied to Israel, not to the general reception of the Gospel among the Gentiles. But they can't have it both ways. If it is wrong for the Dispensationalists to recognize progressive revelation in distinguishable Divine economies, then it's also wrong for them to do so.

The Freedom-to-Choose Factor

God made a sovereign decision to give man the freedom to make a choice concerning the Gospel. Peter explained that the LORD withholds judgment because He is not willing that any should perish, but that all should come to repentance (2 Peter 3:8-9). But in order for mankind to have the freedom to accept the Gospel, he must also have the freedom to reject it.

Herein is the reason why there is such evil in the world today: God has allowed man the freedom to choose to do evil so that he can also have the freedom to choose to believe the Gospel. God could stop evil immediately. But to do so, He would have to annihilate the whole human race. That is the only way God can stop man from choosing to do evil. As long as mankind is alive, there will always be those who reject God's grace and choose evil.

This is why the Lord Jesus delays His coming. When He returns, it will be to judge the world and set up His Kingdom. But until then, the Bible teaches us that the world will become increasingly hardened to the message of grace as the time for Christ's return approaches. This will not happen because of some flaw in the Gospel, nor because of a lack of spiritual power in the witnesses, but rather because of the hardness of the human heart. The LORD intends to allow the human heart to fully demonstrate its hardness in history. This is why there are distinguishable periods of history in which God has tested man's response to progressive revelations of His will.

This is also why victory in this age is measured in terms of causing the whole world to HEAR the Gospel presented in the power of the Holy Spirit, and discipling those who believe it. Nowhere does the Bible teach that preaching the Gospel will convert so many people that the world-system will be brought under subjection of God during this age. That is always presented as the exclusive work of the King-Messiah at His coming in power and glory. It is only then that the Lord will judge the Christ-rejecters (Matthew 25:31-46).

PARABLES ABOUT COUNTERFEIT BELIEVERS

The broad course of history between Christ's ascension to the Father and His Second Advent to the earth is clearly revealed in the Lord Jesus' parable of the Sower and the parable of the Wheat and Tares. In all these parables of Matthew Chapter 13 the Lord Jesus is only dealing with the broad characteristics and trends that would develop between His First and Second Comings. He is not giving a detailed outline of all the events of prophecy that would take place in this period. At this point, Jesus was still dealing primarily with prophetic events as they applied to and affected Israel. I say this because the Reconstructionists teach that since there is no mention of a worldwide Tribulation or a Rapture of the Church in this parable, there cannot be one. Those intervening events are taught later in the Olivet Discourse (Matthew 24 and 25), the Epistles, and Revelation.

In the parable of the Sower, Jesus taught that receiving **the word** about the kingdom (the seed) did *not* depend upon the way it was sown, *nor* upon the quality of the seed, *but rather* upon the condition of the soil. Jesus described four different kinds of soil, but declared only one of the four as being good soil. It is only in the good soil that the seed takes firm root and produces lasting fruit. (See Matthew 13:3-9, 18-23.)

"Taring" Up the Gospel

The parable of the tares is even more revealing about the course of this period. *Tare* is actually the word *darnel,* which is a weed that so closely resembles wheat that it is almost impossible to distinguish it until fruit-bearing time. Only true wheat produces fruit, the darnel does not. The Bible emphasizes that the main point of the parable is to teach about the *tares* phenomenon (verse 36). The Lord Jesus interprets the parable for us:

> **"And his disciples came to Him, saying, 'Explain to us the parable of the TARES of the field.'**

> **"And He answered and said, 'the ONE WHO SOWS good seed is the Son of Man, and the FIELD is the world; and as for the GOOD SEED, these are the sons of the kingdom; and the TARES** [darnel] **are the sons of the evil one; and the ENEMY who sowed them is the devil, and the HARVEST IS THE END OF THE AGE** [Israel's age was in view]; **and the REAPERS are angels.**

> **"'The son of Man will send forth His angels, and they will gather out of His kingdom all**

stumbling blocks, and those who commit lawlessness, and will cast them into the furnace of
fire; in that place there will be gnashing of
teeth. Then the righteous will shine forth as the
sun in THE KINGDOM of their Father. He
who has ears to hear, let him hear'" (Matthew
13:36-43, NASB; compare this with 25:31-46).

Between Christ's Ascension and the Second Advent,
the devil is continuing to infiltrate believers with his counterfeit ministers and disciples. The apostle Paul graphically revealed what the **tares** symbolize:

"For such men are false apostles, deceitful
workmen, masquerading as apostles of Christ.
And no wonder, for Satan himself masquerades
as an angel of light. It is not surprising, then, if his
servants [ministers] masquerade as servants [min-
isters] of righteousness. Their end will be what
their actions deserve" (2 Corinthians 11:13-15).

Just as darnel looks almost exactly like wheat, the
counterfeit believers closely resemble the real ones. This
kind of deception and infiltration of God's people is said
to *continue and* increase right up until the LORD'S return
to the earth.

This parable predicts exactly the same judgment as the
one prophesied by Jesus in Matthew 25:31-46. The LORD
will gather all the Gentile survivors of the Tribulation, and
will separate the believers from unbelievers. The unbelievers will be cast directly off the earth into judgment.

Only one third of Israel will survive, but all who do will be believers, according to Zechariah 13:1, 8-9. However, there will be a judgment of evaluation for the surviving remnant, according to Ezekiel 20:33-37.

Here is another Scripture that predicts exactly the same continuous increase of evil until the Second Advent of Christ as the parable of the wheat and tares:

> **"For the secret power of lawlessness is already at work; but the one who now holds it back [the Holy Spirit] will continue to do so TILL he is taken out of the way [the Rapture]. And THEN the LAWLESS ONE [the Antichrist] will be revealed, whom the Lord Jesus will overthrow with the breath of his mouth and DESTROY BY THE SPLENDOR OF HIS COMING. The coming of THE LAWLESS ONE will be in accordance with the work of Satan displayed in all kinds of counterfeit miracles, signs and wonders, and in every sort of evil that deceives those who are perishing. They perished because they refused to love the truth [the Bible] and so be saved. For this reason God sends them a powerful delusion so that they will believe THE LIE and so that all will be condemned who have not believed the truth but have delighted in wickedness"** (2 Thessalonians 2:7-12, NIV).

Many errors in the Dominion teaching are pointed out by this passage.

The First Error

Most Dominionists teach that the Church will have bound the activity of Satan and established dominion over the world-system at the time of the Lord Jesus' return. In fact an essential part of their eschatology teaches that Jesus will not return until this has been accomplished.

This passage teaches the very opposite. Far from being bound, Satan will reach the pinnacle of his deceptive powers, and will deceive most of the world by the time of the Second Coming. In fact, this passage explicitly teaches that *it is the personal return of the Lord Jesus Christ in power and glory that directly brings about the destruction of Satan and his masterpiece, the Man of Lawlessness who is the Antichrist* (2 Thessalonians 2:1-12).

The Second Error

This points to another doctrine of the Dominionists that is corrected by this passage. They teach that there will not be a personal Antichrist, only a spirit of antichrist. David Chilton wrote, "Antichrist is a term used by John to describe the widespread apostasy of the Christian Church prior to the fall of Jerusalem. In general, any apostate teacher or system can be called 'antichrist'; but the word does not refer to some 'future fuhrer.'"[68]

The Thessalonians passage blows Chilton's argument completely out of the water. The passage teaches that

---

68 David Chilton, *Paradise Restored: An Eschatology of Dominion* (Tyler, TX: Reconstruction Press, 1988), p. 5

although **"the power of lawlessness was already at work"** in Paul's day, there will nevertheless be at the time of Christ's return a person known as **"the Lawless One."** Satan himself will possess him. Satan will give him all of his power and authority.

This is the same person described in Revelation 13:1-10. The **apostasy** that **the Lawless One** will bring with him is described in 2 Thessalonians 2:7-12 as the awful climax of the continued growth of **"the mystery of lawlessness"** that was already at work in Paul's day. Once again, this mystery of lawlessness could not have been destroyed in AD 70 as Chilton claims. This passage clearly predicts that it is the LORD's personal return that destroys both the **mystery of lawlessness** and **the Lawless One**. So whether we call the Lawless One the Antichrist or whatever, he is Satan's masterpiece who will take over the whole world for three and a-half years just prior to the Lord Jesus Christ's personal return.

Again the Scriptures are very clear about the conditions of this age: **"We know that we are children of God, and that THE WHOLE WORLD SYSTEM (κόσμος) is under the control of the EVIL ONE"** (1 John 5:19). The parable of the tares teaches the same thing as 2 Thessalonians: It is the sons of the Evil One who will increase until the Second Coming of the Lord Jesus Christ.

A Parable About Evil's Explosive Power to Spread

Jesus' parable of leaven makes this point even more

clearly, **"The kingdom of heaven is like leaven, which a woman took, and hid in three pecks of meal, until it was all leavened"** (Matthew 13:33, NASB). The Dominionist interpreters constantly emphasize the Bible's elaborate system of symbols. This is the foundation of their whole method of interpretation. But they depart from their own principle when it doesn't serve their purpose. They try to make the symbol of **leaven** in this parable refer to the Kingdom of God and how it will spread to take dominion over the earth. However, there's one big problem with that interpretation—**leaven** in the Bible *is always used as a symbol of evil's explosive power to spread.* It is never used as a symbol of good.

This was the whole point of the Feast of Unleavened Bread. This is why the Israelites were commanded to purge all leaven from their homes before the Passover feast. It was also the symbolic reason why they ate unleavened bread during the feast season (see Exodus 12).

Leaven is used as a symbol of the corrupting power of sin and evil in both Galatians 5:9 and 1 Corinthians 5:6. Paul interprets leaven as symbolic of evil in both passages.

Therefore, Jesus is teaching in this parable that Satan would permeate the world with deception and evil before His return. Jesus again confirms this point while teaching about His elect crying out for justice and relief from per-secution just before He returns: **"However when the Son of Man comes, will He find faith upon the earth?"** (Luke 18:8). In the original Greek, this question assumes a negative answer. The original text has a definite article before **faith,** which in context means **"this kind of Faith."** The idea is that there will not be this kind of strong faith when He returns to earth.

The Third Error ·

The Dominionists also teach that the prophecies of Matthew 24 and 25, and Revelation 6—18, which teach about an unprecedented time of catastrophe just before Christ's Second Advent, were fulfilled in the Roman destruction of Jerusalem and Israel in AD 70. They teach that there is not going to be a period commonly known as "the Tribulation" that preceded the Second Advent. As we have seen, 2 Thessalonians Chapter 2 certainly presents another picture. (More will be said on this later.)

The Great Commission

The Great Commission leaves the numbers who believe the Gospel to God. Jesus commissioned us to preach the Gospel, not to convert. That is His job.

"Thus it is written that the Christ should suffer and rise again from the dead the third day; and that repentance for forgiveness of sins should be proclaimed in His name to all the nations, beginning from Jerusalem. You are witness of these things" (Luke 24:46-48, NASB). **"But you shall receive power when the Holy Spirit has come upon you; and you shall be My witnesses both in Jerusalem, and in all Judea**

and Samaria, and even to the remotest part of
the earth" (Acts 1:8, NASB).

"And Jesus came up and spoke to them,
saying, 'All authority has been given to Me in
heaven and on earth. Go therefore and make
disciples of [ἐκ=out of] all the nations [τὰ ἔθνη in
Greek=the gentiles], baptizing them in the name
of the Father and the Son and the Holy Spirit,
teaching them to observe all that I commanded
you; and lo, I am with you always, even to the
end of the age'" (Matthew 28:18-20, NASB).

Nothing in these Great Commission passages implies
that we will convert the world and take dominion over it.
We are commanded to go out in the power of the Holy
Spirit and to proclaim the Gospel. We are told to make
disciples from *out of* all the Gentiles. You can't disciple
nations, you disciple individuals. So the Greek word
translated *nations* should be understood in its most frequently used sense—*Gentiles.*

This is the same Greek term used in Matthew, **"But
when the Son of Man comes in His glory, and all the
angels with Him, then He will sit on His glorious throne.
And all the nations** [τὰ ἔθνη or *the gentiles*] **will be gathered before Him; and He will separate them from one
another, as the shepherd separates the sheep from the
goats . . ."** (Matthew 25:31-32, NASB). This is a passage in
which the eternal destinies of the Tribulation survivors are
decided. Only individuals have eternal destinies, not nations.

As previously noted, the nature of world evangelism is portrayed in the parable of the Sower. The reception of the Gospel message is not shown to depend so much upon the power with which it is presented, but more upon the receptivity of the human heart, which was illustrated in the parable by the four different kinds of soils. This is why the great evangelist and apostle Paul said:

"But thanks be to God, who always leads us in His triumph in Christ, and manifests through us the sweet aroma of the knowledge of Him in every place. For we are a fragrance of Christ to God among those who are being saved and among those who are perishing, to the one an aroma from death to death, to the other from life to life. And who is adequate for these things?" (2 Corinthians 2:14-16, NASB).

You see, triumph is not presented as everyone accepting the knowledge of Christ, but rather giving everyone a chance to hear about it. We continue to be a sweet aroma to God whether our witness is accepted or rejected.

Now, it is on this very point that the Dominionists greatly err. Their definition of victory is to bring the whole world under the dominion of God. David Chilton puts it even stronger: "The Gospel will convert the world." He means by this that virtually the whole world population will be converted. I wish that this was possible, but God Himself says that it is not. And it is not because the

Church fails, but because the heart of man becomes progressively more hardened to the Gospel.

It is easy to see why the Dominionists make this error. They misapply to the Church passages that clearly refer to the Kingdom that Christ Himself will set up at His Second Coming. Since all the Scriptures that refer to the Messiah's Kingdom speak of virtually everyone in the world being believers, Dominionists assume the Church will have converted these people. But the Scriptures clearly show the reason for this future situation—Christ will purge the world of unbelievers at the judgment that takes place on earth at His coming (see Matthew 25:31-46).

Mockers of the World, Unite!

The apostle Peter makes a very appropriate prediction concerning this issue. He speaks of mockers within the Church just before the Tribulation. They will say, **"Where is the promise of His coming? For ever since the fathers fell asleep, all continues just as it was from the beginning of creation"** (2 Peter 3:4). This sounds very much like what I've heard from Amillennialists, Postmillennialists and Dominionists.

Most Dominionists say that Christ won't come for some time. "His coming," Chilton says, "could be as much as 50,000 years away. We need to get to work and bring God's Kingdom upon the earth. Then Christ will come. So it's not God's will for us to be looking for signs of His coming."

I believe that the LORD gave us a very specific pattern of world events that would function as prophetic signs to tell us when Christ's coming is near. If we are actually in the generation that will see them all fulfilled, then it is of utmost importance not to be seduced by a false optimism. The generation that saw the First Coming of Christ was rebuked for not recognizing the prophetic signs of the time (Matthew 16:1-14). The major reason for Israel's failure to recognize and believe in Jesus as the Messiah was their failure to interpret prophecy literally or normally.

There are many more prophecies concerning Christ's Second Coming than His First. And they are illuminated by the example of Israel's failure in the First Coming.

Take care that you are not led astray by a teaching that says we are going to conquer the world and that Christ's coming is a long way off. No matter how good and positive that sounds, it is not the truth. Over and over again in the New Testament we are commanded to be **"looking for the blessed hope and the appearing of the glory of our great God and Savior, Christ Jesus . . ."** (Titus 2:13). We are even told there is a crown for those who love and long for Christ's appearing (2 Timothy 4:8).

Jeremiah and the Positive-Confessing Optimists of His Day

There are many parallels between this movement's reasoning and the reasoning of the people in Jeremiah's time. Jeremiah was commanded to give an extremely negative message if judged by the human viewpoint. He was sent to a proud people who had rejected God's Word and refused to repent. Even though God continued to offer Israel forgiveness if they repented He predicted to Jeremiah that they would not repent, and that they were surely going to be destroyed by the Babylonians. Here is an example of one of Jeremiah's more "nonpositive" prophesies:

> **"Furthermore, tell the people, 'This what the LORD says: See, I am setting before you the way of life and the way of death. Whoever stays in this city will die by the sword, famine, or plague. But whoever goes out and surrenders to the Babylonians who are besieging you will live; he will escape with his life. I have determined to do this city harm and not good, declares the LORD. It will be given into the hands of the king of Babylon, and he will destroy it with fire'"** (Jeremiah 21:8-10).

Now, you can just imagine how popular this prophecy was. Jeremiah was telling the Judeans to surrender to the Babylonian enemy. To human reason, this was considered defeatism at best and treason at worst. "The LORD would never counsel His people to surrender to their enemies," they reasoned.

So prophets rose up and predicted things that were more "positive" and "inspiring" to the people's ears. This is how the LORD responded to them:

> **"Do not listen to what the prophets are prophesying to you; they fill you with FALSE**

HOPES. They speak visions from THEIR OWN MINDS, not from the mouth of the LORD. They keep saying to those who despise me, 'The LORD says: You will have peace.' And to all who follow the stubbornness of their hearts they say, 'No harm will come to you.' But which of them has stood in the council of the LORD to see or to hear his word? Who has listened and heard his word? . . . I have heard what the prophets say who prophesy lies in my name, They say, 'I had a dream! I had a dream!' How long will this continue in the hearts of these lying prophets, who prophesy the delusions of their own minds?" (Jeremiah 23:16-18, 25, 26, NIV).

The "macho" prophets of optimism of that day discounted Jeremiah's message and branded him a "pessimist," a "loser" and a "traitor." They even labeled him a false prophet, beat him, and locked him in prison stocks. But no matter how pessimistic, negative, and defeatist Jeremiah's message sounded to those who were operating by human reason instead of God's revelation—WHAT GOD SAID HAPPENED!

"Machismo" versus Spirituality

The "macho" Dominionist prophets of "optimism" should take heed to this message from Jeremiah, for it sounds very appropriate for them.

The lesson is this: God's Word does not always line up the changing popular fads of human reasoning. From the human viewpoint, it was "humanly unreasonable" for God to destroy a nation and a land that He Himself had created and preserved. An order to surrender to the enemy was totally contrary to normal human passions of patriotism and manly courage. Yet those who believed God's Word and surrendered survived; those who didn't were horribly slaughtered.

More to the point at hand, the idea that things are going to get worse and worse as the time for Christ's return draws near may not fit in with the popular teachings of the Dominionist movement. But this is what the Scriptures teach clearly and repeatedly.

The only way to come up with a different meaning is to give many prophetic passages an allegorical meaning. Or as a few Charismatics have said, "I have received a special Divine revelation about this." It is always dangerous to reinterpret the Bible so that it fits the bias of a newly acquired system of thought.

However it should be carefully noted, *God's prophets were seldom considered to have a "positive message" by the recipients of their prophecies of judgment.*

But as then, so now! We have many claiming to be prophets who speak in the name of the LORD. They bring messages that "tickle the ears" of those who have swallowed an erroneous concept of what success for the Church really is.

Contend Earnestly for the Faith

The *LORD* through Jude commands us **"to contend earnestly for the faith which was once for all delivered to the saints"** (Jude 3, NASB). It is in this spirit and under this constraint that I have written this book.

If—just if—this is indeed the time for Christ's return, then this new view will ill prepare believers for the events that may be very close at hand.

CHAPTER TWENTY-THREE

The Pre-Wrath Rapture of the Church

*A*nother recently put forth argument concerning the timing of the Rapture is the *pre-Wrath Rapture*. Dr. Marvin Rosenthal champions this view and has attracted considerable attention. But the pre-Wrath Rapture just doesn't line up with Scripture. The pre-Wrath Rapture theory contains all the theological problems and interpretational confusion endemic in the post-Tribulational view, plus a few unique problems it brings to the table as well.

Too Many Tribulations...

Rosenthal postulates three divisions of the Tribulation Period. The Tribulation, argues Rosenthal, begins with the first three and one-half years, or the first four seal judgments. Then he separates out what he calls the Great Tribulation, beginning with the fifth seal of Revelation 6:9-11. This begins at the midpoint of Daniel's Seventieth Week and concludes at some point near the end of the seven-year period. Rosenthal calls his third division the "Day of the Lord," as described by John in Revelation 6:12-17. The "great multitude" of Revelation 7:9-17 is the Church, which will be Raptured somewhere between the sixth and seventh seals. That puts the Rapture after the Tribulation, but just before the Second Coming of Christ. In Rosenthal's pre-Wrath view, there is no clear separation between the two events.

The Problem[s] Are . . .

To follow Rosenthal's theology, we must draw a line between the Great Tribulation and the Day of the Lord. There can be no overlapping of the two events. This conclusion doesn't stand up well under the light of clear Bible teaching.

"Blow the trumpet in Zion, and sound an alarm in My holy mountain. Let all the inhabitants of the land tremble, for *the day of the Lord is coming*, for it is at hand. A day of darkness and gloominess, a day of clouds and thick darkness, like the morning clouds spread over the mountains. So there is a great and mighty people: *There has never been anything like it, nor will there be again after it . . .*" (Joel 2:1-2, NKJV).

"At that time Michael shall stand up, the great prince who stands watch over the sons of your people, and *there shall be a time of trouble such as never was since there was a nation, even to that time.* And at that time, your people shall be delivered, every one who is found written in the book" (Daniel 12:1, NKJV).

"For then there shall be such a great tribulation, such as has not been since the beginning of the world until this time, no, nor ever shall be" (Matthew 24:21, NKJV).

These verses clearly state that there will only be ONE time of Tribulation such has **"not been since the beginning of the world."** After all, the Great Tribulation is presided over by the Antichrist, who the Bible promises will be the conduit for Satan's wrath. So how could the wrath of Satan against human society come even close to the Wrath of God against the whole earth? And if the Great Tribulation is a time unlike any other, and the Wrath of God is another time later, then it follows that the Wrath of God is somehow less terrible. The apostle Paul viewed the Tribulation as **"wrath in the Day of Wrath [Day of the Lord]** *and* **the revelation of the righteous judgment of God."**

When Does the Wrath Begin?

Rosenthal says the Rapture takes place just before the imposition of God's full Wrath against the earth. According to Rosenthal, the Rapture would then take place sometime around the breaking of the sixth seal. But as I've already pointed out clearly in Chapter 17, the opening of the second seal in Revelation Chapter 6 sees the destruction begin. At that point, the rider on the red horse takes peace from the earth, and the slaughter begins. By the time the sixth seal is broken (Rosenthal's Rapture) considerably more than one fourth of the global population, roughly 1,500,000,000 people, have perished. I think it's safe to infer that, at this point, God is somewhat more than mildly upset.

Michael Not Strong Enough

It should also be noted that, in order for Rosenthal's view to work, the Restrainer has to be Michael the Archangel, and not the Holy Spirit. For Michael to be the Restrainer, he would have to be the "restrainer of lawlessness" down through the entire Church Age. Angels are *created* beings, with none of the attributes of the Godhead. Angels are eternal, but so are we. The qualities of omniscience, omnipotence and omnipresence would all need be in play in order for Michael to fill the bill. The Bible makes it clear that, although Michael is among God's most powerful angels, he is no match for that old serpent, Satan.

But even the archangel Michael, when he was disputing with the devil about the body of Moses, did not dare to bring a slanderous accusation against him, but said, **"The Lord rebuke you!"** (Jude verse 9).

Without Michael the archangel cast in the role of Restrainer, the rest of his scenario starts to come unglued. Only the Holy Spirit has the qualifications necessary to fit the description of the Restrainer of whom Paul wrote. Once He is replaced by Michael, well, you just can't get there from here.

Rosenthal's view also destroys the doctrine of *imminency*, the doctrinal view that "no man knoweth the day or the hour." The pre-Wrath view requires that the sixth seal be a forewarning to the unsaved that the Day of the Lord and the Rapture of the Church are at hand. This "one last chance" theology is popular, but it doesn't line up with the Bible. First Thessalonians 5:2 tells us the **"Day of the Lord will come like a thief in the night."** When was the last time you heard of a burglar warning his victims when he would be burglarizing their home?

Not A Great Enough Multitude to Qualify

Rosenthal identifies the "Great Multitude" of Revelation 7 with the saints who will be Raptured before the Day of the Lord. That means only the saints alive during the Tribulation would be included. But Paul tells us in 1 Thessalonians 5 that **"the dead in Christ shall rise first."** The elder says in Revelation 7:14 that **"these are the ones who come out of the great tribulation and washed their robes and made them white in the Blood of the Lamb."** The present tense use of the word translated "come" indicates these saints do not come out simultaneously, but rather, enter Heaven the old fashioned way—they die first! At the Rapture, **"we who are <u>alive and remain</u> will be caught up with Him"** as a simultaneous, global event that reaches back from the point of the Rapture to the first believer who ever lived. The Bible promises *him* a new body, too! And it all happens at the same time.

Turn It All Around and It Works!

For the pre-Wrath Rapture to work, the Church must be raptured in conjunction with the Second Coming of the Lord. That means that the Second Coming and the Rapture of the Church are not distinctly separate events. But Jesus taught the opposite. He promised that all believers will be removed from earth and will be in Heaven at the Marriage Supper of the Lamb during the Tribulation period. All unbelievers will remain on earth during the Tribulation period to experience the judgment of God. At the Second Coming, the unbelievers will be removed for judgment (separation of sheep from goats) and the believers who survived the Tribulation then live on during the Millennial Kingdom period and repopulate the earth. So for the pre-Wrath Rapture view to be valid, virtually the whole of the Olivet Discourse needs to be compressed into a single event and read in reverse order.

I Will (Sometimes) Leave or Forsake You

For any view of the Rapture that leaves the Church on earth during the Seventieth Week to work, we also have to accept the fact the Bible lied. Jesus promised that He would send a Comforter (the Holy Spirit) who would guide us until He returned. He promised that He would never **"leave or forsake us."** Second Thessalonians Chapter 2 clearly says the Restrainer must be removed to allow the incredible evil of the Antichrist free reign on earth. So, to accept a pre-Wrath Rapture, we'd have to rewrite Jesus' promise to read something like: "I will never leave or forsake you, except during a time of trouble unlike anything the world has ever known. So, when you need Me most, I won't be there. But the rest of the time, you can count on Me as usual. Oh, and by the way, when you really, really need comfort, forget it! I'm removing the Comforter to allow unchecked evil to run your world, so don't count on Him, either!"

Summary

So we find that both the overall chronology of prophecy concerning the Tribulation, as well as the chronology of the Book of Revelation, does not fit the pre-Wrath Rapture view. There is no way to cram all of the Divine wrath into the last moments of the Tribulation.

I believe, therefore, that we can trust God's promise in these days of ever-increasing turmoil, **"For God has not destined us for wrath, but for obtaining salvation [deliverance] through our Lord Jesus Christ"** (1 Thessalonians 5:9).

So we are to keep on believing God's promises, **"and to wait for His Son from heaven, whom He raised from the dead, that is Jesus, who delivers us from the wrath to come"** (1 Thessalonians 1:10).

The following chart will give some idea of the difficulties of this position.

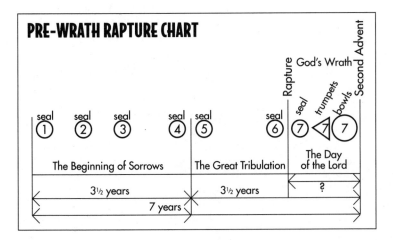

Another Problem

*E*ven though the Holy Spirit is definitely the Restrainer of 2 Thessalonians Chapter 2, there is another issue to settle.

There are two possible ways of viewing the Holy Spirit's ministry as Restrainer. One is that He restrains directly and personally apart from the Church. The other way is that He restrains through the agency of His present personal residence in the Church.

As might be expected, Gundry leads the few who hold to a personal and direct restraining role of the Spirit apart from the Church. (I think it is important to say to the reader at this point that though I haven taken personal exception to Gundry throughout this book, it is done with a healthy respect for his evident spirituality and scholarship.)

Gundry observes, "We have no warrant to infer from the residence of the Holy Spirit in the Church that He cannot work independently from the Church or that He limits Himself to the Church as His sole sphere or medium of activity. Neither in the present passage nor in any other do we catch so much as a hint that restraint of the Antichrist and of the mystery of lawlessness forms one of the purposes for the Spirit's residence in the Church."[69]

Actually, I believe that Gundry misses part of the issue in his statement. I agree that the Holy Spirit, being an omnipresent and omnipotent person, cannot be limited to

---

69 *Ibid.*, pp.126-127

working only through the Church in which He personally dwells.

The Holy Spirit through the Church does exercise a restraint upon the world. We are both the salt that preserves and the light that illuminates the world, but equally important is whether there are certain ministries the Holy Spirit performs in the world because the Church is still in the world. When Jesus first predicted the birth of the Church, He promised, **"upon this rock [that is, the profession of faith in Him as the Son of God and Messiah] I will build My church; and the gates of Hell shall not overpower it. I will give you the keys of the kingdom of heaven; and whatever you shall bind on earth shall be bound in heaven, and whatever you shall loose on earth shall be loosed in heaven"** (Matthew 16:18-19).

If the post-Tribulationist and pre-Wrath views are correct, and the Church does go through most of the seven years of Tribulation, then this promise cannot be kept. First, the Holy Spirit stops restraining Satan and his activities. Second, the mystery of lawlessness is allowed to go rampant and the great apostasy takes place. Third, the Roman Antichrist is unveiled. Fourth, the Antichrist is given complete authority over believers. **"And it was given to him [Antichrist] to make war with the saints and to overcome them: and authority over every tribe and people and tongue and nation was given to him"** (Revelation 13:7).

It Just Doesn't Work

There is no way to reconcile the above prophecy with the promise given to the Church, if these saints are from the Church. If the Church is on the earth during this period, Satan and his Antichrist will totally overpower it.

Furthermore, Jesus made another solemn promise to the Church that is even stronger: **"all authority has been given to Me in heaven and on earth. Go therefore and make disciples of all the nations, baptizing them in the name of the Father and the Son and the Holy Spirit, teaching them to observe all that I commanded you; and lo I am with You always, even to the end of the age"** (Matthew 28:18-20).

In the light of this promise, it is a divine necessity for the Holy Spirit to restrain apostasy and the Antichrist until the end of this Church age, which terminates with the evacuation of the Church. Otherwise, the Church would have been wiped out long ago.

All of the things which occur during the Tribulation are consistent with this view. The Tribulation becomes the hour of the power of darkness. The false apostle and ministers within the false church throw away all truth from God's Word and embrace the Antichrist as their leader. There is no more restraint. The world will be totally under Satan's authority.

The Holy Spirit will still work as He did in the Old Testament. He will not be gone from the world, but His unique ministries in, through, and for the believer will be removed with the Church.

Mid-Tribulationist Relfe erects a straw man concerning this issue and then tears it down in her abrasive style, "If the church is to be raptured before the Tribulation, and 'he' the Holy Spirit is taken out at this time, as pre-Tribulation espouses, how would those many Tribulation Saints with whom Antichrist makes war (Daniel 7:21, Revelation 13:7) get converted?"[70]

No informed exponent of pre-Tribulation believes what she attributes to him. The Holy Spirit will endow the 144,000 chosen Israelites with the same kind of power He did the prophets in the Old Testament. In fact, two of the mightiest prophets from the economy of law will return to shake up the world. The Holy Spirit will convince men of their need of salvation, bring them to faith, and regenerate them as He did from the beginning of man's sin.

But the unique Church economy ministries of indwelling, baptizing, sealing, gifting, and filling of every believer will be removed with the Church. This is consistent with all that is revealed of the average Tribulational believer's level of spiritual insight, knowledge and maturity.

Gundry rejects this idea of a "reversal of Pentecost." He says that since all these ministries of the Spirit were given on the basis of the finished work of Christ, they cannot be removed. But there is nothing in Scripture that says the conditions of one economy cannot be removed

---

70 Relfe, op. cit. pp. 216-217

for a greater Divine purpose and then returned at a later date.

This point is graphically illustrated by another similar Divine action. The whole system of animal sacrifice required by the Mosaic Law economy is set aside in the present economy. The writer of the epistle to the Hebrews shows point by point how this system was fulfilled in the one sacrifice of the Messiah Jesus. Yet we find in Ezekiel Chapter 40 that animal sacrifice will be reinstituted in a memorial sense during the millennial kingdom.

Since the Tribulation is the final seven years of Daniel's prophecy of 70 weeks of years, and since the first 69 weeks of years were under the conditions of the Mosaic Law economy, it stands to reason that the same conditions must return for the final week. Thus the present ministries of the Spirit must be removed.

The Purpose of the Day of the Lord

The purpose of the Day of the Lord is the last part of Paul's argument that proves it has not yet come. Paul says, **"And then [after the Restrainer and the Church are removed] the lawless one will be revealed, whom the Lord Jesus will overthrow with the breath of his mouth and destroy by the splendor of his coming. The coming of the lawless one will be in accordance with the work of Satan displayed in all kinds of counterfeit miracles, signs and wonders, and every sort of evil that deceives those who are perishing. They** perish because they refused to love the truth [the Bible] and so be saved. For this reason God sends them powerful delusions so that they will believe the lie and so that all will be condemned who have not believed the truth but have delighted in wickedness" (2 Thessalonians 2:8-12, NIV).

After the Restrainer is taken out of the way, Satan will be allowed not only to bring in the Antichrist, but to counterfeit the miracles of Messiah Jesus through him. The same three words that are used to describe our Lord Jesus' miracles throughout the Gospels are used in verse 9 to describe Satan's activity through the Antichrist.

The Beginning of God's Wrath

The mid-Tribulationists, pre-Wrath teachers, and the post-Tribulationists argue that God's wrath doesn't come upon the world until late in the Tribulation. As mentioned before, all three views agree that God promised the Church would not experience His wrath.

Because of this, the mid-Tribulationist says that God's wrath doesn't begin until the last three and one-half years of the Tribulation. The pre-Wrath people and the post-Tribbers maintain that God's wrath doesn't fall until near or at the very end of the Tribulation. All of these positions are predicated on the assumption that God's wrath is only expressed in a physical judgment.

I believe that this passage predicts the wrath of God is poured out in the spiritual realm to a horrifying degree from the very outset of the Tribulation. (Physical wrath follows shortly after.)

Just look at the terrifying direct judgments of God noted in this passage:

God allows Satan to counterfeit the miracles of the Lord Jesus in order to deceive the world into following the Antichrist. This will cause men to lose their eternal soul, not just suffer some physical pain. (If this isn't an expression of Divine wrath, what is?)

The unbelieving world will be opened to **"every sort of evil that deceives those who are perishing"** (verse 10).

"God sends them a powerful delusion so that they will believe the lie" (verse 11). **"The lie"** probably refers to the Antichrist's claim to be God. This is a direct expression of wrath from God upon the whole world.

These expressions of God's wrath in the spiritual realm are much more terrifying to me than any of those predicted for the physical realm. Those who disagree need to hear the words of Jesus who said, **"And do not fear those who kill the body, but are unable to kill the soul; but rather fear Him who is able to destroy both soul and body in hell"** (Matthew 10:28).

Paul's Final Proof

Paul assures the Thessalonians that they are not in the Day of the Lord because its purpose is to deceive and bring to destruction all those who rejected God's truth and the Gospel. Since they have received and believed the truth, that Day is not for them. They will be removed with the Restrainer before the two events that set the stage for the Day of the Lord.

Paul closes his argument with God's purpose for the believer: **" But we should always give thanks to God for you brethren beloved by the Lord, because God has chosen you from the beginning for salvation through sanctification by the Spirit and faith in the truth. And it was for this He called you through our gospel, that you may gain the glory of our Lord Jesus Christ"** (2 Thessalonians 2:13-14). We should always be praising the Lord for His grace that has delivered us from the wrath that is soon to come.

In conclusion, the Thessalonian letters teach believers that God has not destined us for wrath, for Jesus is going to deliver us from the wrath to come (1 Thessalonians 5:9 and 1:10). But God has called us to gain the glory of our Lord Jesus Christ (2 Thessalonians 2:14).

In these days of growing darkness, what greater hope can we focus our hearts upon than these promises? The Rapture, thank God, is not a hope for the dead, but for the living.

Interlude Between Rapture and Beginning of the Tribulation

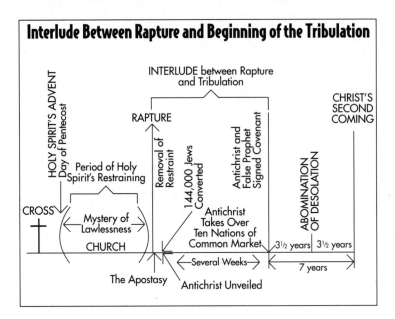

TWENTY-FIVE

VANISHED
Into Thin Air

EPILOGUE

On a Personal Note

$\mathcal{I}$ have never been more thankful to God for the personal hope of the Lord's return for the believer before the coming world holocaust. I had unwittingly begun to take this wonderful truth for granted.

It breaks my heart as I pour over world events, day by day, and see how rapidly the world as we know it is moving toward a catastrophic end.

- Experts say that we are headed for a global economic collapse. Third World countries keep piling up massive debts. They can't even pay interest, much less principal on their loans.

- Many jobs lost in the latest recession will never be restored—experts speak of a whole generation being unemployable because of the painful change from the industrial age to a new technical age of uncertain destiny.

- The Arab-Israeli conflict continues to smolder with the constant threat of igniting the fuse of Armageddon.

- Russia, one of the mightiest military powers in history, continues to be a menace to the world with its political/economic instability coupled with a vast arsenal of weapons of mass destruction just waiting for a dictator to use them.

- Nuclear weapons capable of destroying all life on earth continue to be produced at the rate of approximately six warheads per week.

- "Star Wars" type technology rapidly moves toward lasers and death rays of unimaginable lethality.
- China, with more than one fourth of the world's population, continues to prepare for war.
- Super strains of diseases thought vanquished by antibiotics are rapidly appearing.
- Deadly new viruses are emerging from various places.
- AIDS continues to spread across the planet.
- Global weather patterns continue to change. Storms of unprecedented force are striking in new places around the globe.
- Lawlessness is rampant.
- Bizarre killing rampages are multiplying among our teen-agers.
- Schools have become among the most dangerous of places for our children.
- Rapes are epidemic.
- Gang rapes occur while average citizens look on and do nothing.
- Jails are filled to overcapacity with hardened criminals of all kinds.
- Drugs are virtually a staple of the modern society.
- Traditional families are almost nonexistent.
- Murders with no real motive are commonplace.
- Serial killers are appearing everywhere.
- Famines continue to expand over large sections of the world's population.

- Volcanoes, long dormant, are exploding into life.
- Earthquakes continue to increase in frequency and severity.

To the untrained ear, this may sound like unrelated bad news. But to the student of prophecy, it all fits into a precise pattern that was predicted long ago. This pattern clearly shows us that the Lord's coming for His Church is very near.

In times like these, the hope of the Rapture should be a very practical force in our lives. It should motivate us to gain a combat knowledge of the Bible in order to be able to face the perilous times that precede the Tribulation. It motivates me to win as many to Christ as possible before it's too late. I want to take as many with me as I can. Although I grieve over the lost world that is headed toward catastrophe, the hope of the Rapture keeps me from despair in the midst of ever-worsening world conditions.

The one who knows that Jesus Christ is in his heart and has the sure hope of the Lord's coming for him before the Tribulation is the only one who can face today's news and honestly be optimistic.

My prayer is that this book will help you to have a certain and sure hope of the Lord's any moment return. Maranatha!

I hope to see you at that great reunion in the sky!

Hal Lindsey

About the Author

*H*al Lindsey, named the best-selling author of the decade by the *New York Times,* was born in Houston, Texas. His first book, *The Late Great Planet Earth,* published in 1970, became the best-selling nonfiction book of that decade. As of this date, he has written 18 books with total sales of more than 35 million copies worldwide. He is one of the few authors to have three books on the *New York Times* bestseller list at the same time.

Mr. Lindsey was educated at the University of Houston. He served in the U.S. Coast Guard during the Korean War. After the service, he served as a tugboat captain on the Mississippi River. During this time Hal came to a personal faith in Christ through reading a Gideon's New Testament. Several years later, Mr. Lindsey graduated from Dallas Theological Seminary where he majored in the New Testament and early Greek literature. After completing this graduate school of theology, Mr. Lindsey served for nine years on the staff of Campus Crusade for Christ, speaking to tens of thousands of students on major university campuses throughout the United States, Canada, and Mexico.

He presently travels to speak at conferences all over the world. He continues to write books and produce video and audio tapes.

He also co-anchors a weekly television news show called the *International Intelligence Briefing* on KTBN which is viewed around the world.

If you wish to order tapes or videos of messages by the author, write or call:

Hal Lindsey
PO Box 4000
Palos Verdes, CA 90274
1(800)Titus 35 or 848-8735

Use the same address or phone number if you wish to contact the author concerning a speaking date or a tour to Israel.